PORTRAIT OF OXFORD

Portrait of
OXFORD

HAL CHEETHAM

ROBERT HALE · LONDON

ISBN 0 7091 2415 5

Robert Hale & Company
63 Old Brompton Road
London S.W.7

For

KAY, ANN, DAVID
and
JULIE
with love

PRINTED IN GREAT BRITAIN
BY EBENEZER BAYLIS AND SON LTD.
THE TRINITY PRESS, WORCESTER, AND LONDON

CONTENTS

ILLUSTRATIONS

PICTURE CREDITS

Julia Cheetham: 1 to 11, 12 and 19 (top pictures) 13, 14 and 21 (lower pictures); remainder by John Smith, of Banbury

MAPS

AUTHOR'S NOTE
AND ACKNOWLEDGEMENTS

This book represents one man's reaction to Oxford; the name, the place and the people. It was written after some delving, some reading, a good deal of walking about and a great deal of listening to what was going on. It is therefore a very personal view, a portrait whose colours are heightened by prejudice and tinged with a certain emotion. If you like, with a sort of love, for although a few individuals may have good reason to hate this city, none can be indifferent to its infinite diversity.

If only a little of 'the indescribable something' that is Oxford filters through these pages—its beauty and ugliness, triumphs and disasters, antagonisms and strange dichotomies, its mists rising off water meadows, its sense of time past in time present—then this is as much as any writer dare hope for.

Without the willing help of many friends and aquaintances, my task would have been made far more difficult. My thanks go especially to Jane Edmonds, of St. Hugh's, who gave me the woman's angle on undergraduate life, read most of the text in draft, and was kind enough to chuckle in the right places. To Andrew Ronay, of St. Catherine's, who talked of athletics, introduced me to his college and Vincent's, and toted me around Oxford on days when cricket and cool beer in The Parks were almost irresistible counter-attractions. To John McLaughlin, of Queen's, for his considerable encouragement, and to Gordon Chesterfield for an astonishing toleration. To my daughter Ann, who told me about C. S. Lewis and to my son David, who gave me the low-down on collegiate plumbing. To those colleges which afforded me the privilege of dining in Hall and—with some surprise but with little hindrance—allowed me to wander about their purlieus unchecked. To John Smith, whose camera went into unexpected places and came out with such excellent pictures, and to A. D. Peters and Company for permission to reprint the extract from Hilaire Belloc's *A Moral Alphabet* which appears on page 87.

The final thanks must go to my wife, Julia, who took the rest of the photographs and was in turn chauffeur, critic, proof-reader and guiding hand. But for her tact, firmness and endless patience, this book would not have been written.

Hornton,   H.C.
Oxfordshire

I

MAY NIGHT

Midnight. May Night. The last train for Oxford, sliding away from the strange smells of Paddington. Proceeding with caution past fairy-light signals. Crawling among the steel networks of Royal Oak. Gently jolting over points and crossings. Gaining confidence, gaining speed, getting a move on. Acton, West Ealing, the Ruislips flickering by. Dark suburban jungles left behind. Speed increasing, coaches swaying, heads nodding, to and fro. Rattlety-tat through Slough and Langley, wildly trumpeting, waking the neighbours, careering onwards. Over the moonlit savannahs, through the Taplow backwoods, into the badlands of Maidenhead. To climb the hump of the Chilterns. To take by storm the Goring Gap. To burst with a shout upon the dim, mysterious hobbit regions of Cholsey and Moulsford. Where sweet Thames runs soft between the hollow hills, gently flowing from the city of Isis. Into whose station this train will shortly come, shuddering to a stop alongside Number 3 Platform. Onto whose stones delicious Miss Dobson stepped delicately down. So long ago.

But first the halt at Reading General. An interminable ten minutes. Loading and unloading. People descending. Silent, thankful farewells. The nod to erstwhile companions, those poor passengers for Oxford. A wilting bunch now, thinned out to a countable few. Who rub at windows and peer into the gloom. Who consult watches and groan. Who think of 30 miles to go. Who see Time dragging himself along, a very cripple. Who taste hot oil and choke on diesel fumes and wish they had caught an earlier train. Who hear at last and with relief the sounds of departure.

Who now settle to the second half of a yawning journey.

Luggage creaks quietly on the racks, anonymous as its owners.

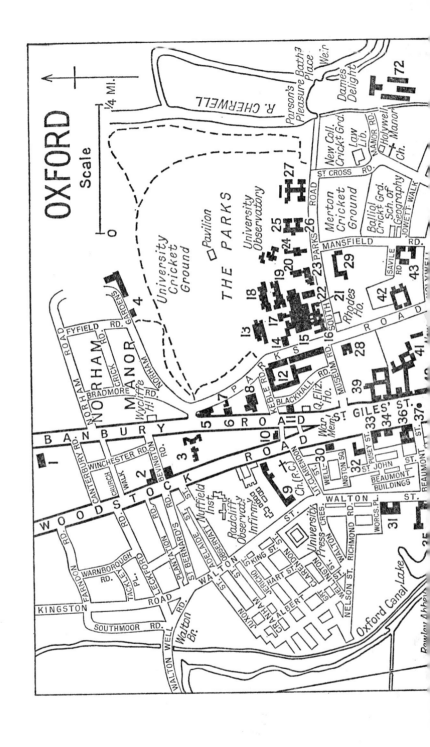

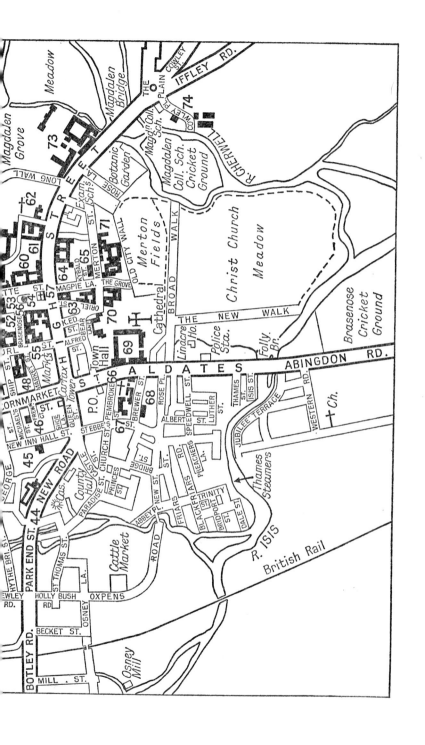

Briefcases, battered and brand-new. Handbags and hold-alls. A kitbag. Three rucksacks, one portfolio, one typewriter. A box. Two masonic aprons in slim self-conscious wallets. Bright plastic carrier-bags lumpy with late-night shopping. Books casually pitched about. A brown-paper parcel of grotesque shape. One trombone in canvas cover.

All of which variously belong to this present bunch of tired travellers. To academics and students. To office workers who have been doing overtime, or doing the town, or both. To a theatre-loving housewife. To a priest, a solicitor's clerk, a couple of shop stewards. Belonging to these and to some twenty other less determinable individuals, sitting, snoozing, sprawling, drooping in their seats.

Up front, a youthful chorus of mixed voices chants a cheerful song of protest. "We Shall Overcome," they sing, and it's past midnight. A man nearby tightens his mouth in dark disapproval. Vague dreams of punishment, corporal and capital, drift through his mind. A faint smile appears on his face as he savours these secret middle-aged thoughts.

For the hundredth time, an anxious woman wonders whether Ron will come to meet her. Whether, indeed, Ron ever got the message. And even if he did, whether Ron managed to start the car works at Cowley and is hopeless with cars. She sighs: that's Ron. Worrying the miles away, she weighs the chances of getting a taxi out to Kidlington.

Two undergraduates from St. Catherine's, two half-milers, are on their way back to college. A meet at White City and a meal in Soho has left them in mellow mood. Somewhat ingenuously, they talk of wine and women, subjects in which their lack of experience is betrayed by a frequent repetition of well-worn clichés. Short of words, they move onto the safer ground of athletics. Conversation now revolves around best times, leg muscles, olive oil, beer, torn tendons, Olympics, the faint hope of being put up for Vincent's next term. Also the dire necessity— 'But dire, me old mate!'—of getting down to some serious work. By which they mean still more jog-trotting in track suits around The Parks and evening work-outs at Iffley Road.

A shaggy don from Balliol smiles indulgently. A few hours ago, he was delivering a paper before a meeting of one of London's more learned societies. It was well received. Very well received.

KEY TO CITY PLAN ON PAGES 10 AND 11

And afterwards, the right people said the right things. A good evening! "An Assessment of Classical Influences in some Romaunsch Dialects of the Grison." No wonder the don is pleased with himself. In this present warmth of mind, he is fully prepared to look kindly upon the follies of the world in general and to accept the follies of these youths in particular.

Whether this acceptance would extend to the magazine in the hands of the Queen's College freshman across the carriage is to be doubted. The undressed and highly nubile ladies on its covers suggest not. Such publications are not to be found in Balliol's Senior Common Room.

Nevertheless, the young man from Queen's, resplendent in college scarf, is studying some remarkable photographs with frank enjoyment. And this much to the disgust of a lean person in the opposite seat who emerges from ascetic solitude with a loud and deprecating sniff. Making no apparent impression, he casts furtive glances towards the magazine with its vicarious feast of flesh. Looking up suddenly, the Queen's man catches the wandering eye, grins broadly, offers to pass over the article for closer inspection and is rewarded by a violent shake of the head as the other dives blushing for safety into the pages of his paperback. The undergraduate reads its title and pulls a face: The *Summa Theologica* of St. Thomas Aquinas. One of *those*, he thinks.

Yet he is wrong. The lean person is not a theological swot; an apprentice parson of frightening intellectual capacity. Nor even a man remotely connected with church or university. Tomorrow, or later today, will find him pedalling on his rounds, collecting weekly insurance premiums from a hundred little houses in Cowley and Headington.

Nowadays, it is all too easy to mistake the man who is up at Oxford for the man who lives in Oxford. Town and Gown travel together and look very much alike. Dons are frequently mistaken for farmers. Bricklayers in their Sunday best have the abstracted air of history professors. Even Vice-Chancellors look like ordinary mortals. On tonight's train, the man hiding behind *The Financial Times* is neither bank manager nor stock jobber but a fellow of All Souls, whose recent study of Bismarck's early years is adding to an already considerable reputation. Conversely, the splendid girl in thigh boots and with-it gear, clear-eyed and lofty-browed, is something of a deceiver. Her thoughtful mien may be that of a young genius from Somerville, all set to take a brilliant double First. In fact, she is just as likely to be the girl who dishes up meat pie and chips at one of the Cowley canteens.

Such cases of mistaken identity are as common in Oxford as elsewhere. Probably more so, since two separate populations have lived here for at least eight centuries and for most of this long period have been easily recognizable as such. But the distinction between the two, between the academic and commercial worlds, the Gown and the Town, is not so clearcut as it used to be. Certainly not in the matter of external appearance. One may say that this building is a college and that a shop, but who, meeting them in the street, is to say that this man is a don and that a shopkeeper? Put one inside a carrel of the Bodleian Library and the other behind a counter in Cornmarket Street and the problem is solved. Take each away from his habitat and it is once again anybody's guess as to who is who.

In short, the processes of democracy have done their work. In a city which once fought fiercely for the divine right of kings and whose academics clung just as fiercely to ancient tradition and privilege, it is now seen that everyone tends to look everyone else. And that everyone dresses as well, or as badly, as everyone else. Man-made fibres and plastics rule the world, Kleenex is universal and Marx is less important than Marks and Spencer. Heresy runs rife. They, and not he, have become the Great Levellers.

Not so many years ago, the term 'Oxonian' was limited in use to "past or present members of the university". This definition, indeed, had behind it the weight of no less an authority than the great Oxford English Dictionary. To the proud townsman, it has been one of those small assumptions that makes him become red and militant. If a man born and bred within sight and sound of Tom Tower is not an Oxonian, then he would like to know just who is!

But whatever the dictionary (published by the University Press, of course!) may say, the word has become more truly generic. Nowadays, it is freely used to describe anyone who happens to live in or around the city.

On the other hand, there are purists who claim that the native *genus oxoniensis* is now extinct; as dead as the university museum's stuffed dodo, that rare old bird which so fascinated Lewis Carroll. It has been pointed out that today's Siamese twin worlds of

Town and Gown are both inhabited by the motliest of crews. And that with its teeming cosmopolitan mixture of emigrants, immigrants, tourists and transients, twentieth-century Oxford is a microcosm of nineteenth-century America. Certainly one finds here the same meeting and mingling of all sorts and conditions of men, the same babble of tongues.

So who, in this context, is your true Oxonian? The ancient don who has dined in hall every night for fifty years? The solid, elementary school, third-generation citizen who has spent a working life in some stolid, unexciting job? The housewives of Summertown and Littlemore? The assembly-line worker from British Leyland who stays so long as the money is good? The undergraduate who comes with high hopes, who is not disappointed and who leaves with a terrible reluctance? The man— and there are many such—for whom the Oxford experience is something never to be forgotten?

There can be no single answer to questions of this kind. All these people may be Oxonians. Conversely, none of them may really belong. For it is not enough to live in Oxford, for a year, for nine terms, for a lifetime. One must also be *of* Oxford. And to be this, it is necessary to establish some sort of *rapport*, even to be a little in love with the place. To be, like Chaucer's clerk, truly "of Oxenforde" is a distinction not to be earned by mere residence.

To speculate upon the affinities of the passengers coming up on our late-night train might still leave the problem unresolved. Without doubt, a majority would consider themselves to be Oxonians. The Balliol philologist, the All Souls' historian and several other collegians would be shocked if the title were denied them. So, too, would a number of townsfolk who are not a little proud of 'being Oxford' as far back as they and their granfers can remember. One man, indeed, is able to trace his local origins back to 1752 when one of his forbears, a 'plaisterer', repaired ceilings at Christ Church. Although a true townsman, he nevertheless quite enjoys the thought of this and other college connections. He once had a great-uncle who worked as a 'scout' at Brasenose. His mother's second cousin was a bedmaker and later a cook at Jesus. And from time to time, his own trade of joiner takes him inside academic precincts in an old-style coming together of Town and Gown.

Town and Gown.... This fading phrase was once much favoured at Oxford, but has long been out of fashion. In the aftermath of two great wars, the words have acquired a quaint and almost archaic quality. The twin Oxfords of trade and learning may still exist but within the memory of many people living, they have changed nearly beyond recognition. Both in themselves and in their relationship to each other, Town and Gown are new worlds, albeit evolved out of the old. The modern situation can be expressed in the modern word: co-existence. For living amicably together is what the two halves of Oxford have finally achieved. Over the years the sharp divisions have been blunted. There has been a blurring of raw edges, a rounding-off of corners, a smoothing down of spiky attitudes, a shifting of stand-points too long entrenched in the frozen ground of tradition.

In general, most people have come round to approving necessary change. As paper bastions crumple one by one, there are some regrets, inevitable protests. But it takes many sighs to make a storm and little breezes from the past do no great harm.

In Oxford, of course, the past exists; has existed. History stands about the streets. Brick and stone is soaked with the stuff and so, for want of a better word, are large numbers of the more receptive Oxonians.

On 'gaudy' nights and at college dinners, old customs matter and come into their own again. Over the toasts and in their cups, dons delight in remembering the good old days they never really knew. But having read their common room histories and steeped themselves in the past, they find no difficulty in getting back there. This is not to suggest that the time game is for academics only. Most visitors try their hands at it. Tourists and day trippers use their guide books as touchstones to romance and are already half-haunted before they step down from the bus. In a city like Oxford, the ghosts are everywhere and the past can be entrancing. Fortunately, perhaps, it holds no one in absolute bondage anymore.

Not, one would think, tonight's travellers. For them, journey's end and a warm bed are by now a mercifully short few minutes up the line. The train leans against the big junction curve at Didcot and rushes towards Appleford Halt. In a cutting here, one grim Victorian winter, the London train ploughed to a standstill among mountainous snowdrifts. Its passengers, mostly university people, forced a way through to Didcot station, there to spend the night and half the following day round a blazing fire in the porters' room, munching cheese and pickles and swigging down gallons of strong ale miraculously produced by the ever-reliable company servants of the majestic old Great Western Railway.

Ninety years ago, that same snow lay thick in the Oxfordshire lanes until the middle of May. Yet like so many things hereabouts, the winters have changed their pattern. It is May again, and warm, with a sky full of stars. And in the orchards of Radley and Nuneham Courtenay the snow is made of apple blossom.

Not far, now, and on the home stretch, time lost has been recovered. The train runs below Bagley Wood, follows the Thames towards Hinksey's suburbs and with factories, furniture depositories and old gasworks coming into view, throbs its way into the Great Wild Western station almost on table time.

Carriage doors bang chunkily. Someone groans. A straggle of tired folk drag along. All sorts of people walk down this platform; many famous, a few notorious, their faces familiar from the papers and television: politicians coming to speak at the Union; actors for the pre-London tryout of a new play; pop stars hired for one of the Commemoration balls. The nobs and the nobodies come and go. Some to stay at the 'Randolph', some to be lodged in their old colleges. Some to flats in Summertown, to semis in Rose Hill and Headington, to council estates at Cowley, to digs in Holywell Street or the Woodstock Road. Some to the favoured villages around the city: to a modernized cowman's cottage at Wheatley, a converted barn at Toot Baldon. And many to the enclosing calm of quadrangles, up twisting stone stairs to old sets of rooms in ancient Oxford buildings: to Oriel, Magdalen, Exeter, Merton and all the others whose names are music.

They all go home and the station shuts up shop until morning. At this time of night, most of the city is asleep. Town sleeps and Gown sleeps but here and there the body politic heaves and stirs and makes noises. Some of its parts have to go on working round the clock. From the ring road comes the distant hum and mutter of traffic. Shift-work factories hiss and snarl. Police cars and an ambulance rush with sirens wailing to a three-car pile-up on the northern by-pass. With one last blare of the horn and two passengers, the late train goes clacketting on its way to Banbury.

At Godstow, the weir smashes itself endlessly into white foam, a continuous roaring. All about the dreamland of Christ Church Meadow, the forked tongues of Isis and Cherwell gleam and murmur in brief moonlight.

Up in town, quick footsteps echo sharply, bouncing between the high walls of Blue Boar Street. A lone policeman surveys the one-o'clock world of Carfax, that famous crossroads at which students and citizens clashed many times in bloody medieval combat. Come morning, its four streets will shudder with the weight of a monstrous load of traffic struggling for right of way, hooting and screaming with impatience: cars, pedestrians, buses, bicycles, delivery vans, pantechnicons, huge articulated trucks cursing each other and topping with bad language the unendurable volume of ear-battering, nerve-stretching, soul-destroying noise.

For the moment, it has the blessed quiet of a nocturne. The young and slightly nervous British bobby sighs audibly. But the near silence is soon broken. Two wild boys on motorbikes bounce over Magdalen Bridge and roar full throttle up the curve of the deserted High Street. And all up the High, that purlieu of knowledge and learning, the blast of unsilenced engines hits college walls with a shattering sound. The night breaks apart. Leaded lights rattle in their iron frames. Shaky floors tremble. From Queen's to University College, from Oriel to All Souls, dead-to-the-world dons turn in their beds and long-dead ones turn in their graves. At Carfax, waiting, the policeman's boyish face assumes a terrible aspect. The traffic signals are at red. He will have them!

Yet before he can say "breathylizer" the lights flick to green and the noise-mongers are through and past and on their way with a last derisive burst. Cheated of lawful prey, the bobby glares fiercely at a mild and inoffensive tutor, trundling sedately home from a late bridge game in his old black Morris.

Like many old towns, Oxford is held ever tighter in the throttling grip of the internal combustion engine. And here the motor-car not only chokes the streets but its production also dominates the local economy. Short time at the Cowley factories would be a serious matter. If ever they were to close down it would be a major disaster. One half of Oxford has been called the English Detroit. The other, the academic core of the place, somewhat amazingly manages to retain something of the atmosphere of a medieval monastery. Or to be more accurate, of a series of monasteries, since tight within its walls, each college is something of a small intellectual order. Black-habited as occasion demands, the members come and go in pursuit of knowledge and other things as they have done for hundreds of years, though nowadays with far more freedom. Alone and unchaperoned, women can now visit the men in their rooms and contrive to stay within the masculine ramparts until a surprisingly late hour. There is already more than talk of certain colleges planning to admit male and female undergraduates. The university, it is pointed out, is co-educational. Why, therefore, should its constituent colleges not be the same? One mixed hall of residence for post-graduate students of both sexes has recently been opened.

In spite of these considerable relaxations of old rules, fearsome spikes and broken bottles set in cement remain on top of many a college wall. But climbing over them and avoiding the Proctors' 'bulldogs' after midnight parties is not the sport it was of old. These terrible hazards are now more likely to be pointed out to visitors as no more than amusing survivals; curious evidence of the puritanical restraints imposed on earlier generations.

College gates are still closed at night, of course. Yet this often seems to be a token acknowledgement of tradition rather than a serious attempt at security and restriction. The majority of colleges now issue keys—if these are necessary at all—to genuine late-nighters, and there are very few which fail to operate a tolerant system of passes in or out.

Nevertheless, the monastic atmosphere can still be felt, particularly in the close-packed huddle of old foundations lying between the Broad, the High and Longwall Streets. For however secular their present purposes, old cloisters still look very much like old cloisters. At a late bonging of bells, even in the 1970s, many big doors in Oxford are shut with an uncompromising bang. Outside, the traffic can roar its muffled head off. Inside is an away-from-the-world quietness, a calm in which people can eat and think and drink. And not infrequently be merry.

It is quiet now, but occasional gleams of yellow light from behind small-paned windows show that some people are still awake. A sharp sweet scent of tobacco plants drifts into a quadrangle from the Fellows' Garden. Pacing slowly round is an odd, solitary figure. In Oxford, one does not ask why. Big elms rustle in the night breeze. The deer in Magdalen Grove move restlessly, look skyward and settle down again. From a dim staircase come shouts of laughter and noisy goodnights as a convivial evening finally breaks up and takes itself off to bed. A few lights go out; a few still burn on. In a dormered room under the leads, a man yawns over his books and finds that logic in the small hours is a puzzling, not to say illogical subject. Tomorrow—no, today—he is down for a tricky interview with his tutor. Of late, the tutor has not been pleased with him. Not far ahead are those unpleasant examinations known to the trade as Schools. He yawns again, trying to concentrate. The words dance about the pages. Sing Hey for Hume! Sing Ho for Hobbes! And to Hell with Kant! He closes the book with a bang. He wishes they had never been born.

Two o'clock and a fine night. Three o'clock and a fine night. Once upon a time the watch came calling the hours but calls them no more. Cats rummage in dustbins behind the Randolph Hotel. The young policeman leans against a wall. Playing hide-and-seek among islands of cloud, the moon sails into the clear for a while. Pale light floods the town. Towers, domes, spires stand white as bone against the sky. Shadows become sharper. In St. Giles, the gothic Martyrs' Memorial stands crisp as an etching. Round the corner in Broad Street, an iron cross set in the roadway glints dully. This X marks the spot where the three bishops Ridley, Latimer and good Thomas Cranmer were burnt at the stake for their beliefs.

At the bathing place of Parson's Pleasure, the river flashes like a silver fish. Long before the emergence of the permissive society, the university allowed its young men to bathe naked here. Sometimes in moonlight; for Oxford in moonshine can still be a magical place, full of dreamings.

The dream and the reality must nowadays live together: the old dream fixed and remembered in stone; the new reality in brick, concrete and glass, rising high and spreading wide in every direction. But the very heart of the place still lies inside the rectangle formed by the old city walls. Within these original confines is a maze of lanes and squares and little alleys. Here are winis and passageways older than Nine Men's Morris, more medieval than the mummers. Here can be found Brasenose Lane, Kybald Street, The Turl, Magpie Lane, Logic Lane, Catte Street, The Grove. Some kink and bend their way along ancient college boundaries. Others, their names remembered but their route forgotten, were built over and lost long ago: Little Jewry, Pennyfarthing Street, Seven Deadly Sins and Slaying Lane: dim ghost ways trodden by men who were boys when Agincourt was won.

There are other and less romantic places in Oxford. Paradise Street, ironically named, leads to Her Majesty's Prison, although there is nothing about this gaunt pile to merit the term majestic. A jumble of gloomy buildings inside dirty grey walls houses an overcrowded population of law-breakers. Held on remand, or serving their time, or awaiting transfer to more salubrious gaols, they sleep within sight of dreaming spires and hopelessly hope for the best.

Erected in the 1840s on the site of the old Oxford Castle, the prison is rightly described by James Morris as "a small but awful place". On and off, wrong-doers have been 'sent to the Castle' for incarceration, execution and other punishments for something like 800 years. Its long record of hangings comes right through to modern times. And hangings in Oxford were a not infrequent public spectacle, approved by those in authority as a useful deterrent in the fight against crime. It has to be borne in mind that until the early years of last century, murder was only one of a large number of misdemeanours for which men, women and even children went to the gallows.

There has been some kind of fortress here ever since William the Conqueror's liegeman, Robert d'Oilly, threw up the tump of Castle Mound in 1170 and stuck his first massive keep on the top. Little of his work remains. The keep has disappeared, together with the massive walls. All were thrown down by a Roundhead army during the Civil War. Only the big square Norman tower of Robert's chapel of St. George-in-the-Castle survives and is incorporated into the prison buildings. The Mound, which once dominated the western approaches to the city, now seems insignificant. Dwarfed by modern constructions, it stands weedy and unkempt by the side of New Road. If it were not for the guide books, visitors would give this 'castle' no more than a passing glance.

In a group of prefabricated huts not far away, the local Simon House operates every night and through the night, giving food and shelter to wrecks and derelicts, offering compassion to society's rejects. For a few shillings a week, the leader of this small Simon Community copes with drunks, drifters, dead-beats, alcoholics, drug-takers, vomit, violence, misfits and mild forms of madness. Good citizens sleep while volunteer helpers, undergraduates among them, do the chores. Not all their tasks are pleasant. At four o'clock on this May morning, two second-year students watch an old man take swigs from a medicine bottle of diluted surgical spirit. Foul-mouthed and aggressive, he has rejected tea, coffee, food, talk, some sympathy; wanting, he growls, none of their bloody help. Drink, sleep, oblivion are his lot.

Men like this form the bottom layer of Oxford's night people, the social silt that has drifted downwards to the ocean floor. In 1967, Simon workers found fifty of them in the city "sleeping rough every night, lying in derelict buildings, in telephone kiosks, along canal towpaths...". Such men can hardly sink lower. If they move at all, it has to be upwards. This, at least, is what the Simonites work for and hope for.

It is in organizations of this kind that the social conscience of some Oxford students finds expression. Sit-ins, placards, picket lines, heckling, noisy demonstrations and writing slogans on walls are not the only ways of protest.

So the night wears on. In London, the last hour before dawn has already come and gone. The morning papers are on their way from Paddington. A dull line of light in the east brightens as, willy-nilly, Oxford is spun forward to meet another day. The moon is down and the city is still in darkness; but not for long. Daylight comes sweeping over the Home Counties like a pale tide, washing along the rides of Epping Forest, pouring through the hill gaps of the Chilterns, flooding over the fields and valleys of Berkshire and Buckingham. Lagging behind, the sun, red-faced, lumbers up the old coach road from Wheatley, climbs Shotover Hill and takes a first peek through the trees at the sprawling place below.

At this hour, at this distance, from this height, Oxford is still a beautiful city. Above the water meadows, mists stir and swirl. The tips of tall chimneys gleam gold. The old town shimmers.

On the first day of May, every year, this is the moment that a thousand early risers wait for.

May morning, at Magdalen Bridge, is something to be seen once, heard once and remembered many times. The silent choir-boys shivering behind stone parapets at the top of Magdalen's graceful tower. The friendly, curious crowds chattering far below. On the river, all around the bridge, a bright and gently heaving carpet, punts packed gunwale to gunwale, stem to stern, covering the Cherwell from bank to bank, full of men and girls.

And as the sun heaves into view and lays a first shining finger on the highest pinnacle, there is a brief cheer from the crowd, a false start, a little laughter and then the half-heard, ghostly singing of *Te Deum Patrem Colimus* the traditional May Day hymn. The clock strikes six. There comes a great clashing of bells, young and joyous.

May morning. Not to be forgotten.

II

IN THE BEGINNING

Several geological ages ago, a warm shallow sea covered Oxfordshire, the Midlands and most of southern England. There were reefs and lagoons and coral islands. Sharks and squids and large ungainly fish searched for prey. Fearsome reptiles were lords of the world. On convenient tidal shelves, oysters lay unswallowed and unsung. Where British Leyland now makes motor cars, the timid shrimp disported itself. Cockles clung to the spot on which Blackwell's Bookshop was to be built. Some 150 million years were to pass before an undergraduate threw a champagne party in his rooms. Or was thrown into the Isis by grateful friends. Or indeed, before there was an Isis into which he could be thrown.

The long, slow saga of this tropical ocean is written in the rocks. It is spelled out in the stone of which the older colleges are constructed. The petrified riches of the past can be found in the worked-out quarries of Wheatley and Headington. There lie ammonite and nautilus, fossils with names like jewels whose sediment floated down to form the layers of that faraway marine floor.

For immense spans of time, little else happened. Then gradually, land heaved itself upwards. The waters sank and receded. In the west, the Cotswolds took shape. To south and east the chalk slopes of the Berkshire Downs were revealed. Sea channels formed between the reefs. The rudimentary hump of Shotover Hill put in an appearance. The rain hissed down continually, pouring across the new inclines, splitting into a myriad streams, gushing into wide sluggish rivers. Where Oxford was to have its beginnings, there was already a familiar network of watery veins and arteries. And, no doubt, the same "dank, miasmal air", the same "heavy, damp and enervating atmosphere" complained of by endless generations of scholars.

The Romans never settled here. Yet they must have taken a good look at the place. After the establishment of their main base at Londinium, they can hardly have failed to do the obvious thing. Which was to move up the Thames Valley, following the course of the river until they reached its confluence with the Cherwell and came upon the site of the future city.

It is not difficult to imagine that some legion commander, viewing this tongue of dry land in the fork of the rivers, sent a very favourable report back to headquarters. Its location in the heart of England was good. Communications were excellent. From the defence point of view, the site was superb. Encompassed on three sides by water; open only to the north; a nightmare of swamps and marshes all around: what could be better?

We shall never know who made the big decision to turn Oxford down. We cannot even be certain that its use as a fortress was ever seriously considered. All we do know is that there was never to be an Oxonium on the great military route from London to the west: no town, no fort, no camp. Not even a humble posting station.

This is not to imply that the Romans made their reconnaissance in an empty countryside. Men had been living in the area for centuries before they came. When the legionnaires first halted by the Cherwell and gazed around at "the almost unbroken expanse of wet land surrounded by thick forest" they were no doubt secretly observed by the original Oxonians. These were men of the late Iron Age. In the early years of the Christian era, at least half a dozen of their settlements were dotted about in what are now the suburbs of North Oxford. And they had been preceded by a succession of earlier cultures. Shaggy Stone Age men lived here, leaving axes and flint implements behind them as evidence of their hunting and fishing activities. The stocky Beaker people came from the Rhine and the Danube, bringing with them and leaving behind their characteristic pottery. Later still, the Celtic invaders, Bronze Age folk, took over. In an Oxford meadow was found a kit of elaborate tools used long ago by one of their bronze-smiths.

Clearly, these less sophisticated people found the locality to their liking. They were thriving hereabouts long before Rome was founded. The arrival of the legions is more likely to have been a nuisance than a major disaster. These Britishers, after all, were not dug in behind some massive earthwork, ready to do or die. They had no Maiden Castle to defend. There was no need to engage the newcomers in bloody battle. The Romans would not be greatly concerned about the activities of a hundred or so natives. They could be brushed aside, or loftily ignored. *Veni, vidi, vici* had to be kept for the big, the worthwhile occasion.

As to why Oxford was avoided by the invaders, we can only hazard guesses. It has been argued that a series of grim defeats on water-girt sites caused them to shun such places. Yet Cambridge, on the road to nowhere and with nothing to offer strategically, was also watery. And there the Romans built the big walled town of Durolipons.

But whatever the reasons, they gave Oxford a very wide berth and to this day, no trace of Roman occupation has ever been found in the city itself.

By the end of the fourth century, this Rome and Colonial period was virtually at an end. The legions were withdrawn and the skies of history darkened. It can only be assumed that the few folk living on and off "that narrow strip of gravel" at Oxford carried on for a while with their traditional pursuits. No doubt they still did their bit of fishing and got on with their simple farming. And they may well have begun to drive their few cattle across the ford that is popularly supposed to have given the town its early name of Oxenforde.

There was still no town as such. A scattering of Romano-British homesteads and a hamlet or two represented the nearest approach to urban life. Trying to portray this Oxford of the Dark Ages is not so much a matter of painting a picture as trying to complete a jigsaw, many of whose pieces will always be missing. For nearly 500 years, facts are hard to come by and what went on must be largely conjectural.

At the beginning of the thirteenth century, that imaginative old rascal, Geoffrey of Monmouth, dreamed up some spectacular fictions concerning the origins of the City and University of Oxford, putting forward theories that are at once charming and totally invalid. He claimed, for example, that Oxford was founded by Memphric 'King of the Britons' at least 1,000 years before the birth of Christ. The next step, he said, was the establishment of a seat of learning. This was accomplished in a truly classical manner by 'Brutus the Trojan', grandson of Aeneas, the hero of Virgil's *Aeneid*. Brutus brought to England twelve Greek philosophers and settled them in the town of Cricklade (originally called 'Greek-lade'!). These were followed by twelve Latin scholars who lived for a time in nearby Lechlade (a corruption of 'Latin-lade'!). These most unlikely persons soon moved to Memphric's Oxford, calling it 'Bellositum'—the fair place.

So this old story goes and for generations was seriously believed.

During the Dark Ages, the name of Oxenforde had occasionally cropped up, although there was still no 'history' in the conventional sense of the word. During the eighth century, for instance, the city's patron saint, St. Frideswide comes into the picture for the first time. The daughter of an Oxford princeling, she was chased across the Thames by King Algar, an importunate suitor from Leicester. She was about to suffer the fate worse than death when a convenient bolt of lightning stopped him in his tracks and blinded him. In understandable gratitude, Frideswide founded a nunnery and in due course was canonized. Christ Church was built on the site of her Anglo-Saxon convent mentioned in the tale and St. Frideswide's Priory was a flourishing house until the dissolution of the monasteries in 1523.

It is not until the tenth century, however, that Oxford moves into recorded history proper. From 912 onwards, it becomes possible to tread on increasingly solid ground. The great Anglo-Saxon Chronicle records this as the year in which King Edward the Elder, son of Alfred the Great, took possession of "London-byrig and Oxnaforda and all the lands owing obedience thereto . . .".

In short, Oxford exists and by now we are among a succession of kings whose names and deeds appear in contemporary accounts. Unlike King Arthur, Alfred the Great is no legendary figure. King, soldier, musician and scholar, he was a man of many parts. But contrary to a tenacious and ancient tradition, he played no part at all in the founding of the university. Alfred died in 899, at least two centuries before Oxford's first scholar clerks appeared. What is far more probable is that he had a hand in the building of the first real town here. Unlike their Roman predecessors, the Saxons were quick to recognize the military potentialities of the site. In their struggle against the Danish invaders a strategically-placed fortress in central England was essential. Alfred needed a key point upon which his forces could be pivoted; an easily defended spot with good access to and from other parts of the country: a place, moreover, that might be used as an alternative capital if London was threatened or became untenable.

Oxford offered all this and more besides. It is no coincidence that the city has many times been a royal stronghold and the seat of government. During the Civil War, when Charles I and his court occupied the colleges for nearly four years, his commanders had no difficulty in basing their elaborate system of fortifications upon the natural defences of the old waterways. Outside the walls, Isis and Cherwell were still the same formidable barrier they had always been. And except in the dryest summer, the surrounding meads could become a vaporous marsh.

Such swamplands must have reminded that earlier king, Alfred, of his impregnable 'Isle' of Athelney in faraway Somerset, from whose sodden depths his army marched out to shatter the Danes at the Battle of Edington. It seems fitting that the great king's jewel, dug up at Athelney in 1693, should now rest in the Ashmolean Museum for all to see.

Whatever he may not have done, it is quite probable that he *was* involved in the creation of Oxford—the town, if not the gown. Before his death, the place had become the vital border fortress we have mentioned, standing in a sort of no-man's-land between the Saxon kingdom of Wessex to the south and the fierce Danelaw to the north. Between the two ran the Thames, a natural boundary and major defence line on which London and Oxford were the key positions.

The place did not grow gradually, from village into town and then into an important city. This first Oxford was built all in one go, and very quickly. Before the Danish invasions, there was not much here beyond a small religious community and a rough agricultural settlement, both standing on a bit of gravelly land raised above the marshes. What Alfred saw when he arrived cannot have been very much different from the scene which had greeted the Romans, 700 years before. But now the pressure was on. Wessex had to be held. Urgent political and military demands had to be met. One of the main needs was for the establishment of the strong base at the "oxnaforda"—the only spot for miles at which the Thames could easily be crossed.

So the walled town of Oxenforde was created. It appears to have been built quickly and in one continuous operation. As such it was the first 'new town' to be seen in England since the days of the Roman occupation. Documentary evidence of its construction may be scant, but the regular geometry of its original streets is clear evidence of an overall master plan. This grid-iron layout of the Saxon town can be recognized without difficulty in the heart of the modern city, where traffic forces its way along routes 1,000 years old.

At this point in time, the dim beginnings of the university were still below a distant horizon. Even the coming of the Normans was still a century ahead. Yet it is from the later hard facts of Domesday Book that the pre-Conquest importance of the town can be inferred. Years before Robert d'Oilly began to build his castle, Oxford was already a prosperous place. Moreover, it had already seen action enough and acquired history enough to merit many references in the chronicles of the period. We can read of the meetings and treatings of kings; of councils of war and peace; of counsels of hope and despair; of royal births, marriages and deaths. And of royal murders.

True history relies on written records and reliable records are firmly attached to dates. From now on, the story of Oxford is increasingly peppered with them. In 1009, the Danes put the town under siege. The following year they had another go and tried to burn it down. In 1013 they were once more hammering at the gates, but in 1015 the game was declared a draw and peace talks were held with Edmund Ironside, the Saxon King. In 1018 his successor Canute held a spectacular *gemot*, or parliament, in Oxford, mainly to show the world who was to be boss man.

The citizens must have been well accustomed to these affairs of state and royal comings and goings. They witnessed the coronation of Canute's bastard son Harold Harefoot in 1037. Three years later they watched his funeral procession pass slowly through the town. Only a few months before the Battle of Hastings, Edward the Confessor called yet another great council of state. Whether his successor Harold, last of the Saxon kings, ever visited Oxford, first among Saxon towns, is a matter for conjecture. What is beyond doubt is that by the time the historic watershed of 1066 arrived, so had Oxford. The Town was firmly established. But many years were to pass before the Gown arrived—those early scholars who "found Oxenforde a busy prosperous borough and reduced it to a cluster of lodging houses . . .".

III

DOMESDAY AND OTHER DIGRESSIONS

When the Normans came, Oxford was already a substantial town. By the standards of those days it was sizeable, prosperous and possessed of civic pride in no small degree. Affairs of state had been discussed and decided within its walls. It was a favoured meeting place of monarchs and the occasional seat of government. In a mint set up in the time of Alfred the Great, Saxon coins of Saxon kings were still being struck by Saxon moneyers. Royal decree had vested in the freemen of the 'burh' all rights to Port Meadow, that vast and still existent grazing mead. The citizens had some reason to be proud.

The town had good defences, although it may be misleading to talk of 'walls' so early in its history. In a country shaggy with forest, earth-filled stockades were more usual than masonry. Such fortifications were primitive but could nonetheless be formidable. It is probable that the Oxford of Saxon times was encompassed by defensive palisades of this kind. Certainly, there were towers and four gates to mark and guard the approach roads from the outside world. And at a sufficient distance, the twisted girdle of rivers and streams continued to provide their age-old protection.

Within the town, all was hard work and noise and bustle. In periods of peace, Oxford had managed to thrive. Men learned to make the most of their limited opportunities. Long accustomed to the comings and goings of the great, the townsfolk were now adept at meeting the needs of courts and camp followers. To one and all the knee was bent, the cap doffed, the forelock tugged, the bill sent in. It is little wonder that when the scholars eventually appeared, these stolid shopkeepers and tradesmen not only welcomed them with open arms, but proceeded to rook them left, right and centre.

Life was rough but reasonably organized. Justice existed.

Traditional ways of doing things were codified into some semblance of law. Good habits were thus preserved and bad ones penalized. Courts and moots of various kinds dealt with complaints and misdeeds. Nor were these concerned merely with the local inhabitants. Oxford had become the focal point of a wide surrounding area. A weekly market brought in countryfolk and produce from scores of villages. The town was also a place of pilgrimage, for in the big priory that bore her name the sacred bones of St. Frideswide were enshrined. On well-placed sites, no less than eight smaller churches ministered to the spiritual needs of a growing community—an early indication of the city's close association with the Church. The recognition of Oxford as a religious centre was later to play no small part in attracting the first scholars. In these middle years of the eleventh century, learning and the priest walked hand in hand. Men turned to the Church for knowledge and enlightenment: indeed, it was their only recourse.

The total population at this period can only be guessed at. It seems likely that at least 3,000 people, and probably more, actually lived within the confines of the town. We can picture the streets lined with low buildings, mostly wattle and daub, rough timber and thatch. In this setting, it is not difficult to conjure up the medieval scene: the tanners and weavers, bowyers and arrowsmiths, shoemakers and blacksmiths plying their trades; the butchers and bakers shouting their wares; the fighting boys, haggling wives, arguing countrymen; their common speech the language of Beowulf and all making up a miscellaneous music of yelps, screams, gurgles, clanks, bangs, scrapings, slicings, howls and twangings.

Except in imagination, nothing of this remains. And of the 1,000 or more buildings recorded in Domesday Book, next to nothing, These original Englishmen were carpenters rather than masons. They used stone for their churches but built almost everything else in wood. A few post holes here and there are the only traces of their domestic architecture ever to come to light. The sturdy tower of St. Michael-at-the-North Gate, with its little Romanesque windows set high in thick rubble walling, is the oldest building in Oxford and the last above-ground evidence of the Saxon town. Deep below present-day car parks and cellars lie the fragments of other and possibly greater buildings of the time. When

Magdalen Tower from the Botanic Garden

bulldozers move in to clear a site for redevelopment, the hopes of local archaeologists rise. But precious little and little precious has so far been found.

On the other hand, we can be fairly sure that the basic plan of Saxon Oxford is preserved in the main streets of today. From the central crossing of Carfax—the 'four ways' of 'Quatre Foix' or 'Carrefours'—four roads at right angles to one another ran down to the city gates. The gates have gone, but the roads remain. It seems that their general line has changed little in 1,000 years. High Street and Queen Street (once called Great Bailey) led to the east and west gates. Cornmarket terminated at North Gate, where St. Michael's tower did duty both as belfry and bastion against attackers. St. Aldate's, so named not after a saint but in token of the Old Gate or Aldgate standing here, dropped down through this east gate to the river and the traditional 'oxenforde' at Folly Bridge.

As yet, of course, there was no bridge, nor was any built until the closing years of the twelfth century. This led to one of the silliest arguments—and there have been many—ever put forward in support of Oxford's claim to being the older half of Oxbridge. Fords, said someone, existed before bridges were thought of. Oxford therefore existed before Cambridge. In wisdom is folly!

Soon after the Battle of Hastings, William the Conqueror sent one of his fighting barons to occupy the city. No doubt this stern soldier, Robert d'Oilly by name, arrived with a sufficient show of chain-mail to do whatever was necessary in the way of sub-jugation. Any resistance would have been crushed very quickly. In 1071, the fearsome walls of Robert's *donjon* were already rising above the town, soon to dominate the whole area.

There is some mystery about the state of Oxford at this time. Just before the coming of the Normans, it was certainly the pros-perous place described earlier. Yet within a few years, when William's surveyors were collecting their facts and figures for Domesday Book, it was flatly recorded that nearly half the houses were 'waste' and unoccupied. The population had shrunk to less than 1,000.

Clearly, some major disaster had occurred, but what really happened and exactly when can never be known. It is one of those baffling enigmas that tease historians. Various theories have been put forward. It is often suggested, for example, that the

3

Saxon tower of St. Michael-at-the-North Gate, the oldest building in Oxford

town may have been ravaged by pestilence or its people put to the sword. We cannot rule out the possibility that the new regime was directly responsible. Jealous of its rights and rather too independent, Oxford may well have found to its bloody cost that the Normans would stand no nonsense from Saxon churls. Needing to establish their new authority with firmness and speed, these fierce Frenchmen were never averse to using terror and exemplary hanging as methods *pour encourager les autres*.

Whatever took place did not much deter Robert d'Oilly. He was soon pressing ahead with a large-scale construction programme in which the chief project was the building of his castle. In the absence of a convenient hill, he picked a site on the western edge of the town, close to the Thames. A deep moat was dug, fed by the river and a number of tributary streams. Excavated soil was dumped and piled to form the little eminence of Castle Mound, now so sadly neglected. On its top, Robert erected a big circular keep, linking it by thick walls to a series of defensive towers. One of these still exists, grim and grey, as St. George's Tower, now part of the dismal complex of Oxford Gaol. In consequence, very few visitors ever see the dim and dramatic crypt of the one-time chapel of St. George-within-the Castle, founded for members of the College of Secular Canons of St. George, while the castle was still being completed.

Other churches began to appear. Some of the older Saxon buildings were demolished to make way for grander structures in the more sophisticated Norman manner. Still others were enlarged or modernized and although much of this work has been pulled down in its turn, Oxford still retains enough of Norman architecture to show what the French masons were capable of.

Along Queen's Lane, the small church of St. Peter-in-the East has a fine chevroned doorway and perfect crypt, full of squat columns and big cushion capitals carved all over with strange beasties. In St. Cross, Holywell, the little sanctuary is again Norman and more work of the same period can be seen in the churches of St. Thomas the Martyr and St. Ebbe's. At Iffley, once a separate village but now a suburb, St. Mary's church is a splendid example of English Romanesque. The rich liveliness of its carvings is a tribute to the humour and inquiring nature of the age in which it was built. But all pales before the late-Norman magnificence of the nave and choir of Christ Church—*Aedes Christi*—the city's cathedral and also the chapel of 'The House', as Christ Church College is called. No other college in the world possesses such a setting for its ceremonies.

All this building activity within a comparatively short time suggests that the town quickly recovered from its mysterious dereliction. The number of inhabitants was once more increasing. It is likely that many of them were pressed into unwilling service in furtherance of Robert d'Oilly's plans. Once the castle was nearing completion, further vast quantities of stone must have been quarried and carted in for his task of reconstructing the city walls. The old earth and timber stockades were gradually replaced by impressive permanent fortifications. With their bastions, towers and gatehouses, they remained intact for centuries; a solid comfort to the townsfolk and an enduring background to their lives.

There is now little to show for all this immense labour. Partly rebuilt in the thirteenth century and constantly repaired thereafter, the walls lasted on into an age which no longer needed them. To a society which could smash down the monoliths of Stonehenge, crumbling walls were no more than an encumbrance. Their last useful purpose in Oxford seems to have been as a ready source of cheap building material for the local masons.

Although most of these old defences have gone, their layout and extent has been determined with some accuracy. From old records, from foundations uncovered during building operations, and from those few sections of wall still standing, it was not difficult to piece together the complete plan. The total length of the walls was about a mile and a half. One can no longer undertake the circular tour by walking all round the battlements, as at Chester. But many of the older streets closely follow the line of the walls, and it is easy enough to circumnavigate the whole area of what was successively the Saxon, the Norman and the later medieval city.

A good starting point is St. Michael's Church, in Cornmarket. The North Gate stood here, its wide arch spanning the street. A warren of dark rooms above became the borough lock-up, the infamous Bocardo from whose tiny windows poor prisoners lowered baskets and even their hats, begging alms and victuals from the crowds below. From the Bocardo, men and women were led out to be whipped, stoned, pilloried, hanged. Or, as the martyred bishops in the reign of Bloody Mary, to be burned to death in Broad Street. It was for long a place of fear and few can have regretted its passing. When it was finally pulled down, the name of nearby Bocardo Lane was quickly changed to St. Michael's Street. A rather genteel echo of the past exists in the 'Bocardo Lounge' of a restaurant close by.

Still narrow and crowded as of old, Ship Street, which begins at St. Michael's corner, was once part of a continuous roadway that hugged the wall for nearly the whole of its course round the city. This lane—it was not much more—formed a means of rapid communication in times of siege and especially when defenders had to be rushed to threatened points. The present street goes only as far as The Turl. The original Bocardo Lane formed another length, while a third can be found in Merton Lane near to the Examination Schools. The rest is buried, mostly under colleges.

The strangely named Turl which now usefully connects the High and the Broad is an ancient footway that once led to a little archway in the north wall. Many writers have supposed that its name originated in the 'twirl' or 'twirling gate' that was set like a turnstile in this small hole in the wall. Pedestrians were able to leave or enter the town through this postern, but there was no way through for cattle or carts or anything of great bulk. The actual gate was demolished in 1722, but the name survives.

From Turl Gate, the wall continued eastwards through the sites on which Parker's Bookshop, the Ashmolean Museum and the Sheldonian Theatre now stand. Very near to the Bodleian Library at the top of Catte Street, it connected with the tower of Smithgate. Like the Turlgate, this was another minor archway used only by foot passengers. These smaller openings must have been punched through the north wall at a comparatively early date. They indicate clearly the direction in which the city first began to expand beyond its original boundaries. The first colleges and most of the halls which were to develop into later ones stood within the walls, but before 1350, Balliol, Queen's and Trinity— then Durham College—had already been built outside and Broad Street was beginning to take shape into something like its present form. Footways like The Turl and Catte Street would provide easy intercommunication yet could be quickly closed off in troublous times.

Catte Street, from which some of Oxford's finest architecture can be observed, was called by this name for more than 600 years. In the nineteenth century, however, certain well-meaning Victorians changed it to St. Catherine's Street. A local historian with a famous Oxford surname, H. E. Salter, campaigned for years to have this and other medieval street names restored. The town council proposed to do this in 1897 as a way of commemorating Queen Victoria's Diamond Jubilee, but the project was abandoned. Later, the university took up the matter with a little more success. During the nineteen-twenties Grove Street and Grove Place became Magpie Lane and Kybald Street once more, while St. Catherine's finally reverted to twelfth-century Catte Street.

Beyond Smithgate, the wall continued fairly straight to the north-east corner of the city. Its line ran roughly parallel with Holywell Street, which was built a few yards outside. Where this street makes its sharp right turn into Longwall, the Morris Garage building marks the location of the corner tower at which the wall changed direction to run southward down to High Street. In some old stables on this site, at the beginning of the present century, the man who was to bring a revolution to Oxford built his first motor cycles. Within fifty years William Morris, later Lord Nuffield, was to be largely responsible for transforming a sleepy university town into its second self: the big, bustling industrial centre of today.

But Morris did not tear down the walls, nor could he do much to basically alter the exclusive world of academic Oxford. He broke down barriers, but never broke through into that closed community of learning. Indeed, he may not have wanted to. His own formal education was limited to a boyhood at the village school and two nights of a course in engineering design at what is now the Oxford Polytechnic. Later in life, he developed an almost pathological dislike for university graduates. His only real interest seemed to lie in making a lot of motor cars and a lot of money. And, once made, the money was something to be given away. It was almost as though he found the stuff distasteful.

William Morris, Baronet, first and only Baron Nuffield, first and only Viscount Nuffield, Doctor of Civil Laws *honoris causa* of the University of Oxford, multi-millionaire and benefactor extraordinary has also been called "a pathetic figure", the "dullest

and saddest" of characters and "a Philistine to the core". He gave
immense sums to the university he had little time for. Nuffield
College was his own creation. He endowed professorial chairs,
founded scholarships, put up the cash for research fellowships,
offered hand-outs to colleges whose finances were strained, built
medical schools and laboratories. Rather late in the day, the
university gave him a D.C.L. in 1931 and followed this up in
1937 with an honorary Master of Arts degree. Gown was late
but Town was later. It was not until 1951 that he received the
freedom of the city for whose prosperity he was so largely
responsible. In spite of all his achievements, he was always a poor
little rich man, "kind to children, but arid and sapless . . .".

Perhaps symbolically, the yard of his premises in Longwall
backed on to the only section of the city wall still standing more
or less as originally built. It was a nice twist of fate that placed
Will Morris on one side and the dons of one of Oxford's oldest
colleges on the other. In those days the future tycoon was far too
busy to bother with bookish men. And for their part, the learned
ones were quite content to pursue the even tenor of their way.
They were vaguely aware that Morris was the chap who kept
the bicycle shop at 48 High Street. Their musings may have been
occasionally disturbed by the rattle of his machinery over the
college wall. But in their wildest dreams, they cannot have foreseen the part to be played by this small and single-minded man
in the shaping of things to come. Safe inside the high and solid
stonework flanking their walks and pleasaunces, they could take
comfort in a sense of enclosure and the remembrance of things
past.

It is from the academic side, from the delightful gardens of
New College that the best view of the old fortifications can be
had. That they should remain intact in this place is no accident.
Nor is it due to the efforts of early preservationists like that other
William Morris, who had such a splendid time in Oxford with
his pre-Raphaelite chums.

The wall stands preserved here because of a solemn undertaking given by William of Wykeham, the famous founder of this
"New St. Mary College of Winchester in Oxford". As part of
the bargain made when the site was purchased, he promised that
those parts of the defences lying within college precincts would
be kept in good repair for all time. City walls have long been an

anachronism, but for nearly 600 years New College has scrupulously honoured the agreement made in 1380.

Running south from Longwall Street, the wall crossed High Street at the East Gate. In horse and coach days, this was the point at which royalty and visiting celebrities usually entered the city. From Wheatley, the old London road climbed wooded slopes to the highwayman haunt of Shotover Plain before dropping steeply through Headington to the Cherwell. By the river, Magdalen Bridge and the magnificent tower of Magdalen College were the great prelude to many a triumphal drive up "the stream-like windings of that glorious street" known to every generation of undergraduates as The High.

Five years after the victory of Agincourt and a century before the tower was completed, Henry V rode down from Shotover with a flashing retinue of knights. Kings had come this way before him and many more were to come after; queens of England, too. The first Elizabeth made two royal progresses to the city. Until her namesake, the Queen Mother, was entertained at Christ Church in 1946, she was the only woman—as well as the only queen—ever to have been officially wined and dined at the high table of an Oxford college.

The East Gate was pulled down in 1771. A bottleneck in an otherwise wide and busy thoroughfare, it was for long an impedance to traffic. A succession of inns and hostelries afterwards occupied the site, the latest of which, the Eastgate Hotel, stands at the junction of The High with Merton Street, once called Coach and Horses Lane after an earlier tavern. The line of the wall closely follows what is still no more than a lane to the sudden corner now marked by the very modern 'lodging' of the Warden of Merton College. It then continues along the side of the college gardens to the south-east corner of the old defences, before turning westward across Merton Fields in the direction of Christ Church.

Some portions of the wall still survive here, as at New College. They have defined Merton's southern boundary for more than 700 years. Like William of Wykeham, the founder, Walter de Merton, entered into certain undertakings when he bought his original plot of land. At first, a strip of ground inside the wall was "retained by the king, that access might be had ... by soldiers in case of war ...". By a document signed on 30th

August 1266, however, permission was given for the college to
extend its site right up to the wall, on the understanding that
provision was made for "posterns under the walls on the east and
west, for access in time of war . . .".

It is interesting to note that until the completion of the Fellows'
Quadrangle nearly four centuries later, no buildings at all were
erected on this important piece of land. Even today, what
remains of the old wall is left untouched and helps to support the
garden terrace. From the field path below, known as Dead Man's
Walk, there are splendid views across Christ Church Meadow to
the rivers. This walk, incidentally, is said to take its name from
an incident in the Civil War. The dead man was a certain Colonel
Windebank, put up against the wall and shot here by Prince
Rupert for daring to surrender Bletchingdon, a village north of
the city, to the Parliamentary forces.

The wall was vital to Oxford's defence for a very long time.
It is therefore not surprising to find that many agreements as to
access, upkeep and other matters, were made from the twelfth
century onwards. Not all were so scrupulously observed as those
entered into by Merton College and New College. From time to
time the authorities had considerable trouble with property owners
who placed their own personal interests before the security of the
town as a whole. The monks of St. Frideswide's Priory, on the
site of which Christ Church now stands, were always something
of a problem.

In 1285, for example, it is recorded that the prior had wantonly
"thrown down the battlements of the king's wall across the
courtyard of St. Frideswide, behind which men used to pass and
to stand for defence of the town; had appropriated it for the
monastery court, and had built instead a plain wall upon which no-
one could go . . .". A hundred years later, another prior, John de
Dodworth was "threatened by the mayor, the chancellor of
Oxford and many scholars" because he tried to stop the townsfolk from using a gate in the city wall which happened to stand
on priory land.

Some of these priors seem to have been over-proud men and
at times irritatingly obtuse. Laws made for laymen were not
made for them. Kings were by God appointed, but so were
priors, by God! In Oxford, St. Frideswide's had been a religious
site since early Saxon times. The first little church, burnt down

by the Danes in 1002, had housed the bones of a patron saint. For all their military precision, even the Normans had sufficiently respected the sanctity of priory land to build the city wall around instead of through them.

Part of the evidence can still be seen. Merton's section of the wall continues behind the garden of its next-door neighbour and one-time tenant, Corpus Christi College. At what was once St. Frideswide's churchyard and is now the Canons' Garden of Christ Church Cathedral, the wall made a big detour around the boundaries of the old priory, not really getting back onto a direct course until it reached the South Gate. At the college of Christ Church the nineteenth-century Meadow Building backs onto the longest length of the deviation. The position of this Victorian-Gothic barrack block in relation to Merton and Corpus Christi shows just how far the Normans had to depart from the straight and narrow in order to accommodate the prior and his brethren.

Guarding the main road to Abingdon, the ancient South Gate straddled St. Aldate's Street until the early years of the sixteenth century. It was probably the first of the city gates to be demolished and only a powerful man would have had the temerity to order such destruction. Such a man was Wolsey, until his downfall the favourite of Henry VIII and in his day one of the most influential figures in Europe. When he decided to build his grandiose 'Cardinal College' on the site of the priory, the old archway was a nuisance and seemed likely to spoil the architecture. So down it had to come.

For nearly 500 years, the stretch of St. Aldate's between Carfax and South Gate was known as Fish Street. Beyond the gate, the road continued across marshy ground as a causeway, raised above flood level on a series of low arches. Although not a bridge, these became the 'Grandpont', the name still given to the residential district around Folly Bridge and south of the river. During the twelfth and thirteenth centuries, however, Fish Street—alias St. Aldate's—was at first simply 'Jewry' and later 'Great Jury Lane'. The names have a fairly obvious origin. Vital for the supplying of money to the privy and public purse, many Jews crossed to England with William the Conqueror. Until they were expelled from the country in 1290, a considerable Jewish community thrived in Oxford. There was no ghetto as such, but their favoured quarter lay immediately to the east of St. Aldate's, centred upon a synagogue which was built close to the corner of Blue Boar Street.

As in Norwich, York and other towns, these early financiers built themselves substantial stone houses, far superior to the simpler wooden dwellings in which most of the population lived. The Blue Boar Inn, which stood for centuries after on the site of the present municipal library, was one of them. Unidentified fragments of others are probably hidden within the fabric of some of the colleges. None survives intact. It is certain, however, that several 'Jew Houses' became 'halls'—those fore-runners of the colleges in which groups of self-governing students lived hostel-fashion under the surveillance of a 'principal'. There are records of a 'Jacob's Hall' and a 'Moyses Hall' being rented out for this purpose. And early in the thirteenth century, even the city guildhall was owned by 'Moses, the son of Isaac . . .'.

In medieval Oxford the long-bearded Jews were familiar figures. Frequently mocked, everybody's scapegoats, they were often the victims of unofficial persecution. Sometimes they were goaded into hitting back, answering blow with blow, insult with insult. When racial feelings ran high, they had good cause to be fearful. Grudgingly tolerated, they must always have led uneasy lives.

In spite of all, they prospered. Their chief business was money and at making it they had long been expert. They lent out gold at exorbitant rates of interest, thereby incurring the enmity of all who had to borrow from them. Poor students, penurious nobles, the university itself, all stood in their debt. That they managed to thrive was due only to the fact that they were an essential part of the economy and as such, had the continuous—if reluctant—protection of the throne.

After the general expulsion, they were not seen again in Oxford for more than 300 years. In 1650, that old gossiper of Merton, Anthony Wood, noted in his diary that: "Jacob, a Jew, opened a coffey house in the Parish of St. Peter in the East, and there it was drank by some who delighted in noveltie . . .".

When Jacob's medieval forebears departed, streets and buildings with Jewish associations gradually acquired new names. The synagogue disappeared, not to be replaced until Victorian times. Great Jury Lane became 'le Fysshe Strete', for here now was the liveliest trading area of the town where fishmongers set up their stalls on Oxford's twice-weekly market days. There were so many of them, and the Christian demand for "fresh fish on fast days and Friday" so great, that the street was often completely blocked. A coroner's inquest of 1320 gives an account of a particularly messy killing among the roach and eels and pikerels of Fish Street. A man running in panic towards Carfax to escape the sword of an attacker was unable to get clear "because of the tables of the fishmongers". But in the event, it was the pursuer who was slain. Finding the way barred, the intended victim also found courage. He stood his ground, turned the tables in more ways than one, and promptly ran the would-be killer through.

The naming of streets in accordance with their principal trades is a natural and universal custom. Until the end of the thirteenth century, The Broad (a comparatively modern title) was always Horsemonger Street. Slaying Lane, hugging the wall beyond South Gate, was where the butchers had their slaughter houses. In 1556, they moved in a body to Butcher Row—now part of Queen Street—the city fathers having provided stalls for them in the roadway. Beasts were killed in the street and here it was decreed that "the bochers of the City shall enjoy their standings in the new Shambles, paying xxiiii shillings a year for every shop . . .".

Meanwhile, the old shambles in Slaying Lane stood empty until Oliver Smyth, three times mayor, bought some of the buildings and turned them into a brew house. The lane thereafter became Brewer Street. On the west side of Cornmarket Street, a passage once called Drapery Lane needs no explanation, nor does Cornmarket itself, known to earlier generations as Northgate Street. The actual 'market' was an open-sided structure put up to protect sacks of corn from the weather. It stood in the middle of the street from 1536 to the time of the Civil War. In 1644, when the city was still the king's headquarters and seemed likely to be put under siege, Royalist soldiers pulled the building down, the leadwork of the roof being melted down for bullets.

It is not surprising to find a few old streets in Oxford with names of academic origin. As far back as 1275, for example, there is mention of a Schools Street, part of which—as the narrowest part of Radcliffe Street—still runs up the side of St. Mary's, the university church. On both sides of this little lane were once situated "most of the schools or lecture rooms used by the 'Regent Masters' in the Middle Ages . . .'". Here also was a tightly-packed group of those early 'halls', some of which later became colleges. At least eight of them were crowded together along the cobbled footway. St. Thomas, Brasenose and University Halls eventually developed into Brasenose College. Across the street, Black Hall, Glass Hall and Staple Hall were demolished in the eighteenth century to make room for Radcliffe Square and James Gibbs' magnificently domed Camera.

Some of the 'academic' streets have disappeared completely, or have changed their names. Civil School Lane, where Roman Law was taught, was swept away when Wolsey started to build his great Cardinal College. Vine Hall, another student house, gave its name to a lane which has long been hidden beneath the later buildings of Christ Church. Its last remaining length is now the uninspiring Alfred Street, which joins The High opposite to the Mitre Hotel.

Other streets, such as New College Lane, Oriel Street and Queen's Lane took their titles naturally from the colleges they served. And at least one name originated in the age-old desire of the scholar for peace and quiet in which to con his books. Market Street, once lined with 'halls', used to be known in medieval days as Chayne or Cheyney Lane. The name arose from iron chains which were hung across each end of the roadway, their purpose being to prevent noisy traffic from entering. The chains were first mentioned in 1315 and were still in use three centuries later.

All these lanes and thoroughfares lay within the wall. Except for a few isolated buildings, there was little outside development until the time of the Tudors. Broad Street, which next to The High is Oxford's finest street, was not even paved until 1674. Before this, it was little more than a rough dirt road. After the horse traders had taken their touting elsewhere, the name of Horsemonger Street was forgotten and it became Canditch, mainly on account of the town ditch that stank and stagnated in the shadow of the north wall. Across this rutted way stood a mere handful of scholastic halls, set among a scattering of smaller houses. Until the sixteenth century, the only other structures of importance along the future Broad Street were the early buildings of Balliol and the monastic foundation of Durham College, later to be re-named Trinity. Like the colleges that followed them, most of the halls were clustered thickly together inside the town. At the time of the founding of Merton, the first college proper, there were over 100 halls and hostels in the city itself, but no more than half a dozen outside.

In this perambulation of the walls, historical browsing has taken us half a mile and several centuries off course. To complete the circuit, we must push back in time through these shouting streets of medieval Oxford to the smells of Fish Street and the South Gate. From here, Brewer Street *alias* Slaying Lane precisely follows the wall as far as St. Ebbe's Street, once called Little Bailey because of its proximity to the Castle. At this point there was long ago still another postern in the wall, this one known as Littlegate. Like all the other gates, it has not survived, but the name is preserved in that of a street nearby.

When Brewer Street was built, it ran so close to the wall that development was possible only on the south side. On the other, the walls rose abruptly; an uncompromising man-made cliff which became the boundary of Broadgates Hall, the forerunner of Pembroke College. Until Victorian times, the top of the walls formed part of the college terrace, at one end of which was perched a charming stone 'pagoda'. When Dr. Johnson was in residence as a 'poor servitor' of Pembroke, this gazebo was used as a summer common room and, to judge by old engravings, a most delightful place it must have been.

From Littlegate, the wall swung across open land to link up with the West Gate and outworks of the castle. Nowadays, the line is ill-defined and may be completely lost when the modern rebuilding of the St. Ebbe's district is completed.

The old wool roads from the Cotswolds came into the town through the West Gate, the site of which is at the end of Castle Street, near to the yard of the prison. It was in this twilight area, now joyless but then green and pleasant, that the first Franciscan friars settled in England. In 1224, nine of them travelled from Pisa and established a community that was to flourish in Oxford for more than 300 years. With the brethren of other religious orders, the Grey Friars played an important part in the growth of the university.

These Franciscans erected their original buildings on a plot of ground that lay between Church Street and the city wall. Henry

III sent for the roof of their chapel a number of oak beams cut from trees in his royal forest of Savernake. Soon afterwards, they were presented with a large house close by, one of the many dwellings built with their backs to the wall. The gift was made subject to various conditions, one being that the friars were to keep their particular length of the fortifications in good repair. This was a serious duty placed upon the occupiers of all 'mural mansions' within the city. The rule applied to everyone, whether humble householders or large corporate bodies like New College or Merton. Within a year or two, however, the brothers were relieved of the obligation to repair, the responsibility then being assumed by the town authorities.

In 1244, finding themselves short of space, the friars managed to acquire a considerable stretch of land on the other side of the wall from their house and other buildings. This brought problems. The city wall now ran right through the middle of their property and divided it into two parts, each of which was quite inaccessible from the other. The difficulty seemed to have been overcome when permission was given for them to demolish the offending ramparts, providing that "a crenellated wall like the rest" was built around the whole of the new area in continuation of the defences. The same procedure had been adopted at St. Frideswide's, years before.

The brothers made a start on demolition and went as far as to make a large breach in the walls. At this stage, if there was not actually panic in the ranks, they must have realized that neither themselves nor their finances would ever stand the strain of erecting several hundred yards of brand new city wall, complete with bastions and battlements. Prudently, they decided to leave well and the wall alone. The two halves of the friary were quietly connected by a little gateway! But they did not entirely escape liability for their depredations. The king made them close up the breach, decreeing that one side of the big new church they were planning must be placed so as to fill up the gap. In consequence, its interior was always of an awkward and irregular shape.

The early records of Oxford are full of such accounts. Disputes, lawsuits, agreements and disagreements abound and few people were more litigious than the friars. Minor irritations frequently sparked off major explosions. Small differences expanded into great and sometimes farcical issues. The recording quills of the clerks fairly flew over the parchment, providing a basic source of information for future historians.

Much of their additional land beyond the wall was turned by the Franciscans into walks and gardens. Their new church was large and impressive. Its founder and chief benefactor was Richard Plantagenet, Duke of Cornwall, 'King of the Romans' and brother of Henry III. When he died in 1272, his heart was placed in a casket and buried before the high altar. The bodies of noblemen and ladies rested nearby. And by tradition, that most famous of friars, Roger Bacon, was brought to his long home here.

The House of the Grey Friars grew in size and importance, receiving many gifts and legacies from prominent citizens who were later to be interred beneath the floor of the church. Not long before the general dissolution of the monasteries, Dr. London, the 'visitor' sent by Henry VIII to inquire into its condition wrote of "this great huge house" that had "pretty islands; well wooded; one fair orchard and sundry pretty gardens and lodgings . . .".

But the end was not far off. Once prosperous, the eighteen friars still in residence were now very hard up. Most of their plate and jewels had already been pawned or sold. They had even torn up water pipes, melting them down and selling the lead to raise ready cash. In 1538, the visitor was reporting that the friary contained "much ruinous building".

There was much dilapidation and neglect, and this is hardly to be wondered at. Throughout England the same chill wind of change had also been blowing. In Oxford, where monastic establishments were remarkably thick upon the ground, their occupants had good reason to shiver. For most of them, the coming Reformation spelt revolution and for all of them the end of a world was at hand.

The Grey Friars shared in the universal dismay. Like Belshazzar, they had seen the writing on the wall. After their house was closed, they were dispersed. Some received a little money in compensation. Others were offered church livings. One became a physician. Another, after rising to eminence as Chancellor of Wells, fell from grace and was burnt at the stake for heresy.

Within a short time, all was in ruin. The conscientious Dr. London had suggested that the valuable site and its buildings might become the centre of a fulling industry. This, he said, "would marvellously help the town, and give them great occasion to fall to clothing ...". William Stumpe, a rich clothier, had recently rented Osney Abbey, only half a mile away, for a similar purpose. There, it was his intention to set up weaving shops for the employment of no less than 2,000 people.

Both projects failed to get under way. Later, a tannery was erected on one of the 'pretty islands' but the extensive friary buildings quickly fell into disuse. Before long, the once-great church was a heap of rubble. And by the beginning of the eighteenth century, its pleasure garden or 'paradis' had become a wilderness of weeds, though still known to the townspeople as the 'Paradise Garden'.

Today, a sadly neglected rectangle of drab houses called Paradise Square stands where the friars once took their ease. Somewhere beneath cracked paving stones may still lie the heart of a king, the bones of a genius. We shall never know. The whole area is being re-developed out of all recognition. By the time this book is printed, the only link with the past may be a neat plaque on a concrete wall. Or there may be nothing to tell of what was once here.

Other religious orders in and about Oxford suffered in the same way as the Franciscans. Houses belonging to the Dominican, Carmelite and Austin Friars were all suppressed in their turn. Outside the town, the famous and aristocratic nunnery of Godstow, the priory of Littlemore and the twin abbeys of Osney and Rewley were soon forced to close their doors. Some of their properties were bought by the colleges. Others were taken over by local tradesmen and merchants. It was also a time of rich pickings for entrepreneurs who, like William Stumpe of Malmesbury, saw the chance of a quick fortune.

Godstow became a picturesque ruin and has so remained. Of the two abbeys, scarcely a stone is left standing. Rewley is a name and a single shattered arch, lost in wasteland between the railway and the Oxford Canal. A depressing cemetery occupies the site of Osney. Long ago, both abbeys looked across open fields and water meadows towards the watchful towers of the castle. In the twentieth century, their ghosts have nothing for company but main line trains, goods yards, coal wharfs and a forest of electricity pylons.

Christ Church Cathedral

Gothic at Christ Church

With its moat, its great *donjon*, and its formidable battlements, the castle of Robert d'Oilly formed an impressive salient at the western end of the town. He was careful to link up his own walls with those originally built by the Saxons.

Under Nuffield College quadrangle is a section of the Norman moat. It was filled in long ago, but the first buildings of nearby St. Peter's College were erected on 'The Mounts'—great heaps of excavated soil piled up there when the moat was being dug in the eleventh century. They are still clearly recognizable.

Outside Nuffield College, the line of this deep dike is marked for some distance by the slow curve of Bulwarks Lane. Until the end of the eighteenth century, this meandering footway was Bullocks Lane. It had nothing to do with either ramparts or cattle, but was so called "from one Bullock, that carried the rubbish of the city there and built him a house in 1588 ...". At the end of George Street Mews, the sharp kink in the lane is where a postern stood. It was through this opening in the wall, which here dropped steeply into the waters of the moat, that Master Bullock's refuse carts passed on their way to the city dump beyond.

East of Bulwarks Lane, the walls can be picked up again in St. Michael's Street—the old Bocardo Lane—which ran just inside them. There was another postern gate here, at the junction with New Inn Hall Street. Of very ancient vintage, this street has had more names in its long history than any other in Oxford. The earliest records refer to it as North Baly. It then became successively Little Bayley, The Seven Deadly Sins, New Inn Lane, New Inn Hall Lane and was finally given its present title at about the time of the Napoleonic Wars.

There are logical reasons for most of these names. The 'Bayleys' reflect the proximity of the street to the castle. New Inn Hall was a student house rebuilt in 1476 on the site of the older Trilleck's Inn and is now the College of St. Peter-le-Bailey. But no-one has yet discovered how The Seven Deadly Sins came about. Did those early scholars who, according to Roger Bacon, "shocked the whole world with their vices" have something to do with it? Was the name merely that of an alehouse which they frequented? Or were those deadly sins a group of seven mean cottages that stood across the way from Trilleck's Inn? In the latter case, one may speculate as to the professions of their occupants, but in any case, the truth is uncertain!

4

Tom Tower, Christ Church

St. Michael's Street runs as far as Cornmarket, the site of the North Gate and the Bocardo Prison. Domesday, defence works and these many digressions end, as they began, at the oldest bit of building in Oxford: the sturdy tower of St. Michael-at-the-North Gate. Simple, strong and Saxon, it was built for battle as well as bells. Part of the original city and its life, it remains as such today.

The shape and size of that faraway Oxford has been traced at street level. So close to the ground, however, it is not easy to visualize as a whole. The bird's-eye view beloved of modern planners is necessary if we are to see the complete picture. Fortunately, this is possible without recourse to wings or helicopters. There are several high places—St. Mary's church tower is one and the cupola of the Sheldonian Theatre another—from which the essential all-embracing view can be obtained.

Half-closed eyes and a little imagination can wonderfully expunge the impedimenta of the contemporary scene. The sky and the distant hills are timeless and within the wit of man, the twists and turnings of old streets nearly so. The mind is soon carried back to the Middle Ages; to the period in which the university began to grow.

IV

THE SEEDS OF WISDOM

Why Oxford? How did a university come to be here? What made this small medieval city so attractive to scholars? Why should it be preferred to perhaps a dozen others, all offering similar opportunities? Did Oxford have some special, undefinable magic of its own?

Answers to these questions can only be uncertain. Modern universities are founded but ancient ones, like buildings revealed in a clearing mist, are seen gradually to emerge. In the Middle Ages, some cities provided the right sort of air for the growth of scholarship; a soil into which the seeds of wisdom could send their roots. Oxford happened to be one of these places.

At the beginning of the twelfth century, however, it was far from being the only town in England with an atmosphere of learning. Schools it certainly had, and some small fame as a teaching centre. But in possessing these things, it was by no means unique. At Cambridge, the monks of Barnwell Priory had already established a reputation as sound teachers. Religious houses at Stamford, Reading, St. Albans, Canterbury, Northampton and Winchester were equally well known for their instruction. London had many monastic schools and must surely have seemed the most likely city of all to follow the lead of Paris in becoming the home of a great national university. In the event, there was to be no London University for another 600 years. If the capital had early ambitions in this direction, they were soon overshadowed by the growing prestige of Oxford and Cambridge.

Yet the Oxenforde of this time could claim no particular enchantment. Its spacious days as the tilt-yard of philosophers, the dreaming ground of poets, were still far ahead. It was not yet the nursery of greatness. Nor had it even begun to acquire any of its strangely seductive aura, that later mystique which enfolded it as the land of intellectual heart's desire.

Promising young men who wanted to sit at the feet of the famous went elsewhere. They were drawn to Salerno and Bologna; to Padua, Toulouse, Montpellier. Or, like Roger Bacon and Thomas à Becket, they made their way to Paris where all the great masters taught and the fabulous Abelard could be heard expounding his "rational theology".

Paris, not Oxford, was then the convenient Mecca of aspiring English clerks. Thousands of them passed through the schools of the Île de la Cité. Here, they formed one of the 'nations' of which most medieval universities were comprised. Together with Italians, Spaniards, Greeks, Germans, Netherlanders, Scots, Irish and native Frenchmen they made up the *universitas*, the scholastic guilds, later the *studium generale*, that prototype academic community of which all were members, whatever their country of origin. Babbling drunk, these early undergraduates cursed and argued in their mother tongues. Stone cold or near sober, they conversed in the universal language of Latin, spoken by all, understood by all. And on the left bank of the Seine, *la rive gauche* then as now, they crowded into the lodgings of what is still the 'Latin' Quarter.

English scholars must have greatly enjoyed life in France. Their best masters were celebrities. No better teaching was to be found anywhere. The clash of disputation, the meeting of minds, the mixing of races produced a heady ferment that seems to have been quite irresistible to those early seekers after knowledge. The Dark Ages were at an end, the horizon bright. Men of letters as well as men of action were now walking the corridors of power. Kings were beginning to realize that mastery lay in intellect rather than muscle. Europe was experiencing a pre-Renaissance and Paris had become the intellectual centre of the world.

By comparison, an education in England still seemed rather redbrick and homespun. Paris represented glamour and excitement while Oxford and Cambridge were often regarded as bucolic backwaters. Such unfair notions persisted for many years. Long after the two English universities were highly successful going concerns, "the finest scholars still sought to go to Paris . . . and few great pre-Reformation teachers had failed to study on the Continent . . . .".

Youth, as always, hankered after the taste and colour of foreign parts. Rich men, seeking for their sons what the world thought best, were quick to send them across the Channel.

This is not to suggest that all scholars who went abroad were wealthy. On the contrary, some were poor to the point of wretchedness. But in those days, penury was no detriment to youthful ambition. Hard-up students with good brains were always being subsidized by the Church, for after all, the chief aim of medieval education was the continuous production of orthodox clerics. For those who failed to get the backing of monastery or abbey, there was the honourable alternative of 'working one's way through college'—a system as common in twelfth-century France as it was to become much later in twentieth-century America. And as a last resort, the really poverty-stricken could always fall back on begging; a widespread practice that was frowned upon but generally tolerated.

So it cannot be said that Oxford of the early days was a sort of second-best study centre for those who could not afford to attend a foreign university. Getting off to a good start, Paris was both famous and fashionable. But England's turn was soon to come. Paris was already giving something of itself to Oxford and was to give much more. Sometime before 1117, Theobald of Étampes, a Frenchman calling himself a 'Master of Oxenforde' was lecturing on the scriptures in a school set up by the monks of St. Frideswide's. He was the first of several such 'masters' whose names have been recorded. Robert Pullen, a Devon man, came over from Paris in 1133 to teach theology. He was followed a few years later by the jurist, Vacarius, brought from Bologna to lecture on Roman Law, the modern subject of its day.

There must have been many others, bringing new ideas, new methods, a new outlook. Paris and Bologna were the archetypal universities of Europe, by now becoming well organized and largely self-governing. And with its embryo colleges already taking shape, Paris, in particular, was to provide both model and inspiration for the future development of Oxford and Cambridge.

Emigrant teachers were not the only academics to come from Paris to England. Once their formal education was completed, it was natural that the majority of English scholars should return home. When—as in many cases—their years abroad had been paid for by the Church, home meant the religious house which sponsored them. So young and not-so-young men took themselves and their gowns and their degrees to abbeys, monasteries and priories throughout the length and breadth of the country. Rich youths returned to the lands of their fathers, sometimes sadder, always a little wiser, having escaped at least the ultimate effects of sword-play, drink, general dissipation and that French disease which Parisians insisted on calling *la maladie Anglaise*.

Some, however, came to Oxford. Here were good monastic schools, growing in size and importance, the demand for teachers becoming more and more insistent as students clamoured for instruction. Theobald lectured to groups of 100 at a time. The student population steadily increased—some of them "a mob of wild, half-starved boys". Wild or not, they wanted to hear what Theobald and his contemporaries had to say. So many packed themselves into the little lecture rooms that doors had to be barred and fights were frequently breaking out amongst those unable to get in.

Clearly, a situation now existed very favourable to the formation of a *studium generale* on Parisian lines. The time was ripe. The climate was right. The soil had been well prepared by toilers in the schools. And men who had enjoyed the privileges conferred by that greater scholastic body in France were busily sowing their ideas and enthusiasms.

Seen in retrospect, however, these things are still not enough to fully explain how Oxford, rather than other towns, found itself with a university. Our brief cross-Channel excursion inevitably brings us back to the original basic question: why Oxford?

Simple questions often call for complex answers and this one is no exception. The existence of schools in Oxford and the undeniable general 'atmosphere of learning' are only part of the picture. The rest must be pieced together from a haphazard collection of circumstances, linked here and there by one or two happy accidents and arbitrary decisions. Even at this, much is still vague and a matter for surmise. No one ever said, for example, "The times are propitious, the place perfect—*ergo*—let us found a university here." Such Godlike utterances are reserved for more modern times. In medieval Oxford there was merely a slow awakening to the fact that something new had materialized; that somehow or other, and almost unnoticed, a university had come into being.

It is accepted that the climate of scholarship played no small part in this emergence. Yet as we know, the same sort of academic air existed in other places, some not far away. It follows, therefore, that other factors must have influenced events and it is these differences that we must look for.

To begin with, Oxford in its twelfth-century context was a considerable city. Not so much in physical size, but in its overall status and prestige. Although no longer a vital strategic point on the frontier between Wessex and the Danelaw, it was still economically important. A centre of communications, a prosperous trading borough, ranking ninth in the kingdom in the amount of taxes to be paid to the crown, it was not lightly to be passed over.

Unlike Cambridge, the marsh town once derided by Oxonians as 'that little place in the Fens' whose *raison d'être* as a university city is even more of a puzzle, Oxford was well placed to stay near the centre of affairs. We have already remarked upon its role as 'England's second capital'. The Saxons had made much of the town in this respect and the tradition was continued by the Normans. Its connections with the throne were not weakened by the coming of William the Conqueror. Rather the reverse. After the Conquest, it was quickly favoured by the new line of French kings. Not only was Oxford a useful political focal point —a neutral ground upon which opposing factions might meet— but also a place in which the monarch could relax from the cares of state. It was much to royal liking.

Woodstock, a crown demesne even in Alfred's day, became a hunting lodge and was soon turned by William's son, Henry I, into palace, pleasure ground and England's first zoo. A contemporary account gives us the impression of a kind of medieval Woburn or Longleat: "There were sent from divers outlandish lords: lions, leopards, strange spotted beasts, porcupines, camels and suchlike animals ... to a park enclosed around with stone walls in which the king did nourish and maintain the delights of such creatures."

In the same park, the second Henry did later nourish and maintain creatures of less fearsome aspect. Chief among these was his favourite mistress, the Fair Rosamond, who died at Godstow nunnery and was buried there with loud lamentation before the high altar. For Rosamond, the king built the legendary bower at

Woodstock, setting it safely in the middle of a vast maze. Bower, maze and palace are all gone, the last bits of their ruin being torn down by the redoubtable Sarah, Duchess of Marlborough during the construction of Blenheim.

The lives of Henry I and his grandson were not all animal delights. Indeed, some of their activities are useful pointers to the way things were developing in Oxford. Both were highly literate—a quality which did not always go with kingship—and both were cultured men. Henry I, nicknamed 'Beauclerc' because of his scholarly accomplishments, was always proud of his excellent education. He could read and write Latin with ease, was familiar with the finer points of law, knew something of Old English (still the common language of his people) and as his menagerie at Woodstock witnessed, took a genuine interest in natural history. He "delighted himself much with the air and conversation of clerks", a pleasure even more enjoyed by Henry II.

Besides Woodstock with its 14 miles of boundary wall, Beauclerc also built at Oxford his great palace of Beaumont. This huge complex of buildings stood a little beyond the North Gate. The exact site has not been determined, but it lay roughly between St. Giles and Worcester College. Present-day Gloucester Green with its stinking turmoil of buses occupies what was once part of the palace gardens and the old cattle market that used to be here stood on the site of the royal bowling greens.

With the exception of Charles I, for whom the city served as headquarters for three years of the Civil War, Henry II seems to have spent more time in Oxford than any other English king. Writing in 1483, the early historian John Rous recalls that "the said noble King, a person of great literature, took great delight to abide and inhabit in Oxford . . .". Henry lived mostly at Beaumont, and there were born his two sons, Richard Lion Heart and the less admired John.

Henry, first of the Plantagenets, took over Beaumont from Stephen, last of the Norman kings, whose reign had plunged England into anarchy. Already becoming overcrowded with students, Oxford was the scene of some high drama in those troublous times. In the winter of 1142 Stephen, battling with barons, put the castle under siege. His chief aim was to capture his popular rival to the throne, the dowager Empress Matilda,

Henry's mother and 'Lady of the English'. But to the king's discomfiture, she escaped to Wallingford, clothing herself and four knights in white gowns and making her way on foot for 6 miles across the frozen Thames and a countryside deep in snow. Soon afterwards, the castle was taken by storm and its inhabitants massacred, but the royal bird had flown.

Of Beaumont, nothing is left save a plaque at the end of Beaumont Street and a time-eaten archway in the garden of a house in the Woodstock Road, reputedly salvaged from the ruins. The palace gradually fell into disuse as a royal dwelling and in 1318 was handed over to the Carmelites by Edward II. Narrowly escaping capture by the Scots at the Battle of Bannockburn, the king vowed in gratitude to found a monastery. His princely gift to the White Friars of Oxford was the result.

The friars found the upkeep of this rambling pile something of a burden, although they stayed in occupation for more than 200 years. In 1328 they were asking the mayor to "remove harlots and other women of bad character" from the outbuildings and houses adjoining. Later, they were letting off rooms to secular students and just before the dissolution of the monasteries were properly shocked when "a girl of thirteen disguised as a boy was found in the cubicle of one Browne, a scholar...".

Beaumont maintained its royal associations for a long time. Regarded to some extent as a health resort, the brethren provided accommodation for many 'persons of distinction', particularly those who were close to the court. Bishops, abbots and church dignitaries were frequent visitors, as were minor royalties. John Rous, who lived in the days of Henry VI, tells us that the king "did stay in the Carmelite's house at Oxford as in his own palace...".

By 1538, when monasteries were being closed down wholesale, the once-proud Beaumont was already far gone to rack and ruin. The end is a familiar story, common to most of Oxford's religious houses. The prior had let some of the friary lands, sold most of the plate and jewels and had even begun to sell off the great elm trees surrounding the property; all in a desperate effort to stave off disaster. The final chapter was soon written. Land and buildings were sold to a country squire for £388 5s. Except for the refectory, which was used as a parish poorhouse until 1596, nearly everything else was pulled down. In that year, what was left in the way of stone and timber went to the fellows of St. John's College for a ridiculously low price. The ruins must have been very substantial: more than 1,000 wagonloads of material were carted away, most of it being utilized in the construction of the college library and other buildings.

The university was born during the lifetimes of two enlightened kings. This cannot have been entirely fortuitous. Both saw the value of learning. Both were able to appreciate that knowledge is ultimately power. Both recognized that the country could best be ruled through an educated class. Henry I chose his ministers with care and most were men of no mean intellect. When Henry II came to the throne, the realm was administered not by militaristic nobles, but through a growing body of clerks—some of them Oxford trained—who comprised a rudimentary civil service.

Whether the two Henrys ever foresaw a future in which Oxford would be turning out a long succession of statesmen, we cannot know. What does seem certain is their early realization that the trained mind was a key to successful government. This is surely one of the reasons for the continuing favour they showed to the town. The schools were encouraged and patronized; citizen guilds were recognized and protected; privileges were given, charters granted and confirmed. Oxford was marked out as a royal town.

This might well have been sufficient in itself to attract the scholars, for in uncertain times, it was no small advantage to be under the benevolent eye of the king. Even so, students were still to be found in other centres. Stamford, for example, with several monasteries, seventeen churches and hundreds of clerks under instruction, was a serious rival.

What seems really to have made Oxford University inevitable (and for that matter, Cambridge University too) was a deliberate act of Henry II. In 1167, following a quarrel with the French king, Louis VII, all English scholars at Continental universities were ordered to return home.

Simultaneously, Louis expelled all foreigners from Paris, whereupon Henry issued a further decree which forebade Englishmen from going anywhere overseas to study.

The practical result of these royal manoeuvrings was that within a matter of weeks, some 2,000 masters and students were back in England wondering what to do with themselves. After a pause for taking stock, the great majority made their way to Oxford, descending in droves upon a town quite unprepared for such an invasion. Within a few months, their numbers had grown alarmingly, added to by hundreds of frustrated clerks to whom not only Paris, but Bologna, Salerno and the other European universities were also barred.

This army of scholars moved in on Oxford. They occupied the city by a process of infiltration rather than taking it by storm, but took possession just as effectively. The place was overwhelmed, its resources quite inadequate to meet the new demands. The simple scholastic machinery of the old schools seemed likely to break down under the sudden load. Confusion reigned everywhere.

It is not difficult to imagine the scene: the streets thronged with strangers, some in rags, some richly clad, some in outlandish garb but all of them arguing, trying out their Latin, indulging in disputation, flinging high-faluting phrases to the four winds as they wandered about in a vain search for teachers. They must have been regarded with disquiet and amazement by the citizens. This totally unexpected influx may have presented itself as a great opportunity for making money, but it also brought in its train some serious problems. Armies—and this was certainly one—have to be fed, clothed, housed and otherwise provided for. As yet, there were no colleges, few halls and a dearth of good lodgings. Food supplies which were sufficient for a population of 3,500 were not likely to satisfy nearly twice that number. Nor could the economy of the town be altered overnight. Inevitably, prices rose sharply and much to the disadvantage of the newcomers. Already, the first stirrings of enmity between townsfolk and scholars could be discerned.

After their initial dismay, the native Oxonians soon got to grips with the situation. The Oxfordshire man has always been realistic in his approach to life. Here were scholars hungry for knowledge, but even hungrier for other things. Some were poor and therefore a nuisance, but most had some cash in their purses. The Town made sure that as much as possible was transferred to its own. The Gown was going to be made to pay for whatever inconveniences it inflicted. The two were showing themselves as separate entities at a very early date.

So the real beginning of the university was dramatic, if unplanned. Its early years were shaky. More than once, its very existence was threatened by mass migrations of dissatisfied scholars to other towns. In 1209, after a dispute in which King John sided with the townspeople, the whole *studium* "dispersed to Reading and to Cambridge in which latter place many remained"—and there helped to form the nucleus of the sister university. Later there were similar large-scale desertions to Northampton and Stamford. Fortunately, the errant scholars returned, but Stamford was a thorn in Oxford's flesh for many years. The traditional rivalry between them died hard. Not until 1827 were candidates for an Oxford degree released from the absurd necessity of swearing an oath never to give or attend lectures at Stamford!

The university has always been a very human organization. Yet to describe it as such in its early years is both truth and a contradiction in terms. Although it 'existed' well before the end of the twelfth century, it had never been 'organized'. Its growth was organic, but this is something rather different. For a long time, it had no statutes, no officials, no buildings and very little money. Like Topsy, it just growed.

In contrast, the first colleges were without exception formal creations. They were founded by men of wealth and provided from the start with rules of conduct and terms of reference. In all senses of the word, they had structure laid down in advance for the convenience and control of their members.

Of the colleges, more will be said in a later chapter. They were not to come upon the scene for another 100 years. In 1170, which is the point at which we end this one, Oxford University was already in being. It was soon to become even more famous than Paris. This happy outcome of his schemings no doubt delighted Henry II, however much a side issue it may originally have been. Thomas à Becket was murdered but Oxford lived. And as the historian Sir Charles Mallet reflected: 'As Becket lay dead by the altar steps of Canterbury, the life of the first English university began. . . .''

V

THE SEVEN HUNDRED YEARS WAR

So Oxford was overrun by students.

They were a plague of rats, a pack of wolves, a swarm of locusts. They brought disaffection, riot and pestilence. Drunkenness, thieving and lechery were the least of their offences. In their wake came killing, strife and infection. Civic liberties were "trodden underfoot until the city stood alone in its bondage among the cities of Europe". And it was not very long before "the burghers lived in their own town almost as the subjects of a conquering people . . .".

Harsh words, yet some would say scarcely strong enough to describe the developing situation. More than one mayor of Oxford could have prayed for a piper to play the whole scholastic rabble into perdition beneath Shotover Hill. In the centuries that followed, many a freeman of the burgh must have brooded darkly upon the injustice of its fate. Freeman? The very title was a misnomer, something of a laugh. Free to do what? Free to be what?

Free, it would seem, only to serve the scholar, now the dominant force in an economy that had the citizen firmly in thrall. Any freedoms that were going were reserved for the university, "the monstrous cuckoo in the nest" that never stopped growing and was never satisfied.

Like most things in Oxford, this sad state of affairs did not come about overnight. The erosion of civic power was gradual, the enthraldom of the people a slow business. But it went on steadily and at first was quite imperceptible. By the time the townsfolk began to waken up to what was happening, it had already happened. They were tightly held in an academic grip, within which they were to struggle helplessly for 700 years.

It is ironic that only six years before those expelled scholars came scuttling back from Paris, Oxford had been granted its first municipal charter by Henry II. Green, a historian always sympathetic to the common people, says of this moment: "It would have been hard for a burgher, flushed with the pride of its new charter, to have dreaded any danger to the liberties of his borough...."

Yet the danger was real and very near. Henry's petulance in bringing all his students home from France set in motion irreversible processes. However strenuously the citizens tried to kick over the traces—and this they tried many times—they still found themselves fixed firmly between the shafts. And if they dared to take the bit between their teeth, the scholastic body had no compunction about using the whip to show who was master. The town was not their town any more. It quickly became the Town; a separate and lower order of existence whose creatures had to keep their place and their distance.

The Town was a term of general derogation. Usually, a capital letter upgrades a noun. In this case it degraded a town. Oxford "had already seen centuries of borough life before a student appeared in its streets" but a proud past counted for nothing. Like all *conquistadores*, the scholars were arrogant and largely insensitive. If the natives were friendly, life was a little more pleasant. If they were hostile, it was necessary to put them down. Either way, the Gown was not over concerned.

Not until modern times, when Cambridge men lampooned Oxford University as "the Latin Quarter of Cowley" was the balance restored. As late as the 1870s, after long overdue reforms had been carried through against fierce opposition, the town was still "a mere offshoot of the university seeming to exist only by the grace or usurpation of prior university privileges...".

To Victorian academics, as to many before them, Oxford meant the university and that alone. The Gown mattered and was remembered in dull memoirs, common room recollections and anthologies of college gossip. The town hardly existed and the Town was something about which they could make snide remarks. Then, as always, it was made up of louts and yokels, people in trade, shopkeepers alternately dunning and smiling, quaint servants of questionable habits, noises in the street outside and the smell of the great unwashed. Within, the clever men talked of emancipation, Utopia and the great tomorrow and wished the talk would last forever.

John Richard Green listened, said little, but wrote much of the indignities heaped upon town and people, of those academic presumptions that century by century "had humbled the municipal freedom of Oxford to the dust and utterly crushed it".

This is not to say that the Gown was always at fault. On the contrary, the Town often asked for trouble and it was never slow in coming. Youth is quick-tempered and hot for action and the average age of medieval students was rarely more than 17. Clashes between respectable citizens and irrepressible teenagers were bound to occur, with or without cause. At first, however, the newcomers were welcomed with open hands, if not entirely with open arms. After the initial shock of invasion, the townsfolk settled down to making a profit out of the university, "no doubt thinking it would be easy to fleece simple scholars".

For a time, they succeeded. Exorbitant prices were charged for food, clothing, services, accommodation—particularly the latter. All the basic necessities were in short supply and for the scholars at least, the cost of living rose alarmingly.

But the 'simple scholars' were not so daft as some of them might have seemed. They began to kick against the avarice of tradesmen. They objected to paying 43 per cent interest on loans from Jewish usurers, and when rents rocketed to new heights, they complained to the monarch himself. In its excessive greed, the Town had gone a long way towards killing off the geese that were laying golden eggs in its lap. In 1231, the king sent a letter to the mayor of Oxford, warning him that if his fellow townsmen persisted in overcharging in a way that was "heavy and burdensome to the scholars ... they needs must leave Our city, and having abandoned the University, depart from Our land, which We in no respect desire ...".

The message was clear and the king's displeasure obvious. Like his earlier namesake, Henry III had no wish to see the scholars returning en masse to France. Two years before, indeed, "humbly compassionating the tribulation and not small griefs" then being endured by French students, he had made a valiant attempt to persuade the whole University of Paris to pack its bags and come to England.

The offer was not taken up. For a time, however, the Town became a little more circumspect in its dealings with the Gown. It was already beginning to lose out on the high rents racket.

Forming themselves into groups, more and more students were living on a rough co-operative basis, hiring whole houses, buying food in quantity and doing their own housekeeping. Such houses were, in fact, the first 'halls', many of which were later to become colleges in their own right.

In spite of the fierce indignation shown by scholars in the face of this blatant fleecing, there were also other reasons for the bloody brawling between Town and Gown that was now so common. After their first pleasure at the chance of quick profits, the townspeople soon developed a deep dislike of the university and its activities. This feeling, compounded of mistrust, ignorance and hurt pride turned into a smouldering resentment that was always likely to burst into flame. The scholars were strangers, yet they received privileges denied to freemen. When they committed offences against the common law, they were protected by ecclesiastical courts. If a student killed a townman, he was often let off with no more than a few months in prison. A citizen found guilty of murder or manslaughter was hanged without further ado. Increasingly, members of the university became a privileged class. They enjoyed benefits denied to the rest of the community. The royal smile was now turned upon them, rather than on the Town. The Church seemed indulgent to even their worst excesses and guarded them against the just wrath of outraged citizens.

It is small wonder that year after year, generation after generation, there was fighting and bloodshed. Men walked in fear and would not venture out of doors when the sun was down. And even in broad daylight there were high-noon encounters between individuals only too ready to use sword or cudgel.

The historian Rashdall comments: "There is probably not a single yard of ground in any part of the classic High Street between St. Martin's and St. Mary's which has not, at some time or another, been stained with blood. There are historic battlefields on which less has been spilt. . . ."

When riot ran about the streets and Town mobs fought with Gown mobs, this quarter-mile stretch of The High from Catte Street up to Carfax was always the accepted battleground. In the highly charged atmosphere of those days, a single small incident was enough to spark off an explosion of terrifying violence. Quite by accident, a student might stumble in the street and jostle against a townsman. An affray was soon in the making, with each looking wildly about and screaming for support.

One such affair took place in 1263. It began as a minor squabble, observed from a safe distance by an excitable scholar. Seeing fists raised, he ran to St. Mary's church and began to toll the 'Scholar's Bell', always the alarm signal when the Gown seemed to be getting the worst of an argument. Scores of clerks poured out of the inns and halls nearby in answer to the summons. Within minutes, the High Street was a struggling mass of students and townsmen, all doing their best to beat the living daylights out of each other.

The sound of bell answering bell in the university church of St. Mary and the city church of St. Martin must have been dreaded by the peaceable folk of Oxford. By no means all were fractious or desirous of sending opponents to hell. When trouble threatened, they quietly disappeared. The bonging of the riot bells was enough to clear The High like magic as the opposing factions assembled like small armies around the two churches. In the uneasy silence that followed, they glared at their enemy across the empty space before an odd shout or scream broke the spell and sent them charging into battle.

Then once more there was slashing and bashing, broken limbs, smashed heads, gouged eyes, daggers in guts and bruised bodies. Too often, there were dead bodies, for no niceties of conduct were taken into account, no rules of the game. It was played dirty and with a ferocity out of all proportion to the issues involved. These frequent mauls were accepted as part of the pattern of Oxford life, as inevitable as the seasons. Deplored by gentler souls, there were many who saw them as a necessary blood-letting, a release of dangerous emotions, a re-assertion of respective positions. Perhaps because they were partly therapeutic, these battles were more often than not indecisive. Nearly always, victory was claimed by both sides, although the score in terms of cracked skulls and mangled flesh may well have been fairly even. Needless to say, with a greater command of the written word at its disposal, the university's own records tend to wash the scholars whiter than white. We are left in no doubt as to who were the goodies and who the baddies.

In the long run, certainly, the Gown came out well and truly on top. As Ruth Fasnacht points out in her fine history of the

5

The Chapel, St. Edmund Hall
Merton College

city, "every time there was a dispute or riot, the almost invariable result was a further extension of University privileges at the expense of the Town . . .". The Gown may have lost battles, but it was always winning the war.

The really memorable riots took place during the first one and a half centuries of the university's life. They culminated in the deplorable happenings of 1355 when, on St. Scholastica's Day, more than 100 people were slaughtered and such dishonour was heaped upon the town that its people were made to feel the humiliation well into Victorian times. But this was not the end of strife or killing. Like the families in some Shakespearian drama, Town and Gown went feuding on without cease. The pages of Oxford's history are spattered with the blood of unfortunates unlucky enough to be caught up in the quarrelling.

Only the more serious affairs are fully recorded. Lesser skirmishes receive passing mention in letters, court proceedings and other contemporary documents. Down the years, there must have been thousands of minor 'incidents' of which there is no record at all: beatings-up in alleyways; terrified boys out on larks that suddenly turned sour; savage confrontations in ale-houses; desperate running feet and frantic knockings on doors.

The first big riot broke out in 1209 and started an upheaval that almost put an end to the university. The last student killing occurred in 1857, in which civilized year a 'townie' stabbed an undergraduate to death with a butcher's knife.

The trouble of 1209 was set off in typical medieval fashion by the lynching of two clerks for the murder of a local woman. Mad for revenge, a town gang grabbed the first two scholars they could find and strung them up. It turned out that both were innocent and there followed much violence and breaking of pates. The university demanded justice of the king, but wily John, fuming under an interdict placed on England by the Pope, had little love for the Church and its scholars. His sympathies were all with the town and he refused to take any action.

In high dudgeon the whole scholastic community packed up and left Oxford for other towns. For five years, there was no university. Students and masters went to Reading and Maidstone and a large number stayed for good in Cambridge. A few even trickled back to France—the final insult.

The citizens were hard hit by this mass desertion, although it was largely brought about by their own foolishness. It was claimed that no less than 3,000 clerks settled in Cambridge alone. The town quickly felt the pinch. The constant demand for goods and services had suddenly disappeared. Tradesmen geared up to an expanding economy began to fear ruin. The hotheads responsible for that original lynching party were soon being reviled by one and all. But worse was to happen.

Justice may have seemed a long time in coming, but when, in 1214, it finally arrived in the person of a papal legate, there was no doubt as to who was going to come off best. His quarrel with the Pope temporarily patched up, King John ratted on the town. An ordinance from Rome not only inflicted penalties on the citizens for their misdeeds, but rubbed in the salt by granting the university new privileges. The townsmen had to pay in perpetuity an annual fine of 52 shillings for the relief of poor scholars and in addition, provide a feast for 100 of them every year. The dinner was dropped long ago, but the fine is still paid and a yearly cheque for £3 1s. 6d. now goes into the Vice-Chancellor's fund for needy students.

Next, the rents of houses occupied by groups of clerks were to be cut by half for a period of at least ten years, and the rentals of new ones fixed at a reasonable figure by a committee of masters and freemen. Similarly, 'victuals and other necessaries' had to be sold to the scholars at fair prices. In future, there was to be no repetition of the rough justice meted out to the two unfortunate clerks whose demise was the cause of all the bother. Any student arrested in the town for misdemeanour was not to be dealt with by the civil authority, but must now be handed over to the Church for punishment. Meanwhile, those responsible for the hasty hanging were disgraced by having to undertake public penance, in those days no small matter. The final indignity was that every year fifty influential citizens should swear an oath promising to observe all the other indignities.

This ordinance was a package deal much to the liking of the scholars, and in some respects, its provisions were reasonable. The town had not only profited, but had profiteered by the coming of the university. Some control of rents and prices was long overdue. But the first nail to be knocked into the coffin of municipal liberty lay not in this, but in the proposal to place scholars who broke the law outside the jurisdiction of the town courts. Within a short time, clerks became completely immune from lay control and were able to cock a snook at the town in general and its law officers in particular. Indeed, this papal ordinance marked the first step on the road towards the complete separation of Gown from Town.

Suitably mollified, the university—or most of it—now returned to Oxford. The *studium generale* was officially recognized by both king and pope. Within five years it had a Chancellor, the famous Bishop Grosseteste. In the safe keeping of St. Mary's church it had increasing funds, held in the university chest. It also had an increasing awareness of its own importance, a quality that was to develop to an inordinate degree.

Knuckling under, the townsmen observed these developments with some gloom. The more astute probably realized that the papal degree was the real beginning of their troubles, not the end. More controversies, greater riotings lay ahead, and after every settlement still another freedom was whittled away.

In 1248, during the high jinks of May Day, "a noble scholar of good conversation was set upon and mortally wounded by certain burghers". Employing its favourite threat, the university promptly threatened that if justice was not seen to be done, and that forthwith, the scholars would at once "cease from their lectures and settle elsewhere". This was something the townsfolk no longer dared contemplate: the Gown had them on the hook and all they could do was squirm.

A new charter of 1248 laid down that, in future, members of the university would assist the mayor and his officials in the proceedings of the Assizes. Furthermore, at the beginning of his term of office, the mayor had formally to bow the knee in token of the superior power of the scholars. Together with his bailiffs and aldermen and sixty freemen of the burgh, he must go in procession to St. Mary's Church and before an approving congregation "solemnly swear to respect the liberties and customs of the University". No-one seems to have recognized the irony of a situation in which men virtually held in bondage promised to uphold liberty for their oppressors! This mortifying annual ceremony went on until 1856!

Year after year, there were fresh humiliations and the power of gownsman over townsman became more complete. By 1255, the university not only had jurisdiction over those of its own members who committed crimes, but citizens accused of offences against clerks could also now be tried by the Chancellor's court. Continually inflamed by such measures, the wrath of the Town flared up again and again, only to be quenched by contemptuous indifference and put down by even tighter control.

Street fights, large-scale disturbances and mob encounters seemed never ending. Medieval Oxford was not the pleasantest of places in which to live and as the student population increased, that of the town was declining. The Poll Tax returns for 1380 show that the number of inhabitants was already less than at the time of Domesday Book, and this was before England was ravaged by plague. Even some of the scholars were fed up. In 1334 "tired of fighting and disputes" a considerable number of clerks packed up and went to Stamford "there to pursue their studies in peace".

These clerks were northerners and formed part of the Northern 'nation' at Oxford. The division of students into Northern and Southern 'nations' was a traditional feature of medieval universities, where people of many different countries might be gathered together. All shared the common language of Latin and could therefore communicate, but inevitably, there were fierce antagonisms.

Between the English clerks of North and South, there was at best a marked antipathy and at worst open war. The situation was further complicated by the irritating presence of Scots, Welshmen and of course, a lively group of the fighting Irish. To add to the confusion was an increasing enmity between 'secular' and 'regular' students. Like all medieval students the seculars were nominally clerks in holy orders, but they had become less and less under the control of the Church. As the monastic schools gave way to the halls and lecture rooms of the *studium generale*, the secular scholars emerged more as lay brothers than priests. The regulars, on the other hand, were men destined for no other vocation but the Church. They belonged to monasteries and friaries, were tonsured and wore the rough gowns of their orders, and were under close surveillance.

These various allegiances produced violent cross currents and turbulence. North and South hated each other; Scots and Welsh were constantly at loggerheads; all parties had their seculars and regulars and the Irish pitched in happily whenever there was a fight going. Thus, not only did Gown fight Town, but Gown fought Gown with no less vigour. Not infrequently, three or four different causes were being battled out down the length of the High Street in one glorious mêlée.

One of the few things ever to draw Town and Gown together in some sort of alliance was their common and growing dislike of the Church, an aversion that was to end in the Reformation. The Church represented wealth, power and privilege and the way that these were wielded often gave great offence. All over England, anti-clerical feeling had become rife. With its preponderance of ecclesiastics, Oxford was a natural centre of discontent. The historian J. M. Trevelyan tells us: "The rights of seculars were defended against all aggression by hosts of turbulent graduates. . . . When the occasion called, they poured forth to threaten the life of the Bishop's messengers and to hoot at the King's official. . . ."

At the same time, they continued to "bludgeon and stab the mob that maintained the Mayor against their Chancellor . . ."!

Throughout the thirteenth and well into the fourteenth century, the riots went on. The rallying bells of the two churches rang out more and more often. The city church of St. Martin was both vantage point and fortress. If a Town gang was outnumbered by a Gown gang, or seemed to be getting the worst of an encounter, it was the practice to withdraw inside the sturdy tower, lock the stout doors, and from the battlements hurl down abuse and anything else appropriate on to the heads of the frustrated students.

Their own church of St. Mary not lending itself to such knavish tricks, the university complained to the king that the town held an unfair advantage. Edward III was sympathetic and in 1340 the top stage of St. Martin's tower was demolished "so that no longer in times of combat would townsmen retire up there as to their castle, to gall and annoy the scholars with arrows and stones . . .". The tower, minus its upper storey, still stands at Carfax, although the body of the church to which it belonged was long ago pulled down for street widening.

The town made much use of its church during four days of continuous rioting in 1298, when "clerkes and laics" fairly ran amok. A "numberless multitude of country clownes" came in to take part in the fun, but matters took a tragic turn when one scholar was brutally beaten to death. The outcome was a fine on the town of 200 marks (probably some £4,000 in terms of today's values) and seven months of excommunication by the Bishop of Lincoln.

Serious though they were, affairs such as this pale into insignificance beside the events of 1355 and the few hours of madness known forever afterwards as the Massacre of St. Scholastica's Day. For massacre it certainly was, and the date one that would be long remembered in the seven centuries of war between Town and Gown. In three fear-crazed days, the town's frustrations and the overweening pride and ambitions of the university expressed themselves in an orgy of killing and destruction.

VI

DIES IRAE—DIES SCHOLASTICA

Never before had there been such a horrible bloody business. Yet like many previous encounters, it all started casually enough. At Carfax, where the site is still marked by a plaque, stood the Swyndlestock Tavern, much used by medieval scholars. One February day in 1355, a bunch of scholars drinking there complained that the wine was sour and unfit to drink. The vintner said hotly that if they didn't like it, they could lump it. A fierce argument developed. The students may have already drunk more than was good for them; it is even possible that, as often happened, they did not have the wherewithal to pay. The innkeeper made it clear that he would not take any more abuse. And when the clerk Roger de Chesterfield picked up his pot and flung its contents in the man's face, a small riot was in the making.

Thus far, the accounts of the affair put out later by Town and Gown more or less agree. From this point on, however, they begin to diverge considerably. The vintner was beaten about the head with the pot, said the Town. But only after extreme provocation, said the university: the man had given the scholars "several snappish words and much stubborn and saucy language".

The rest of the customers joined in the fun. Blows were exchanged and before long, the riot bells were ringing. Bows and arrows were produced, staves and cudgels brought out. Trying to calm the mob, the Chancellor himself was shot at. Suffering several near misses, he hurried off with dignity tattered but life intact. Greatly outnumbered, the clerks fell back towards St. Mary's where they collected weapons and reinforcements and began to fight back, bashing and cracking until "dark night, at which time the fray ceased, no one scholar or townsman being mortally wounded . . .".

As usual, the set-to had more or less petered out with nothing more serious than a few bruises and breakages on either side. By tacit agreement all went home to bed. Next day, possibly seeking to restore his injured pride, the Chancellor issued a public proclamation, asking both scholars and citizens not "to bear or wear offensive weapons". For their part, the city bailiffs not only warned the people to get themselves ready to fight, but also bribed and persuaded folk from the countryside around to help them in the coming battle.

In the dinner hour of this same day, Anthony Wood recounts, "the townsmen subtilly and secretly sent about four-score armed men into the parish of St. Giles in the north suburb", where they fell upon "certain scholars walking after dinner in Beaumont Fields". This was the beginning of the real bloodshed. Some of the clerks fled to the priory of the Augustine's at St. Frideswide's. Others lost their pursuers among the maze of alleys in the centre of the town. But some were not so lucky. One was murdered outside the walls and several left for dead.

Hundreds on both sides now sprang to arms. The bells rang wildly and outside the gates, which had been shut and barricaded by the students, an army of country people 2,000 strong clamoured for action. The storm soon broke. Gown fought Town through the streets, the scholars defending themselves as best they could "till after vespertide"—at which time the rural mob broke in at the West Gate bearing "a black dismal flag". Their sudden appearance and screams of "Slay, slay! Havock, havock! Smyt fast, give gode knockes!" must have finally demoralized the clerks, in whom discretion was already getting the better of valour.

They withdrew from the fighting as fast as they could, shutting themselves up in their lodgings and lying low. In the streets a reign of terror had begun. The townsmen marched about and broke into one hall after another, smashing and plundering, dragging out terrified students, beating and killing them. Night brought an uneasy quiet and a proclamation from Edward III, then staying at Woodstock. He warned that "no man should injure the scholars or their goods, under pain of forfeiture", but the royal command did little good. King Mob, not King Edward, ruled in Oxford.

The following day, the carnage increased. At an early hour "with hideous noises and clamours, a numberless multitude again invaded the scholars houses, which they forced open with iron bars and other engines . . .". The scene has been likened to some medieval game of Cowboys and Indians, but this was no celluloid calamity. The intentions of the rabble were murderous and they went about the job in earnest. Scores were slaughtered and hundreds maimed. Priests were a particular target: in derision, some chaplains were cruelly scalped before being killed. Others, grievously wounded, were hauled off to the town gaol "carrying their entrails in their hands in a most lamentable manner". The bodies of the dead were thrown into privies and cesspits, buried in dunghills, or left lying in the gutters.

By the evening of the third day, the worst passions had burnt themselves out. Town and Gown took stock. Sixty-three scholars and an unspecified number of townsmen had been killed. There was no count of the wounded, although many must have taken the vicious scars of St. Scholastica's Day to their graves. Nineteen 'halls' had been spoiled and their contents stolen or ruined. Set on fire, shops and houses in various parts of the city were soon smouldering ruins. "The scholars being fled divers ways, our mother the University of Oxon, which had but two days before many sons, was now almost forsaken and left forlorn . . .". Only Merton College, whose clerks had a reputation for quiet behaviour, was left undisturbed. Indeed, Merton became a safe refuge for many scholars whose own halls had been plundered.

Oxford now awaited certain retribution and university and town hastily prepared their own accounts of the three tragic days. Each blamed the other for what had taken place. The mayor complained that the Chancellor was not the only dignitary to have been attacked: he too had narrowly escaped death at the hands of arrogant clerks. Moreover, after the trivial incident in the Swyndlestock Tavern, his bailiffs had politely requested the Chancellor to arrest the students involved in order to prevent further trouble. They had been met with a contemptuous refusal. Instead, some 200 clerks "armed in the manner of war" had attacked the bailiffs, the town sergeants and himself, inflicting various wounds. These bully boys, claimed the mayor, had then swaggered about threatening to set the whole city on fire. In a scuffle, they had killed an innocent child. Undeterred, they had finally set off on a mad progress of looting, robbing and killing, committing the very crimes of which the townsmen themselves stood accused.

In short, all had been affected by the same madness and there seems little doubt that a truly just apportionment of blame between Town and Gown would have been immensely difficult. Justice, however, was for the university alone. For the town, there was only retribution, and a savage one at that.

For more than a year, while a commission of inquiry did its work; the town was placed under an interdict. In effect, this meant that all churches were closed. Sacraments were no longer administered, nor could the people attend mass. Even Christian burial was forbidden, only infant baptism still being permitted. In the Middle Ages this was an awful punishment. Men might hate the priesthood, but they loved Christ and feared the wrath of God the Father. To deny them access, to stop confession and absolution was dreadful in the extreme.

Soon after the rioting ended both scholars and citizens meekly surrendered all their former rights to the king. Within four days, the privileges of the university were restored and a royal pardon given to all erring clerks, who were urged to return to Oxford. Meanwhile, the county sheriff had been dismissed and the mayor and his bailiffs incarcerated in London's Marshalsea Prison. The town paid an immediate fine of 500 marks with an annual penalty of 100 marks to follow and agreed to compensate scholars for all goods and property that had been stolen or destroyed.

This was merely the beginning. In June, with the town already beaten to its knees, a new charter was granted which gave the university greater powers than ever before. Henceforth, the Chancellor was to be virtually in control of most of the town's affairs. He, and not the Mayor, was now to supervise the important business of checking weights and measures at the yearly 'Assize of Bread and Ale' at which prices were also determined. He, and not the town, could now deal summarily with those who sold bad or adulterated food. He was made sole authority in such matters as street cleansing. His officers would in future be able to arrest wrongdoers in the town and bring them before the university court. And lastly, he was now the man to assess the *Quotae*—the taxes paid by that special class of persons directly serving scholars—servants, scribes, illuminators and parchment makers, the hated 'privileged persons'.

If the charter of seven years before had seemed harsh, this one was positively brutal. There was no magnanimous attitude towards the town; no forgiveness of sins; no letting of bygones be bygones; no recompense. On the contrary, the subjection of the citizens to the university and their dependence upon it was now made almost complete. To remind them and their children, and their children's children, of the enormity of the town's offences, they finally had to agree to undertake an annual public penance. Only by doing so could they ensure that the interdict was lifted.

For nearly five centuries, the town was forced to celebrate a solemn mass on the anniversary of the massacre. The mayor, bailiffs and sixty-three burgesses—one for every scholar who had been killed—marched in slow procession from the Guildhall to St. Mary's Church. There, watched by a congregation mostly made up of members of the university, they knelt and prayed for the souls of the slain and offered at the high altar each a silver penny in token of submission.

Except on a few rare occasions, this humiliating ceremony went on until 1825, when it was quietly dropped after the mayor of the day had point-blank refused to take part. Several of his predecessors who took the same stand were brought to heel and heavily fined. *Dies Scolastica* was truly Oxford's *Dies Irae* and a Mosaic revenge seemed only right and proper. So twice a year— once on the Feast of St. Scholastica and once at mayor-making when the town's chief citizen swore to uphold the rights of the university—the people's shame was made into a public spectacle.

There was never to be another massacre, but this is not to say that there was an end of rioting and violence. Far from it. After a few years of comparative calm, street battles were once again resumed and much blood spilt. The war between Town and Gown was far from being over and if scholars were not fighting with citizens, then they were constantly brawling among themselves.

Particular objects of hatred to the townsfolk were the two university Proctors, originally appointed to look after the interests of the Northern and Southern nations. Representing the power and authority of the university, they were not infrequently attacked in the streets by townsmen who thought they had a score to settle. In 1517, John Heynes, a former mayor, induced a group of malcontents to set upon the proctors "about the silent time of night" when they were doing their rounds of the city. Heynes had been accused of selling sour wine and students who tried to set his house on fire had gone unpunished, so undoubtedly, he was a man with a grievance. Arrested after a sharp fight, he was afterwards banished.

A few years later, returning late home from a visit to Osney, a peaceable citizen called Robert Maydeman was beaten up three times by separate gangs of students between St. Peter-le-Bailey and his house in Carfax. Battered and in some distress, he saw a Proctor approaching and appealed to him for help. But the Proctor, merely cracked him on the head with his poleaxe for good measure and went on his way without a word.

The town had its own watchmen who went around at night calling the hours, but the university held them to be men of little account. They were always fair game for the scholars, particularly after drinking bouts. There are records of a big fight which took place in 1520 between the town watch and a mob of students from Broadgates Hall (later Pembroke College). In this affray, one old watchman was killed and several of his companions wounded. The ringleader, a clerk by the name of Thomas Whem, was sent packing from the city, but was allowed to return to his studies the following year after promising to pay compensation and do penance.

The business of the night watch was a constant source of friction. After St. Scholastica, proctors were given the right to 'take up' any citizen who happened to be out on the streets at night without good reason. In effect, a curfew was in force. Townsfolk who indulged in 'noctivagation' and were outside their houses after ten o'clock in summer or nine o'clock in winter ran the risk of arrest. The extreme point of absurdity was reached when the proctors took to arresting the city bailiffs as they went about their accepted job of patrolling the town and keeping the peace.

During the 1800s, the townsmen submitted several petitions to Parliament asking for some easement of these antiquated fourteenth-century rules, but they asked in vain. Privilege, not public interest mattered, and privilege was to be maintained at all cost. One night in 1822, a 70-year-old man was arrested by the proctors "after refusing to be sent home like a dog to its kennel...". He was put into prison for the awful offence of being out in the street after the permitted hours, but being an old man of spirit, refused to take the indignity lying down. He sued the proctors in common law and as the case became something of a *cause célèbre* seemed quite likely to win. But as usual, the university turned the tables and won the right to have the case heard in the Vice-Chancellor's court. Wise to the ways of the academic world, the old man dropped his prosecution and the proctors' powers of arrest were preserved. Not until 1868, when the Oxford Police Act set up "one Constabulary Force for the Whole District" were citizens finally free to walk about their own town as and when they pleased.

Of course, the proctors still exist and continue to indulge in their nocturnal perambulations. They can be seen occasionally pacing slowly up the High Street or The Broad, impressive, in mortar board, gown and white tie and attended by thoughtful bowler-hatted 'bulldogs'. Townspeople are no longer their real concern, however, and their 'taking up' is nowadays confined to taking the names of undergraduates who appear to stand in need of correction or mild reproach.

Although they are said to be adept at picking out undergraduates from ordinary mortals, the Proctors do slip up from time to time. Now and then there is an unwarranted tap on the shoulder for some townsman or startled young tourist. This is understandable, for how can you tell t'other from which nowadays, or either from your legitimate prey? The number of extramural educational establishments in Oxford increases every year: the students of the Polytechnic up Headington Hill look the same as all other students and are a case in point. Their style and manner and appearance all conform to the current non-conformity. In the circumstances, proctors must be allowed their little mistakes. The person wrongly challenged receives an apology and is allowed to go about his business perhaps a little flattered. Even today, there may be some small pleasure in being mistaken for an Oxford scholar.

Vera Brittain told a nice little tale of one of the early women students who was stopped by one of the Proctors late at night. To the traditional challenge of "Are you a member of this University?" she briskly replied: "I'm sorry—I never speak to strange men in the street!" And leaving behind her a flabber-gasted proctor and admiring bulldog, she jumped on her bicycle and pedalled away.

Female undergraduates arrived in Oxford rather too late in the day to take part in riots, although on occasion, their conduct has been noted as riotous. They do sometimes take a vehement part in protest marches and 'demos' in the city, the modern way in which students express their dissatisfaction with the way of things. But unlike the fictional Zuleika Dobson, they do not have the trick of throwing the whole university into a state of chaos.

In the past, however, true women of the town have more than once been the cause of serious disturbances. Anthony Wood, wrote of the happenings on a cold Sunday night in the winter of 1640, "when were assembled hundreds of Layicks together in a riotous manner to disturb the Proctor in the execution of his office against a lewd woman . . .". Big trouble seemed to be developing. "The Citizens caused their great bell as St. Martin's to be rung to draw their company together, as in the time of K. Edw. III, when the great conflict happened. . . ."

In the seventeenth century, many new pressures were brought to bear. It is no coincidence that further riots in 1640 and 1641 took place on the eve of the Civil War. Nor that four years earlier, the dynamic Chancellor, Archbishop Laud, had completed his sweeping reform of the university. New statutes, which still form the basis of its administration, were now confirmed by the grant of a royal charter. Laud was soon to have his head chopped off, but not before his zeal had brought more privileges to the scholars and plunged the town into a gloom deeper than ever before.

The university now had its own coroners; a further usurpation of civic authority. Furthermore, it could take away the bodies of hanged criminals for the purpose of dissection by the professor of anatomy. The Vice-Chancellor was placed in full control of the markets and also the licensing of the city's vintners. In future, no citizen could build himself a house unless he had the prior per-mission of the university, which was also empowered "to make orders and byelaws binding the townsmen in all matters affect-ing the scholars and to enter and search private property as required . . .".

This 'Laudian Code' marked the high peak of the Gown's supremacy, and the low water mark of the Town's shame and subjection. These final discriminations must to many have seemed the last straw. The wonder is that the town did not break out into open mutiny. In fact, Laud's 'Great Charter' also marked for the town a turning of the tide. As Strickland Gibson remarks: "It gave the University all it could desire, but it went too far. . . . No compromise was henceforth possible and civic resistance stiffened. . . ."

From now on, the flow of events slowly began to run in the town's favour. A fight back with constitutional weapons becomes evident. In 1690, for instance, Parliament surprisingly refused to ratify the Great Charter following strong objections to it from the citizens. It may well have begun to dawn on some of them that moral, and not physical force was the only hope of their ever winning the long, sad war.

There were still to be many pitched battles fought in the Oxford streets. In the next 150 years, The High would echo time and time again with cries of "Gown, Gown!" and "Town, Town!" as men from either side were set upon and tried to summon help. But gradually some of the old bitterness was to go out of these encounters. They might be fought no less fiercely, but they would sometimes be fought for simpler reasons: for a bit of blood, for love of a loose maul, or simply because Town and Gown had always fought. In such circumstances, someone sooner or later was bound to ask: why fight?

But not for a long time yet. In seventeenth-century Oxford, mob violence was still something to be feared, although killings were now comparatively rare. It never took very much to change the mood of an Oxford crowd from the jocular to the downright ugly. Local festivals, national anniversaries, royal marriages, civic ceremonies—all in their turn were occasions of holiday merriment that somehow ended in hooligan outbreaks and near tragedy.

Such disturbances continued well into the nineteenth century. Traditional shindigs of various kinds were always a time for indulging in Oxford's favourite blood sport of bashing the opposition. The great St. Giles' Fair, of medieval origin but still held every September, brought the normal business of the town virtually to a stop for days on end. For centuries, the fair brought

The High and Queen's College

Gothic magnificence—New College Chapel

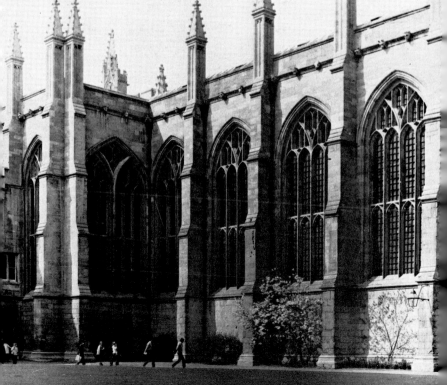

drunken brawls and vicious fighting, with the town lock-ups full of morning-after characters nursing their wounds and grievances ready for the next time.

And after the death of Guy Fawkes, the rival parties never failed to remember 5th November, always a popular battle date, with gangs of students and townies roaming the streets in search of trouble. In 1835 undergraduates went around smashing shop windows and hunting for suitable trophies which they later bore back in triumph to their colleges. The next morning, the basin of the Mercury Fountain at Christ Church was full to overflowing with signboards, door knockers, sundry shop fittings and miscellaneous chinaware.

This famous fountain has always been a popular receptacle for the cooling of hot passions. It was not uncommon for college and town rowdies alike to be pitched unceremoniously into its classical waters. And in the days when ragging was more rife than it is now, many a shivering freshman of 'The House' has made his dripping way across Tom Quad back to his rooms. During the anti-Corn Law agitation of the 1830s when Oxford had its 'bread riots', the leader of a town gang was chucked into the water and held under until he was all but drowned. This time, the tumult went on for three days. Special constables were sworn in by the hundred and it took the presence of a company of soldiers to calm everyone down.

The Reform Bill, perhaps the most hotly contested political cause of the nineteenth century, also brought its troubles. During its passage through Parliament in 1832, there were so many clashes in the streets that the university created a considerable number of 'pro-proctors' in an effort to keep order.

One eye-witness, then a student at Oriel, tells a frightening story of being forced with companions against the walls of Balliol College, there to be hemmed in by a sea of jeering faces. This undergraduate made a grab at a town boy and was immediately felled by a great stone. He was picked up and carried off for dead, but the crowd howled louder than ever. At that moment, old Dr. Jenkyns, Master of Balliol appeared at the door in his robes. If he thought that the mob would be over-awed by this display of academic splendour, he was very mistaken. Poor Jenkyns began to make a speech, but had got only as far as saying,

6

The "telescopic towers" of All Souls

"My deluded friends ..." when one of them knocked him senseless with a piece of pavement.

Royal visits to Oxford have not been without their unplanned excitements. When, as George IV, the Prince Regent finally came to the throne, the scandal of his coronation made him for a time the most hated man in England. The truth about his treatment of the wretched Queen Caroline broke upon the people like a rotten egg, and what came out stank to high heaven. The age in which the Regent lived was prurient rather than prudish, but even so, his lechery had gone too far. The Queen became "the heroine of a popular agitation of almost revolutionary proportions ...".

In Oxford, the Town exhibited an excess of devotion and showed its contempt for the new king by going on a violent rampage. The university, on the other hand, proposed to express its loyalty to royalty by arranging elaborate illuminations. As so often in the past, Town and Gown were diametrically opposed and fought each other up and down the High Street with something of the old fury. Two servants from every college were made into special constables, the proctors' forces were augmented, the Vice-Chancellor read the Riot Act and the nearest regiment of Yeomanry was called in.

These riotings of 1820 were somehow put down without any fatalities. As we noted earlier, the last tragedy of the long war took place in 1857, when a boy from Brasenose, Mervyn Prower, was stabbed to death during the high jinks of Guy Fawkes' Night. From that date onwards, such civic disorders as took place were more contained. On the town's side, truculence rather than terror became the keynote of opposition. The university, for its part, was a long time in losing its ancient arrogance. In the later years of the nineteenth century, a visitor to Oxford recalled seeing at the time of a General Election "the proud sight of rank upon rank of undergraduates advancing to meet The Town with arms linked, clearing The High of all strangers and stragglers, *the first row being led by young noblemen* ...".

It is difficult to resist the italics, and almost impossible not to laugh at the sadness of it all. How, in the face of such ridiculous pomposity a second, or third, or fourth St. Scholastica was ever avoided is a near miracle. Yet generations of late-Victorian dons were to carry such snobberies and pretensions across the chasm of the Great War into the 'twenties. Sir Maurice Bowra reckoned that had it not been for the Education Act of 1944, "Oxford University could hardly have continued to exist".

That Act began a democratizing process which still goes on. It ensured that sooner or later, the Gown would finally know how the other half lives.

VII

A LOT OF LEARNED MEN

Oxford is visited every year by great numbers of people. Most of them arrive with at least some small knowledge of the place. Certainly, they will have heard of a university. Vaguely aware of its fame, many will make immediate tracks for the nearest college, quite convinced that this or that college is 'the university'. Others, not so sure of themselves, may be seen standing about Carfax or the bus station in doubtful attitudes. Slightly bewildered by the immense turmoil of traffic, they consult their maps and shake their heads and begin to wonder whether they have come to the wrong city.

Sooner or later—sooner if your appearance is faintly shabby and therefore reasonably Oxonian—you will be approached by one of these puzzled people. In any of a dozen languages, you will be asked the standard tourist question: "Please—can you direct me to the university?"

To this, of course, there is no proper answer. As they have already discovered, the university is not on the map. And on or off, to furnish them with the necessary directions is impossible. There *are* no directions. Held tight in the cleft stick of a paradox, you can offer no help. Quite indubitably there *is* a university—some would say the greatest in the world. Yet indisputably, you cannot go there, cannot see it. It is not there to be seen: not, at any rate, as one 'sees' Buckingham Palace or Westminster Abbey or the White Cliffs of Dover.

Oxford University has buildings, but is not a building in itself. There is no huge and single classical pile to dominate the townscape, all pediments and porticos and colonnades in the grand Continental manner. You have to see this university a bit at a time, take a bit at a time, creeping round corners, sneaking up alleyways, coming upon it suddenly framed and revealed in the gaps between the most unlikely jumbles of old property. And always, its frequent beauties, its occasional majesty, will take you unawares.

In short, it is a thing of many parts, no one of which takes an absolute precedence over another. Some of its buildings are of great importance. Traditionally, historically, architecturally, the Bodleian Library, the Old Schools, the Sheldonian Theatre, the Radcliffe Camera and a score of others rank high. But neither singly nor together can they be pointed out as 'the university' although the university owns them. Not even the oldest of the lot, the old Congregation House in St. Mary's Church, the heart of the medieval *studium*, is given the overriding title.

Nor, for that matter, are those strange little departments of this and that, humming like beehives in rambles of back-street houses. Nor the pensive quiet of silent researchers in Victorian bay windows. Nor soggy punts abandoned along the Cherwell, the Holywell Music Room, cricket in The Parks, the Ashmolean, the Pitt-Rivers Museum. All these 'belong', are each a part of Oxford University, like the 10,000 blocks, bookstacks, towers, telescopes, offices, officers, literary catacombs, chambers of horrors, computerizations, oddball activities, invaluable assets, wastelands, lines of thought, plans of campaign, considerings of the future, hearkenings to the past.

Ask how you please: "*Bitte—Zeigen Sie mir, wo die Universität ist?*" You see now: it is quite useless. You cannot really see these things. In Oxford, the university is ubiquitous, omnipresent, everywhere, nowhere. It is all around and still not to be seen. It is ideas, talk, books, memories, blood, history, acts of faith, Acts of Parliament, Aristotle, statistics, official reports, poetry, plasma physics, dreams.

It is all things to all its members, but almost nothing to the other quarter of a million people who also live within the area of Greater Oxford. For most of them, the university is another world, and that a world away. What it is and what it does holds little of interest for assembly-line workers and men from the press shops at Cowley. They manage well enough without 'that lot'. Academic excitements and vicissitudes are not their concern. The university is a closed book, a closed shop. Let Them get on with it!

A closed shop, perhaps, but only of the kind suggested by Sir James Mountford when he described universities as "communities of those who teach and those who learn . . .". His definition provides us with a key to the paradox. Writing of the fourteenth-century university, Ruth Fasnacht pointed out that "it consisted of its people—scholars and masters—not its buildings. It was a society, *not* an architectural show. . . ." Basically, the same still holds true.

Society, community; these are words which point to reasons why we cannot go 'looking at Oxford University' in the generally accepted, tourist kind of way. We are trying to discover the nature of a society that has been developing for eight centuries, a community whose prime functions are teaching and learning, a body for whom the pursuit of knowledge at the highest levels is a *sine qua non*. This, and not the sticks and stones, is what it is all about. And this is what countless people who have enjoyed the Oxford experience seem mostly to write about.

'Countless' is by no means an exaggeration. Every man and woman who was ever up at Oxford has held a very personal opinion of the university and a staggering number have committed their views to paper. The steady flow of Oxford memoirs, Oxford poems, Oxford novels, Oxford autobiographies, Oxford ephemera will no doubt continue until Oxford is no more. The bibliography of the university is already vast and unmanageable. The mass of material increases daily with a sort of nightmarish mathematical progression; an explosion of knowledge on the subject of the explosion of knowledge.

Accounts of the university and its affairs are variously dull, lively, boring, witty, sad, scurrilous, bitter, loving and downright ribald. Fortunately, a great many are entertaining, although the humour may not always be intended. Irreverence appears in the most unlikely places, not least in the reader's mind, but where Oxford is concerned, this is as it should be. Pricking over-large bubbles of conceit and taking the starch out of stuffed shirts has been the prerogative of the undergraduate right from the beginning. Few of us are ever the worse for being cut down to size on occasion. The young may acquire some questionable habits, but they do have the happy knack of letting light and fresh air into dark places. Maybe we have good cause to envy those ancient Oxford academics whose amazing longevity has more than once been attributed to their constant contact with students. The secret of eternal youth, it would seem, is to live with it.

Fifty years ago, the youthful C. S. Lewis saw these greybeards and the University as: "A close corporation of jolly, untidy, lazy, good-for-nothing, humorous old men, who have been electing their own successors ever since the world began, and who intend to go on doing it. . . ."

Somewhat earlier, Hilaire Belloc had passed a brilliant four years at Balliol, culminating in a first-class honours degree in history and the Presidency of the Oxford Union. He was to remember his college days in several fine poems, but treated the university with less respect. In 1899 appeared his "Moral Alphabet" in which:

> O stands for Oxford, salubrious seat
> Of learning! Academical Retreat!
> Home of my Middle Age! Malarial Spot
> Which people call Medeeval (though it's not)
> The marshes in the neighbourhood can vie
> With Cambridge, but the town itself is dry
> And serves to make a kind of Fold or Pen
> Wherein to herd A Lot of Learned Men. . . .

For the poet Edward Thomas, killed at Arras in 1917, it was nothing if not "but a spirit of wisdom and grace". Edward Gibbon, however, found it just the opposite.

Coming to the university with high hopes, he found it "steeped in prejudice and port" and left it thankfully. He did not take a degree, which, in those eighteenth-century days of farcical and almost non-existent examinations, was in itself no small achievement.

A hundred years later, passing through the city on one of his rural rides, the great historian's sentiments were echoed by William Cobbett. In typical radical fashion he "could not help reflecting on the drones that the colleges contain and the wasps that they send forth". Something of a Jude, though by no means obscure, old William sourly considered that: "The great and prevalent characteristics of the University are folly; emptiness of head; want of talent; and one half of the fellows who are what they call *educated* here are unfit to be clerks in a grocer's shop. . . ."

Cobbett had reason enough to criticize. For although some of the more blatant abuses of the previous century had been curtailed, young gentlemen of means and leisure were still able to enjoy three pleasantly indolent years at Oxford. They drank, drawled, dressed dandy-wise, womanized, hunted, cut lectures—which, anyway, were few and far between—ignored their tutors, did little or no work and cared not a damn for anything or anybody. Yet somehow, because of a complicated system of malpractices and minor corruptions, a surprisingly large number of these idlers managed to get a Bachelor of Arts degree.

There must have been consternation in the ranks when examinations were tightened up. In 1807, the university brought in new statutes and degrees were no longer to be had for the asking. Lectures were now taken a little more seriously. The introduction of degrees in the first and second class was a novelty, but also a little worrying. They were not always easy to obtain and in 1809, 'thirds' were added, to the considerable gratification of the not over-bright. And by the time *Rural Rides* was published in 1830, fourth-class 'scrape-through' degrees had opened the academic doors wide open. Practically anyone but a near moron could now become a full member of the university and leave it with at least some small show of honour. The drones must have buzzed loud with relief.

Yet although wholesale university reform was still a long way off, Reform with a capital 'R' was very much on the march. For the far-sighted and idealistic, the word was like wine; but for the Oxford Establishment it spelt out rank poison. As a national institution, the university had for centuries enjoyed the official blessing of the State. In the most troublous times, it had never been greatly disturbed, either by crown or parliament. Even after the great upheaval of the Civil War, Cromwell had deemed it prudent not to interfere with its antediluvian workings. Always seeming to be a necessary rock, standing firm against the pounding seas of revolutionary thought, or an ancient monument in a gimcrack world, the university was largely left alone to moulder and manage its own affairs.

Its critics, however, saw the venerable institution in a rather different light: at best it was a useless medieval survival; at worst a corrupt and swollen fruit, rotten to the core. "Oxford and Cambridge", wrote Gibbon, "were founded in a dark age of false and barbarous science; and they are still tainted with the vices of their origin. . . ."

Of course, always where Oxford was concerned, he had an outsize chip on his shoulder. Nevertheless, some of Gibbon's

views on the likely course of future events were to prove remarkably accurate. When the prestige of the university stood at the
lowest ebb and its activities—or lack of activity—stank in men's
nostrils, he said that "new improvements are admitted with slow
and sullen reluctance in this proud corporation. . . . We can
scarcely hope that any reformation will be a voluntary act."

How right he was! When reform, talked about for so long,
finally became an official matter, the diehard representatives of
"the spirit of chartered monopoly" fought reform tooth and
nail. Appointed almost in despair by a government tired of trying to persuade Oxford to do something off its own bat, the
University Commission of 1850 was resisted by the academics
at every step of its inexorable way.

The commissioners, eminent but mild enough men, were
treated as though they were lepers. Every possible obstacle was
placed in their path and they met with everything from insults,
blank looks, lofty indifference and closed doors to open rudeness
and hostility. Variously described as "mischievous", "odious
fellows" and "a great joke" they nevertheless pushed on
conscientiously with their investigations.

The colleges were secretly advised not to co-operate. In the
event, only seven of the nineteen then existing were prepared to
give proper evidence, or to make their records freely available.
At the very first sitting of the commission, there was a serious
attempt by the Vice-Chancellor to stop the whole business before
it had even begun.

He might as well have tried to stop the tide. For once in its
history, the stubbornness of the university was more than
matched by the determination of the State. In spite of much
passive resistance, the work of the inquiry went on. Fortunately,
a number of liberal-minded dons came forward to speak their
minds. The separate testimonies of these individuals helped to
build up 'massive evidence' of the urgent need for reform.

And reform was not long in coming. The commission's report,
known as 'The Great Blue Book' was published in 1852 and
rapidly became a best seller. It was a weighty document in more
ways than one; indeed, it was popularly supposed to have
finished off the Duke of Wellington, then University Chancellor.
On the very last night of his life, he took it to bed with him, saying to his son: "I shall never get through it, Charles. . . ." Nor did

he, although he proved himself "an obstinate university reformer" right to the end.

Always a man for the commonsense view, the Iron Duke had earlier warned his Vice-Chancellor that he would be well advised "not to try and defend the indefensible, nor to stay the inevitable . . .". But Oxford not only fought a hopeless battle against reform, but for some years to come was engaged in an equally hopeless series of rearguard actions. After the main recommendations of the commission had been accepted by the Cabinet, the university was allowed one year's grace in which to come forward with its own proposals for improvement. Heads of colleges were warned by Mr. Gladstone, the university M.P. and already Chancellor of the Exchequer, that unless they stirred themselves, the government would be bound to step in and force action upon them.

With their heads firmly stuck in the sand, however, the diehards still thought that they could hang on to the old ways. Their plan for self-improvement, published in 1853, fell far short of what was required to satisfy the critics and enlightened public opinion. As a result, Parliament passed in the following year the wide-ranging Oxford University Act, a measure which both in letter and spirit embodied nearly all the Blue Book proposals.

The Act was immensely complicated and during its passage through Lords and Commons, clause after clause was bitterly contested. Basically, its provisions covered the government of the university, its discipline, its studies, its finances, and the practices and short-comings of its constituent colleges. For centuries, Oxford had steadily become less and less democratic. Real power lay solely in the hands of the Vice-Chancellor and his 'Hebdomadal Board'—so called from its habit of meeting once every seven days. This body, made up of heads of colleges and the two Proctors had things very much their own way. In theory, the board constituted an upper house, the lower one being known as 'Convocation'. This latter was supposedly a 'parliament of graduates' but was now largely ineffective. It could discuss nothing and do nothing without the prior consent of the Hebdomadal Board, and since this was not often forthcoming, Convocation seemed likely to remain just another of those archaic anachronisms for which the university was noted.

Surprisingly, the Act kept the moribund Convocation in

being but did away with the board, replacing it with a Heb-domadal Council. This involved far more than a mere change of name. Now reasonably democratic, the council was composed of the Vice-Chancellor and Proctors, six 'Heads of Houses', six professors and six ordinary members of the university. There were regular elections in which candidates were properly voted for by a new-style 'Congregation' comprising all resident teachers and senior officials. By some mistake, the medieval 'Congregation of Regent Masters' which should have been abolished was left in existence. Turning the error to good account, this ancient body was re-created as the 'Ancient House of Congregation' and given the job of conferring degrees, a task which it still happily performs.

Although considerably added to over the years this original framework of university government laid down in 1854 survives. Executive power is still exercised by Hebdomadal Council. Legislative function remains the prerogative of Congregation. Convocation—in total a vast, unwieldy and shadowy presence—is seen and heard but does not often make its presence felt.

Now and again, however, Convocation does manage to hit the headlines. When its members elect the Professor of Poetry, for example, fun and games and verbal fireworks are nearly always the order of the day. Letters appear in *The Times*. Placards are paraded. Undergraduates delight in the playful seriousness of their seniors. And when terribly controversial matters raise temperatures in the colleges, hordes of aged clergymen, retired schoolmasters and other fully paid-up members of the club can be seen making a slow but anticipatory progress up The High to some lively meeting of Convocation. Some of them may not have visited Oxford since their graduation, but the scent of battle occasionally proves irresistible.

This proved to be the case in 1960, when it was proposed to abolish Latin as a compulsory subject for matriculation. There was a great storm of protest and high words flew in all directions. Greek had been similarly dropped forty years before and the row sparked off by this 'new and outrageous proposal' was a clear indication of how tenaciously Oxford tries to hang on to its classical traditions.

Once the commonly used language of all lectures and most official university business, Latin is now kept in its place among classical studies, breaking out in public only on such state occasions as degree ceremonies and the splendid annual affair of Encaenia. This word means 'commemoration' and refers to the last festival of the academic year. Held on the anniversary of the dedication of the Sheldonian Theatre, it is just about the most gorgeous get-together the university has to offer. It is the day for remembering Oxford's benefactors and also the day on which distinguished people from all walks of life come to receive honorary degrees. Under the painted sky and gambolling cherubs of the Sheldonian ceiling, the Public Orator makes speeches in his best Latin, lauding the achievements of each 'honorand' before showing him off to a colourfully-gowned crowd and presenting him to the Vice-Chancellor.

They were enjoying their Encaenia long before there was any silly talk of reforming the universities, and they still manage to do so. On this day of all days, the classic muses float overhead on clouds of glory, toga'd professors walk gravely about like Roman senators and the language of Virgil and Juvenal seems the only possible one appropriate to the occasion.

Just as Roman numerals were soon dispensed with as being too cumbersome for the flowings of mathematics, more slowly but just as surely was Latin dispensed with as a medium for the communication of ideas and instruction within the university. Sooner or later, it must certainly have dropped into disuse by general consent, but the nineteenth century gave it one or two definite shoves in the right direction.

A clause inserted into the 1854 Act insisted that discussions in meetings of Congregation should henceforth be conducted in English and not, as formerly, in Latin. If tipsy dons wanted to swap classical quips in the original or ramble on in Augustan periods, they could do so at high table. But in future, they could forget about parading their classical erudition in public places.

So after an apparently never-ending age of status quo, Oxford found itself with a reasonably workably system of internal self-government arranged on reasonably democratic lines. Although to some the changes seemed like revolution, they were, in fact, true reform. Only the rot had been cut away. The worthy and worthwhile was allowed to remain. What James Morris calls "a rambling kind of semi-democracy put together in bits and pieces down the ages" was not destroyed, but was given a more regular shape. Its thinking stifled by the fungus of the past, its forward movement hampered by all kinds of anomalous knobs and excrescences, the university badly needed major surgery. Kicking and plunging, it had to be dragged out of the psychological morass of the Middle Ages for its own good, and for the good of future generations.

Of course, neither this medieval ambience nor the old image disappeared all at once. For many years, Oxford clung determinedly to the faraway past, as it still does in various quaint observances. Even today, the cloister casts mysterious shadows across college quadrangles. A century ago, monastic gloom was not so distant. When her sporting son, Bertie, Prince of Wales, was an undergraduate at Magdalen, Queen Victoria shivered with apprehension at the mere thought of Oxford University, "that old, monkish place, which I have the greatest horror of . . .". Yet for most people, Oxford continued to be a place of pleasantly ancient walls, magic casements and Keatsian romance, all held timeless and preserved in a dimly religious light.

To the opponents of reform, however, the past was no mere Gothick novel. After the University Commission had done its work so well, J. W. Burgon, the old-style Dean of Oriel, wrote in a fit of depression of the great darkness that had come over all the land. "Oxford", he grieved, "has seen her best days. Her sun has set for ever. She can never again be what she has been—the great nursery of the Church. . . ."

Poor John Willie Burgon! Transparently honest, a devout churchman, a tremendous fighter for his beliefs, he would have been at his best back in the fifteenth century, burning heretics or being burnt as one. Essentially humane yet incredibly intolerant, he was that strange dichotomous sort of man not uncommon in early Victorian times. He could rush to sponsor a new Theological School, yet savagely squash proposals for a quite innocuous School of Modern History. He would not accept that knowledge was expanding, nor that a university which had grown up within the Church must ultimately go on without it.

Within the greater context of learning, the attitudes of Burgon and his kind were parochial in the extreme. They stood in the way of nearly every advance. They detested the very word 'progress'. They would strenuously oppose the introduction of even the most innocent 'modern' subject to the curriculum. If they admitted the slightest 'improvement' or gave way by a single inch, they reproached themselves because they "had fallen into the weakness of the spirit of the age . . .".

For them, it was the spirit of ages past that really mattered. Keble, Newman, the higher-than-high-churchmen, Catholic Revivalism, the Oxford Movement, Pugin, the misguided church restorations of the self-styled 'ecclesiologists'—all pointed in one direction only: backwards. It was no wonder that missals and frontals, copes and chasubles were considered so immeasurably more important than physics and chemistry.

This was the thinking of true reactionaries. The attitude of these academic diehards was summed up by Mark Pattison when he spoke of "their unquestioning satisfaction in the old college tutorial system; in one man teaching everybody everything; in the same belief that all knowledge is shut up between the covers of four Greek and four Latin books; in the same humdrum questions asked in the same examinations; and in the same arts of evasive reply. . . ."

To Pattison, who was later to do so much for the education of women in Oxford, the despised 'spirit of the age' was clean, new and exciting. When reform was seen to be working, he spoke for most of the younger dons, interpreting their inner convictions, the temper of the times, and good minds chafing under restraints at once intolerant and intolerable.

In spite of many a backstairs intrigue against him, Pattison eventually achieved his heart's desire. As Rector of Lincoln College, he became head of the house he had served so faithfully as fellow and tutor. He lived on long enough in Oxford to see the university transformed from an essentially medieval concept into a basically modern institution. Towards this change he worked unceasingly. A man of warm heart and deep sincerity, he was greatly admired. This makes it all the more difficult to understand why George Eliot, once a guest in his house, should have chosen to portray him in Middlemarch as that humourless, dry-as-dust pedant, Mr. Casaubon.

Mark Pattison died in 1884, John Burgon four years later. The first was undoubtedly the greater man, yet by one of those ironic twists of fate, it may well be the second who is longer remembered. For as a young undergraduate, Burgon won the famous Newdigate Prize for English verse with his poem "Petra", giving to the world that single stunning phrase: "A rose-red city—half as old as Time!" Fame can sometimes rest on no more than a few words.

Equally quotable, though less poetical, was Burgon's pronouncement on women, made from the pulpit of New College chapel during the course of a Sunday sermon. Glaring at the few females present he thundered out: "Inferior to men God made you, and inferior to the end of time will you remain!" Unlike his old enemy, the Dean was no champion of women's rights. The mere mention of a future in which girls might be awarded Oxford degrees was enough to make him blow his top. The notorious New College sermon was later printed as a pamphlet: "To educate young women like young men—a thing Inexpedient and Immodest".

In the academic manœuvrings of Victorian Oxford, neither Burgon nor Pattison were key figures, though both were important. Each in his opposing way had the interests of the university at heart. Each was sincere, each articulate. Each thought the other a bigot and totally misguided. Although they were fellow Christians, they seem to have regarded each other with a remarkable mutual hatred. Representing two different Oxfords, they stood at a mid-century crossroads and did not like what they could see.

Learned men are blessed with an abundance of uncommon sense, but are often sold short on the commoner variety. Throughout the squabblings of the second half of the nineteenth century, this fact emerges time and time again. Men of immense intellect, sometimes of near genius, are seen completely lost in the most fatuous arguments. It is some tribute to the overriding common-sense of the university as a whole, to realize that what finally came out of the confusion was something which combined the best of both worlds.

The grim facts of university legislation brought reformers and reactionaries together, and to their senses. The colleges, so used to having everything their own way, were firmly put in their places. No one denied their importance in the scheme of things, but in future, mere lip-service to the university would not be enough. Houses now had to pay part of their revenues into a general fund. They were expected to contribute substantially towards teaching and other facilities provided by the university for the good of all.

Professorial chairs proliferated. What Burgon said about the Chair of Chinese "set up by public subscription", in 1875, or the Chair of Celtic Studies endowed by Jesus College a year later, is not on record!

To be a professor was no longer to be a member of a downtrodden race, sneered at as an unnecessary appendage to real teaching. Self-satisfied college tutors who had formerly looked down their noses at professorships began secretly to covet them. And their own college fellowships were not so easily come by as before. Such appointments were now "made to depend more upon merit and less upon personal or ecclesiastical considerations . . .". Who a man happened to know was henceforth to be less important than what he knew. Jobs for the boys were now less common.

The same sort of conditions now applied to most of the great number of scholarships offered by colleges. Originally intended by their donors to help needy students, many lucrative awards had for centuries been closed to all but a favoured few. By order of the University Commissioners, the majority of such scholarships were now made 'open' for competition by all comers. Furthermore, the re-alignment of college finances brought to light an amazing variety of strange old funds and charities whose proceeds were now put to better use. Some went to the establishment of new faculties; some to the provision of new university buildings, and nearly all were applied to the common good.

Although Oxford remained very much a preserve of the Anglican Church until well into the twentieth century, the ecclesiastical bonds which had always held the university so fast were being loosened. 'Dissenters'—that is, Noncomformists—were at last allowed officially to sit examinations and take degrees without having to trace a circumlocutory path around the regulations. Fellows of colleges need no longer take holy orders and, after 1877, they were finally permitted to marry. With the lifting of the hitherto inflexible rule of celibacy and the scrapping of many quite farcical medieval statutes, the last links of the colleges with their monastic past were broken.

The final step towards independence of the Church was taken when religious 'tests' for university membership were abolished by law in 1871. From then on, it was not necessary for students or dons to swear to uphold the tenets of the Church of England.

The Martyrs' Memorial in St. Giles. Balliol in the background

They did not have to be Anglicans. In theory, at least, they did not have to belong to a church at all. It has been said that by 1880, "both Oxford and Cambridge were open to all and sundry, from whatever religion, nation and race . . .".

There was still, however, one race apart: the poor. Almost another hundred years had to pass before the hard-up and the low-born found a real place in the Oxford sun. For in the matter of "the poor and needy scholar", the reforming zeal of the University Commissioners had somehow backfired. In theory, new opportunities were opened up for the under-privileged and less well-to-do. In practice, things did not work out this way. True, the number of scholarships and awards was steadily increased; true, many of the existing ones were made 'open' to all who wanted to try for them. But the subjects and mode of teaching provided in village and grammar schools hardly fitted boys for competitive examinations in the classics which, in any case, were no test of intellect. Even the brightest local lad was up against it when he competed against entrants from the big public schools.

For a very long time, the doors to an Oxford education were effectively barred to members of what were still unhappily referred to as the lower classes. Even the back door was now closed, since the old system of 'servitors' had been abandoned. During the eighteenth century, such men as Dr. Johnson, George Whitefield and Samuel Wesley had found a place at college by becoming little more than servants, fetching and carrying for the more wealthy undergraduates, living off scraps and existing at near-starvation level, picking up an education in between times as well as they could. It was menial; it was degrading—but it had worked.

For Oxford, the Victorian period was the Age of Reform. The revolution did not come until one world war had decimated the academic population more effectively than the Black Death and another had made more than mere words of the doctrine of equal opportunity for all.

7

The Jacobean porch at Oriel

VIII

WEATHER OR NOT

Most people in England talk about the weather, but in Oxford, they talk about the weather more than most. They have been doing so for centuries, nearly always in terms of high disparagement and rarely without good reason. There are endless descriptions of dank Oxonian fogs, of unhealthy steams rising from rivers, of smothering heats and bitter chills, of choking clammy days that seem to last for ever, sapping the will, muddling the mind and draining away the energies of all but the strongest spirits.

Indeed, this 'awful Oxford atmosphere' has been blamed for all the ills that flesh is heir to. Headaches and catarrh; dyspepsia and diarrhoea; fits of black depression, screaming madness and an inordinate number of suicides are all laid at its door. "The climate is ghastly," says James Morris: "It always has been. . . ." Three hundred years ago, Anthony Wood said much the same thing: "Colds become verie frequent in Oxon; many sick; colds without coffing or running at the nose: onlie a languidness and faintnesse. Certainly, Oxford is no goode aire. . . ."

No goode aire! The phrase is as brief and accurate a summing up as you will find. There are probably few cities in the land where you may so often shake in the dog days, or in December, sweat. Even the climatologists will admit that the place can be terribly enervating, "warm and humid in summer; damp, raw, foggy and liable to bitter north-east winds in winter . . .".

And of the Oxford winter, when tourists come not in battalions, but singly, there is usually more than an amplitude. Wrote the long-suffering wife of a visiting American professor: "It wasn't such a bad winter—seen from the vantage point of May. But at the time, there seemed to be an awful lot of February and March . . .!" Long on imagination but sometimes short in

98

memory, a few romantic writers have seen things differently. Those "nasty moorish stinks rising from the meads to the putrefaction of the aire" are poetically transformed into "a dreamlike haze" or "soft mists".

Max Beerbohm, euphemized the notorious fogs into a "white coverlet" and for him the choking stuffiness of high summer became "a mild miasmal air that has helped to produce a peculiar race of artist-scholars, scholar-artists". To be fair, the gently ironic Max was prepared to allow that his lotus land had a certain inherent dampness, a moisture which tended to take away from men their power of action. All the same, what really lurked in the vapours of the meadows, he said, was not rheumatism, but "the true and mysterious spirit of Oxford". Transfer the colleges to the dry and bracing top of some hill, and all would be lost.

But the dream and the reality of Oxford have often been greatly at variance. The famous day on which Lewis Carroll of Christ Church took little Alice Liddell picnicking to Godstow and first told her of Alice in Wonderland was always "that golden afternoon". Rowing upstream, inventing the story as they went along, he clearly remembered: "the cloudless blue above, the watery mirror below, the boat drifting idly on its way, the tinkle of the drops that fell from the oars as they waved so sleepily to and fro. . . ."

'Alice' herself was later to recall "the burning sun of that blazing summer afternoon". It had obviously been a suitably idyllic day for the creation of Carroll's small masterpiece. Unfortunately, the meteorological records for Oxford show that far from being gloriously hot, the "golden afternoon" was in reality rather cool and wet! Alas for romance! Alack for fond memories! And drat those killjoy scientists with their horrid facts and figures!

But the climate of this soggy district must not be blamed for the long succession of plagues endured by the city down the years. Oxford had its share of such visitations, but seems to have been little worse off than many other places. Overcrowding and dirty domestic and personal habits were always the main factor in the spread of epidemics. For too long, sanitation was primitive and drainage systems non-existent. The common receptacle for all unwanted offal was a hole in the ground. Yards and gardens were dotted with reeking cesspits, often placed close to the wells from which families took their drinking water. When one pit was full, you dug another alongside it. The main cesspit of New College was so huge that for nearly 300 years, it needed neither emptying nor enlargement.

And from the early Middle Ages onwards, every house had two lots of occupants: the people themselves and their attendant quota of hidden livestock. The flea and the rat were everywhere and both carried disease. The one fed on human blood, the other on human refuse, and there was no shortage of either. As early as 1300, a letter from Edward I to the High Sheriff complained of "air so corrupted and infected by filth that an abominable ague is diffused among masters and scholars . . .".

By implication, the townsmen were held responsible, but the mode of living of the academics had little to commend it. They were a filthy lot. Nor did their standards of cleanliness improve much with the passing of the centuries. The great Erasmus, who came to the university in 1498, was shocked by what he found in some of the colleges. The floors of most dining-halls were made of beaten earth, strewn with rushes that were only occasionally removed. Trodden into a smelly mess, the bottom layers stayed where they were, sometimes for twenty years or more, "there to harbour expectorations, vomitings, the leakages of dogs and men, ale-droppings, scraps of fish and other abominations, not fit to be mentioned . . .".

The wonder is that through all the colics, poxes and fevers, students managed to live long enough to take a degree. Many did not. In times of serious plague, life expectancy among the young was not high. And although privileged in other directions, scholars were as liable to be carried off by the pestilence as the humblest citizen. Closing college doors and sitting tight within may have been a brave gesture of defiance, but did little to keep death at bay. A better chance of survival lay in withdrawal to the retreat houses established outside Oxford by various colleges.

Having bought up the medieval Hospital of St. James and St. John at Brackley, the fellows of Magdalen made it their refuge whenever the signs of plague appeared. Parts of the old buildings are incorporated into the fabric of present-day Magdalen College School. The scholars of Merton went to Islip or Cuxham. Trinity College had a house at Garsington. Exeter holed up at Kidlington, then distant, green and pleasant, but now all sordid suburb. Much closer to the city was the old leper hospital of St. Bartholomew, founded by Henry I when he was constructing Beaumont Palace. This stood near to the site of the motor works at Cowley and was given to Oriel College in 1328 "for the use of wholesome air in times of pestilential sickness ...". Its remains can still be seen.

A generation later, the university was hard hit by the Black Death. Coming ashore at Bristol, the infection travelled rapidly eastwards by way of Gloucester and the Cotswolds, reaching the city at the beginning of 1349. By March of that year, this lethal combination of septicaemic, pulmonary and bubonic plague was wreaking havoc in the towns of the Thames Valley. Few places escaped. In Oxford, half the priests died and great numbers of masters and students who shut themselves up with the intention of sweating it out fell victim to the horrible disease. In spite of these precautions, "they fared no better than the townsmen, and probably did a great deal worse ...".

Close to the town wall, in what is now the garden of New College, the largest ever of Oxford's plague pits was dug. Within three months, it was full to overflowing with dreadfully disfigured corpses. The living tried to carry on. Those who could do so got away into the countryside, but even in the apparent safety of rural surroundings, the pestilence thrived. Far from being killed off by the cold of winter, the bacillus multiplied and spread.

Inside the city, "those that were left behind were almost totally swept away. The school doors were shut, colleges and halls relinquished, and scarce none were left to keep possession or make up a competent number to bury the dead. ..." At St. Bartholomew's Hospital, the fellows of Oriel must have prayed for deliverance. Maybe they wished that its miraculous relics had remained in their possession: the skin of the saint himself; the bones of St. Stephen; a rib of St. Andrew and Edward the Confessor's magic comb—useful, it was said, for curing bad headaches! It would seem that the only thing missing was a lucky rabbit's foot.

Medically, there was not much to be done. Science had been brought to Oxford by the friars a century before, but its development was hampered by an eternal preoccupation with religion and moral philosophy. No one continued the work begun by Roger Bacon. Monks resorted to prayer rather than potions. The pestilence had long been accepted as one of the grimmer hazards of life. Men saw it as judgement and a punishment for their sins; an expression of the wrath of God. They were stoical, but even so, the Black Death was almost too much to be borne. No earlier visitation had been anything like so savage and virulent. Nothing before had killed off so many people so quickly and so horribly.

In England alone, conservative estimates put the numbers who perished at one and a half million, a figure which represented one third of the entire medieval population. The rest of Europe suffered in the same way. On the Continent, four universities vanished completely. Because it was so dependent upon small groups of aging men, the academic world was "peculiarly sensitive to the impact of the plague. Mortality among men of learning was calamitously high. . . ."

About 7,000 people are thought to have been living in Oxford at this time. In the first half of that awful year, it is probable that some 3,000 of them died. The number of students dropped alarmingly, and continued to decline. By the end of the century, there were reckoned to be no more than 1,000 in residence. A few years later, the total had dropped to a mere 600. Each time the numbers began to build up again, they were reduced again by still another epidemic. Typhus, smallpox and various horrifically-named fevers made frequent appearances. During the Tudor period, the disease most dreaded was the highly infectious 'sweating sickness', a malady which could sweep through the body at an appalling speed. Generally attributed to the fogs and moisture of the native climate, this 'English sweat' was capable of striking down and killing a man in less than twelve hours.

The sickness decimated many urban areas and was a constant drain on an economy trying to recover from the effects of the Black Death. In the thirty-eight years of the reign of Henry VIII, Oxford suffered from 'the sweat' at least seven times. The virus travelled like wildfire and the devastating rapidity with which the infection spread created havoc. Official measures aimed at improving the overcrowded and insanitary conditions in which people lived always came too late. Many old halls had stood ruinous and deserted for generations and were thought still to harbour pestilence. Orders were given for them either to be cleaned up or pulled down, but the work seems to have done little good. A decree of 1584 prohibited the presentation of plays and other spectacles "because of the sicknesse wherewith this Universitie hath oftentimes been grievouslie visited, by reason of the extraordinarie concourse of people at unseasonable times of the yeare . . .".

General isolation of the sick was found to be as effective a way as any of containing infectious disease. Indeed, until medical science began to make progress in the eighteenth century, there was little else that could be done. Houses that had the plague were marked by a cross and their occupants locked inside. Poor folk, both plague and poverty stricken, were sent to a dismal house on the town's Port Meadow, there to recover or, more often, left to die. On the Meadow, and on Headington Hill, were a number of wretched 'cabines' kept in reserve for the yearly victims.

The colleges and religious houses offered their members a natural isolation. This might prevent contact with the outside world, but inside disease could still rage and run its course unchecked. Monasteries and priories suffered heavily. Between 1349 and 1351, nearly half the monks and nuns in England died and the mendicant friars, "descending as angels from Heaven" on priestless and plague-beleagured villages, were reduced to a handful.

Yet in a certain other type of closed community, there was even greater suffering. Men locked up in prison had to lie in the filth and stench and endure their misery, without hope, without relief. Pestilence came in to them and there was no escape. Long before the Black Death, Roger Bacon noted that "the most pernicious infection next to the plague is the smell of the jail when prisoners have been long and close nastily kept . . .".

The most feared of prison diseases was typhus, transmitted from man to man by lice. Commonly called 'jail fever' it was also widely known as 'the black fever' because of the characteristic dusky countenance which developed in the sufferers. This phenomenon gave the name to many so-called 'black assizes' in the sixteenth century, at which prisoners on trial infected judge, jury, witnesses and anyone else who happened to be present in court.

Oxford's most notorious Black Assize took place in July 1577. A local bookseller, "a saucy foul-mouthed fellow" named Rowland Jenkes, was being tried at the castle for issuing "bulls, libels and suchlike writings against our Sovereign Lady the Queen, and against Religion . . .". Found guilty, he was sentenced to have both his ears cut off. The crowd cheered. . . . "But there then arose such infectious damp or breath among the people, that many there present were smothered, and others so deeply infected that they lived not many hours after. . . ."

With 600 others, the Black Assize carried off the Lord Chief Baron, the High and the Under Sheriff, two judges, the Clerk of Assize and the coroner, and all within a few days. But although it was always being recognized that the two city gaols were persistent sources of infection, neither at the castle, nor in the Bocardo at Northgate were conditions improved. The prison reformer John Howard was appalled by what went on at the castle. Cells and dungeons were stinking and crawling with vermin. Men and women slept in their clothes on dirty mats laid on the stones. "It is very probable", Howard reported, "that the rooms in this place are the same as the prisoners occupied at the time of the Black Assize. The wards, passages and staircases are close and offensive; so that if crowded, I should not greatly wonder to hear of another fatal Assize at Oxford. . . ."

Inside or outside gaol, people went in constant fear of being struck down by some fatal malady. There were too many deaths to allow them to forget the nightmare of plague, for which the city always had a bad reputation. The more prudent left, never to return, and even the more flashing spirits could sometimes throw rashness to the winds. In 1571, without having taken a degree, even brave young Philip Sidney left Christ Church rather hurriedly to escape the sweating sickness, preferring death in battle to the obscure miseries of putrid fever.

There seemed no end to these outbreaks. Public health was still very much a private affair, while dirt was a way of life. When James I came to the throne in 1603, there were further disasters, gloomily regarded as a sign from Heaven that the new monarch was not all he was cracked up to be. Sent to make an inspection of the colleges, one of his judges landed in the middle of the latest flush of pestilence. He stayed at the Golden Cross in Cornmarket, mentioning in his journal that this hostelry was "the best in the citie, yet ther wer two howses on either side adjoining, infected with the plague . . .".

This particular epidemic was sufficiently serious to delay the commencement of the Michaelmas Term, which normally started in October. This was put off, first to November, then to mid-December and was finally abandoned altogether. In the end, the academic year became the shortest ever, not getting properly under way until the last week of February 1604. There were so many deaths and such grievous distress, that the citizens petitioned the university for help, asking for weekly contributions for the relief of the suffering and destitute. Collections were made among the colleges and the proceeds handed over to the mayor. "Times were verie sadde," runs an old account, "and nothing but lamentation and bemoanings heard in the streets. . . ."

The disease raged until springtime, having lasted for nine months. It was probably the worst single outbreak of pestilence since the fourteenth century and Oxford became literally a city of the dead. Contemporary accounts tell a familiar tale of churches and colleges closed up; of scholars making for home or shutting themselves away in their academic retreats; of the rich flying into the countryside and the poor folk enduring or being carted off to those miserable huts on the Port Meadow.

The pattern was repeated at intervals throughout the seventeenth century. Still another visitation of the plague marked the accession of the ill-starred Charles I in 1625. Originating in London, it caused such panic among the high and mighty that Parliament removed itself from Westminster to Oxford, bringing king, court and infection in its train. To make room for the unexpected influx, most of the colleges were closed down and the scholars sent off home. This was fortunate, from their point of view at least, since many of the townspeople were to die within the next few weeks.

Ten years later, the court was again driven from the capital by plague, first to Woodstock and thence into the city. The royals were lodged in Christ Church and Merton College, where they seem to have had a pleasantly idle time watching amateur dramatics put on by the students. Strode, the University Orator had written an elaborate comedy which was presented on a temporary stage erected across one end of Christ Church Hall. An ingenious system of moveable scenery was used, some claim for the first time in England. There are delightful descriptions in contemporary writings of "scenic partitions, that could be drawn in and out at pleasure, upon a sudden, and new ones thrust out in their places . . .".

Clearly, this was great stuff, to be rivalled only a few days later by *The Hospital of Lovers* given in St. John's College, and *The Royal Slave* for which Mr. Inigo Jones designed "a curious Temple with the Sun shining over it".

During the Civil War, the city became the King's headquarters and, overwhelmingly Royalist in sympathy, the university was his staunchest supporter. He must have felt that so long as Oxford stood firm, the crown could endure. In 1642, after the Battle of Edgehill, the court and army descended upon Town and Gown, staying for the best part of four years. Officers and gentlemen lived mainly in the colleges. Wives, courtesans and camp followers packed themselves into any house that could offer a spare room or two. As always, the common soldiery bedded itself down in stables or pigsties or anything that provided a roof and dry straw. Cramped within city walls that had renewed their defensive significance, Oxford was bursting at the seams, crowded to suffocation by a grossly expanded population.

It is not surprising that disease was rampant, and the surprisingly nasty habits of the courtiers can hardly have helped. They changed their linen at very infrequent intervals, rarely took baths and were given to spitting, vomiting and relieving themselves in odd corners with little show of embarrassment. After the Restoration, when the Great Plague of 1665 was raging in London, their manners had still not improved. Once more, king, court and Parliament established themselves in Oxford. The scholars were all sent away for six months, and this time, the take-over of the colleges was virtually complete.

Wood, who lived through it all at Merton College, tells us that members of the Merrie Monarch's court were "high, proud and insolent, and looked upon scholars as no more than pedants and pedagogicall persons . . . never regarding that these same had parted with their chambers and conveniences for them. . . ." He found it a great wonder that "we had not the least show of infection or plague among us, no, not even when 8,000 died at London . . ." and especially when: "Though the court were neat and gaye in their apparell, yet they were very nasty and beastlie, leaving at their departure from the colledges their excrements in every corner, in chimnies, studies, colehouses and cellars. . . . They were rude, rough, whoremongers: vaine, emptie, careless . . . !"

Like medical knowledge, clean habits were slow to develop.

The treatment of disease was still based largely on old wives' tales and medieval mumbo-jumbo. Certain classic remedies were stubbornly held to be effective, even though some may well have killed off more people than they cured. Soothing syrups, opiates and poultices were always popular, but for the plague itself, methods and medicines could be weird and varied in the extreme. One medico put all his faith into hot plasters made up of resin, the roots of white lilies and dried human dung! Another plumped for a treacle mixture, at least ten years old, in which the main ingredients were "good wine and chopped-up snakes ...". To have a good sniff at foul odours was also considered beneficial, it having been noted that "attendants who take care of latrines, and those who serve in hospitals and other malodorous places, are nearly all considered immune to infection ...". The sight of plague-haunted people perched over privies, "absorbing with relish the foetid smells", would have been very funny had it not been so pitiful.

But the universal cure-all was blood-letting. It was not for nothing that the old doctors were called leeches. The title persisted, although as the years went by, they became increasingly skilled at bleeding patients by surgical incision. Whatever the illness, to get rid of 'bad blood' at all costs became quite an obsession.

Unfortunately, not all practitioners were over-competent in the use of instruments, with the result that quite a few unfortunates were killed off accidentally. In Oxford, several such cases are on record. In 1657, a gentleman commoner of Balliol, James Powell, died miserably from gangrene after being bled for a comparatively minor ailment. The job was bungled by "one Grundy, an apprentice chirurgion, which having learned the new fashion of striking the vein, missed it and struck an arterie ...". Poor Powell's arm swelling up and festering, Grundy offered to cut it off, but the offer was politely declined and the poor chap expired with thanks.

In spite of the aversion of James I for "the black, stinking fume" and his strenuous efforts to have the habit put down, smoking was long considered to be a great prophylactic. Clay pipes and strong Virginia tobacco were always in greater demand when disease threatened. During the Great Plague, "none that kept the tobacconists' shops had the pestilence and smoking was looked upon as a most excellent preservative, in so much that even children were obliged to smoak ...". The diarist Thomas Hearne once talked to a university beadle who had been a schoolboy at Eton in 1665. This man told him that even the littlest boys "were obliged to smoak in the school every morning, and he himself was never whipped so much in his life as he was one day, for *not* smoaking ...!".

Fire, which often seemed to follow plague, was a constant menace in the now jam-packed city. Colleges kept their own engines, one of which—200 years old and as splendid as a vintage car—can still be seen in a corner of New College cloisters. But after the days of its beginnings, when the wooden town was burned down several times, Oxford mercifully escaped wholesale destruction. The worst outbreak occurred during the Civil War, when within a couple of hours, 330 houses were destroyed in the crowded quarter to the west of Cornmarket. The fire was started by a Royalist foot soldier who happened to be roasting a stolen pig in a quiet back yard.

A few years afterwards, Oxford caught the whiff of an infinitely greater conflagration. On 2nd September 1666 Anthony Wood recorded in his diary the start of the Great Fire of London: "The wind being eastward blew clouds of smoke over Oxford the next day and chiefly on Tuesday, and the sunshine was much darkened. The same night also, the moone was darkened by cloudes of smoak and looked reddish. ..."

Refugees from the capital appeared in the street, wandering and disconsolate, and a number of Cockney tradesmen set up shop. In towns close enough to London to hear eye-witness accounts from survivors, people were thoroughly frightened by the magnitude of the disaster. In Oxford, "everyone being soe suspicious, noe sorry fellowe could pass but they examined him; no gun or squib could go off but they thought it was the fatall blow ...".

Three days after the Great Fire began, people in church listening to a sermon thought they heard someone outside shouting, "Fire! Fire!" Already in a highly nervous state, the whole congregation rushed out in a panic, only to find that a butcher driving oxen across Carfax had been calling the cattleman's "Hyupp! Hyupp!" to his beasts.

By the beginning of the eighteenth century, plague in England had virtually burnt itself out. There were still large-scale epidemics in which many people died, but *bacillus pestis*, the micro-organism that had caused all the trouble, was gone. In its place came a variety of other infections which, in the absence of modern knowledge and skills, often proved fatal. "This month and in one or two months before", wrote the invaluable Wood in August 1690, "there was the griping of the guts common in Oxford, and many dye thereof. . . ." Such agonies might be due to anything from bad water and food poisoning to germ-laden airs drifting from any of a thousand sources of rottenness in the city. Little was done about them, nor could be done.

To some diseases, however, increasing attention was given. Smallpox was a common and considerable killer. Many who survived a virulent attack were at best disfigured and at worst blinded. Although Edward Jenner was not to start his researches into vaccination until 1788, inoculation for the pox had been tried out with some success at least sixty years before. In 1721, experiments were being performed upon prisoners in Newgate and other gaols—surely a pre-echo of Nazi methods in the concentration camps. And in 1774, after eleven guinea-pig prisoners in Oxford Castle had died, Town and Gown got together in an unsuccessful attempt to put a stop to such goings-on.

By 1860 compulsory vaccination had all but wiped out this once widespread affliction. With the Industrial Revolution, however, disease took on new and less familiar forms. Until the coming of Morris Motors, Oxford might not have been much of an industrial town, but it still suffered considerably from the typical nineteenth-century urban scourges. This is not really surprising. Within the old city boundaries, a great part of the population was crowded into crumbly dwellings that lacked drainage, adequate light or air, and a proper water supply. The new workers' quarters in areas such as Jericho were thrown up at a time when buildings byelaws did not exist, and were little better than the medieval middens. Neither habits nor habitat did much to arrest an epidemic, once it took a hold.

'Consumption' and typhoid fever were the two diseases of the period, the one caused mainly by malnutrition, the other by infected food or water contaminated with sewage. In Oxford, even the most genteel areas could be afflicted by a succession of fevers and the young gentlemen in the colleges were often laid low. Sewage was discharged directly into the rivers, some very close to Magdalen Bridge, and the once-sparkling Trill Mill Stream at Christ Church carried so much brown filth that under-graduates ironically named it Pactolus, the gold-bearing river of Greek mythology. There was always "the ancient fishy smell which pervaded the riversides when flood water subsided, and which was so characteristic of Oxford in the Lent Term ...". This stench arose every year from a horrid mixture of decompos-ing plants and town sewage which the floods spread over the fields. It was said that the water meadows might be dangerous to health, but they were marvellous for their bumper crops of hay.

Many of the countless malaises and disorders prevalent during the eighteenth and nineteenth centuries must have arisen from tainted water. Until the time of James I both city and university drew their supplies from wells sunk into the Oxford gravel, and these were never far from cesspits and privies. Public cisterns were dotted about the town, although nearly all have now disappeared.

The first step to be taken towards the provision of a proper water system was taken in 1616. Otho Nicholson, one of the wealthier fellows of Christ Church, paid for the erection of a handsome Renaissance-style conduit house at Carfax. This was fed by spring water collected on Hinksey Hill and brought down in wooden pipes, these being later extended to the colleges and other parts of the town. The conduit supply served most of the colleges until 1865. For long a well-known city landmark, Carfax Conduit had its moments of glory as, for instance, when the spouts feeding the basin "ran claret for the vulgar people" in honour of the visit of James II. Lucky people! The whole elaborate building was pulled down in 1787 to ease congestion at the increasingly busy crossroads. The stonework was then pre-sented to the Earl of Harcourt, who had the conduit re-erected as a garden feature in Nuneham Park, where it still exists.

Various later efforts were made to improve water supplies. In 1694 a company was granted a 900-year monopoly "To erect an Engine and Sistone" on waste land near Folly Bridge "to convey water to all the principal streets and lanes ...". Never a very efficient set-up, its owners were constantly being called upon to increase the efficiency of the ponderous water engine or "to keep their cisterne full in the night tyme" in case fire broke out in the town. Eventually, the whole Heath Robinson arrangement was taken over by the corporation.

The final episode in the long tragedy of Oxford pestilences had nothing to do with water, or weather, or sanitation. The great influenza epidemic of 1918 was due almost entirely to the exhaustions of an apparently never-ending world war. Terrible and widespread, it raged across the continents like one of the pandemic plagues of old, decimating populations and wiping out 20 million people in less than a year. Weakened physically and mentally by four years of war, many Oxonians fell with the rest. By now, there were less than 400 students in residence at the university, but even these few suffered proportionately. In the town, the working-class districts of Jericho and St. Ebbe's paid a particularly heavy toll in lives. Volunteers from the women's colleges did their brave best to help. Girls working in pairs and going from house to house would quite often find whole families collapsed in bed, sometimes with corpses among them.

Plague, sweating sickness, black fever, typhoid, smallpox, tuberculosis, influenza; all have come to Oxford and passed on their way, bringing fear, leaving stark memories of horror endured. It is possible that their impact has made some contribution to that strange 'spirit of the place' that is always being talked about, but this is to be doubted. The only certain thing is that Oxford has survived. And survives.

IX

NO CERTAIN PURSE

Although it has 10,000 students, a considerable staff and some very concrete evidences of existence, Oxford University still has no central physical core. There is no tidy campus, no group of grave buildings of which one can say: this is the university, nor is such a layout ever likely to materialize. These arrangements (and then only on the smallest scale) are seen only in the colleges. And the colleges are *not* the university.

It seems fitting that Oxford and Cambridge, the only universities in the world to have preserved the medieval collegiate system intact, should not only be different but also look different from all the rest. The *studium* of the Middle Ages developed organically rather than geometrically and nowhere can this natural growth be better seen than inside the half-mile circle which is centred on Carfax.

Like the methods by which it diffuses learning, the buildings of the university are spread around. Some are tucked away and hard to find. Some are more obvious. Sometimes they come singly, and in unexpected places, like the Radcliffe Observatory. Others jostle together in clusters and informal groupings, small enclaves of seriousness hemmed in by demanding neighbours or existing on strips of territory grudgingly conceded by the colleges. The best of these, Radcliffe Square, is as near to the heart of the whole business as you will ever get and the lovely dome of its Camera the only obvious centre point you will find.

It is in this tightly-packed area that all the original university buildings can be seen; those component parts of the intellectual powerhouse that is Oxford University. Here is St. Mary's Church, in which the first scholars received their degrees. Here, tacked on to St. Mary's like an extra chancel, is the Old Congregation House,

The Radcliffe Camera

the very first building that the university could really regard as its own.

For at least two centuries before 1320, the year in which Adam de Brome, founder of Oriel College, built the Congregation House, St. Mary's itself had been regularly used for a variety of academic purposes. Forum, court room, examination hall, treasury—in turn it was all these things and more besides. And for all this time, as Edward Thomas wrote, the university "had neither a roof nor a certain purse". The construction of this two-storey annexe marked a great step forward. Although high ceremonial was still carried out within the body of the church, the real business of scholastic administration could now be conducted elsewhere. Oxford University, already rather more than just "a spirit of wisdom and grace" had a home.

It also had a little money. But although financial endowments began steadily to increase in number, another century went by before work was begun on the second building, the famous Divinity School. The magnificent Gothic vaulting of the interior long ago earned for the school the accolade of being "the finest room in Europe" and even today, the honour is not unmerited. To walk inside its marvellous hall for the first time is a breath-taking experience and it comes as no surprise that three successive generations of master masons worked on the job for seventy years before the final stones were put into place in 1490.

This first building complex in and around Catte Street grew with painful slowness. This was partly because the all-important task of teaching devolved more and more upon the colleges, but more so because there was rarely very much cash in hand to carry out elaborate schemes. Initially, the university had ludicrously small funds. In 1240, its only regular income was a settlement of 52 shillings a year. And the earliest recorded benefaction, made three years later was "8 marks per annum"—perhaps £50 in modern terms—from the estate of one Alan Basset. Even at thirteenth-century values, this was hardly a princely piece of benevolence. Later gifts became larger. In 1249, a legacy of 310 marks was received from William of Durham. The money was left "for the maintenance in perpetuity of ten Masters of Arts", but led indirectly to the founding of University College, originally known as 'The Great Hall of the University of Oxford'.

As the years went by, the fame of Oxford increased and many

8

The Chapel, Trinity College
Holywell Music Room, the oldest in Europe

benefactions were made with the specific object of providing necessary buildings. At first, the colleges were considerably more favoured than the university itself, for by founding a hall or college, a man could build his personal monument and thereby achieve some sort of immortality. The names, if nothing more, of Walter de Merton, John de Balliol, Nicholas Wadham—and in a later age, of Lord Nuffield—will be remembered as long as their colleges exist. Other men provided for the expansion and development of existing foundations, building libraries and chapels, and in the process creating some of the world's finest collegiate architecture.

Yet in spite of the general desire of rich men to found colleges, the university was never entirely forgotten. It was soon seen to be developing a power of its own, and serving a grander purpose than any one of its component parts. After the first enthusiastic wave of college founding spent itself (starting with Balliol in 1260, no less than nine were established in little more than 100 years) the university began to share in the general benevolence of the times.

Long before the old House of Congregation was erected, seven of the colleges were already in being and three more had appeared during the building of the Divinity School. All of these scholastic societies were autonomous bodies. The fellows conducted their own affairs without hindrance and within their own walls. They had their own funds, their own libraries, their own churches, their own living arrangements. Somewhere outside was the university, providing a loose organization, some general discipline, essential contacts with higher authority and the power to put troublesome townsmen in their place whenever they presumed to step out of line. But even at an early date it was also recognized that the university provided certain other services. The awarding of degrees—in effect, licences to teach—was important and scarcely less so was the teaching offered in the various schools. Young students, some of whom would one day be members of colleges, had to be looked after.

It is not always realized that, until the beginning of the sixteenth century, the colleges were made up of graduates only, scholars who had already been awarded at least a bachelor's degree. The great body of students lived in halls and lodgings scattered about the city. They belonged to no college. At best, they were attached to an inn or hall licensed by the Chancellor, where their life and work was under the jurisdiction—sometimes no more than nominal—of a principal. At worst they were unattached and left to fend for themselves. Many of these paid a fee to be entered on the roll or *matricula* of an approved master, after which they started on the long course of studies leading to a degree. Even today, every Oxford undergraduate must 'matriculate' by presenting to the university an educational certificate as proof of his competence.

Although very few of the early students were members of colleges, all were members of the university. Boys of 14, wild sparks in their twenties, sober clerks old enough to be their fathers, doddering greybeards: all shared in the benefits of the common weal, differing only in the seniority of their membership. From fluffy-cheeked youngsters to quavering ancients, everyone came under the protection of the academic body which now began to provide more and more facilities for its scholars.

The murder of Thomas à Becket in 1170 and the building of the House of Congregation in 1320 make two useful reference points in the early history of the university. The first symbolized a serious clash between Church and State. The second marked a step on the road to intellectual freedom, to a pursuit of knowledge unhampered by religious prejudice. Though the Church was to have a considerable hand in university affairs for centuries still to come, the scholars took an increasingly independent line. Congregation now met in a secular and not an ecclesiastical house. A pattern for the future had been laid down.

This span of 150 years was certainly the first great formative period in the life of Oxford University. At the beginning, there was little in the way of rules and organization and students had no real sense of 'belonging'. In the end, they had become fiercely loyal, defending their privileges by force of arms and making it clear that they regarded themselves as a state within the State; an island which people attacked at their peril. The Church, out of which the *studium* had evolved, remained a dominating force, but, as time passed, its grip began to slacken. It could not withstand for ever the questioning, independent attitudes of the scholars, among whom were to be found some of the greatest minds of their time.

The Bishop of Lincoln might still be the nominal overlord, but the Masters of Oxford were soon putting up their own man for the all-important office of Chancellor. The university was a growing and a going concern and the masters were the people who had to keep the machine running. Prayers and piety had a natural place in the scheme of things, but practical considerations were of no less importance. The medieval scholar might have been the Church's own creation, but he was now beginning to kick hard against too much religious domination.

Paradoxically, the slackening of ecclesiastical control is first really noticeable during this vital thirteenth century, when the number of religious houses in and around Oxford was reaching its peak. Perhaps the scholars thought that they were getting too much of a good thing. Certainly, there was no lack of new foundations. With the three great houses of St. Frideswide, Osney and Godstow already firmly established, the Church undertook further expansion. In 1282, Rewley Abbey was founded as a place of study for Cistercian monks and was soon to become the largest establishment of its kind in England. Within the city itself, Gloucester College was set up a year later for the Benedictines, to be followed in 1291 by Durham College. Although strictly religious in nature, these houses became an important part of Oxford's increasingly complex educational system.

But the influence of the monks was far less than that of the friars, whose arrival may well have spurred the Establishment on to greater efforts. The first little groups of mendicants began to appear in Oxford as early as 1221, when the Dominicans occupied a few buildings in the Jewry, on the east side of St. Aldates. Three years later, with St. Francis of Assisi still alive, a company of his Grey Friars arrived, settling themselves close to the city wall down by Paradise Street. Hard on their heels came the Austins, the red-gowned Trinitarians and, last of all, the cross-bearing Crutched Friars.

Dedicated to the life of poverty and entirely dependent upon alms, they brought with them few material possessions. But they did possess lively and inquiring minds and knew how to use them. Their numbers were small but their influence was powerful. Their coming was not so much a breath of fresh air as a wind of gale force, blowing through an Oxford already fusty with traditional teachings.

It quickly became clear that poor though they were, these

mendicants were men of no mean intellect. Some were truly great: Adam Marsh, lawyer, statesman and theologian; Duns Scotus, terror of the age and the "subtil doctor" who was sent to found Cologne University; William of Ockham, the Nominalist philosopher; Robert Grosseteste, the first Chancellor, "finest scholar of his time and master mind of the age". And towering above them all, the English Leonardo, Roger Bacon, without question a man of sheer genius.

Scholars of this calibre were hardly likely to be satisfied with the long-established curriculum of the university, based as it was on the ancient 'Seven Liberal Arts and Three Philosophies' of Aristotle. The friars had humanist leanings and their love of nature attracted them to the study of medicine, physics and the other natural sciences. These enthusiasms led to a serious general interest in subjects previously considered to be unworthy of academic attention.

The newcomers were prepared to accept the seven liberal arts—the *Trivium* of Grammar, Rhetoric and Dialectic, with bits of the classics and Roman Law thrown in—and the *Quadrivium* made up of Music, Arithmetic, Geometry and Astronomy. They admitted the importance of the three philosophies; Natural, Moral and Metaphysical. And being above all men of God, they had no quarrel with the over-riding pre-eminence of Theology as 'the supreme science'.

But the friars were already looking ahead to a more exciting world. Chemistry, physics and experimental science were only three of their special fields. It is not surprising that the first School of Mathematics in Europe was established in Oxford. Or that the work of Roger Bacon, conducting strange experiments in his tower on Folly Bridge, should influence the world of scholarship up to the Reformation and beyond.

Yet in spite of their achievements, the friars created a lot of ill-feeling. They were accused of all kinds of malpractice, sometimes not without good reason. One frequent grumble was that being always eager for new recruits, they were given to enticing boys into their orders with promises of easy living and a grand education. In 1358, the university made a serious attempt to put a stop to such practices by framing a statute forbidding the friars to take in any student less than 18 years of age. A more malicious complaint, though not without foundation, was that members of the orders commonly obtained their degrees by influence, rather than by hard work. During the fourteenth century, they became known as 'the wax doctors'. The name was given them because: "They seek to extort graces from the universitie by means of the letters of lords sealed with wax, or because they run from hard study as wax runs from the face of the fire."

There is no doubt that some of them went gossiping in high places and got themselves involved in dangerous matters. Because of their Continental origins, the friars were still thought of as 'foreigners' and in troublous times, were regarded with great suspicion. The Dominicans, in particular, were always being accused of harbouring 'foreign spies'. Certainly, Italians, Spaniards, Portuguese, Germans and, not least, the detested French were among their number. And in 1381 they were actually accused of helping to foment Wat Tyler's ill-fated Peasants' Revolt.

In the world of learning, however, these "eager, impetuous friars" exerted a lasting influence. No-one could deny the power of giants like Bacon whose "adventures of the mind were soon passing into realms hitherto undreamed of". Indeed, it has been claimed that if he, instead of St. Thomas Aquinas, had become the favoured philosopher, the long and bitter struggle between science and theology would have been avoided.

As Albert Mansbridge wrote: "The friars were in the van of intellectual and social advance. . . . Their coming was a clear call to the University to go beyond the purely 'academic' life and the requirements of the organized Church to those which would serve the needs—physical, intellectual and spiritual—of the layman. . . ."

Unfortunately, the call was not answered and it was not until the beginning of the twentieth century that "the true functions of the university were exercised without religious check . . .".

The academic authorities did not much like the friars. For one thing, they were increasingly indifferent to the established customs of the university. For another, they tended to strike out along independent paths which were often right outside the prescribed courses of study. And a more serious challenge was posed by the way in which they were infiltrating into positions of administrative control.

This official dislike of their activities was compounded of many fears and prejudices, but the chief ingredients were considerable envy, a mistrust of anything new and a fear of the unknown. Yet these antagonisms did have useful results. The houses of the mendicant orders offered better facilities for teaching and quiet study than most other places in Oxford. As corporate and self-governing societies, they provided prototypes on which the early halls and colleges could be modelled. It was no coincidence that the first spate of college-building occurred during the great days of the friars.

Nor can it have been a happy accident that during the same period, the university began to reveal itself as a material presence. Roger Bacon died in 1294, Duns Scotus in 1308, William of Ockham in 1347. The Old Congregation House was completed in 1320 and 100 years later the Divinity School was in building. By this time, the friars had been in Oxford for nearly two centuries, but before this finest room in Europe had been finished, their power was clearly beginning to wane. The Renaissance was already in being. Not far ahead was the Reformation, when most of northern Europe was to reject the teachings of the Roman Catholic Church. In England, the Dissolution of the Monasteries would soon sweep away monks and friars alike.

It must have been a bitter time for them. Great humanists, almost revolutionary in their thinking, intensely curious about the nature of the world, the friars had lapsed into comparative idleness. They no longer produced men of genius. Time had caught up with them and the new world they had helped to create was passing them by.

The university, on the other hand, survived the Reformation. It emerged a little bruised, not quite certain of its direction, but still more or less intact. With roots deep in the past and still clinging tenaciously to the 'Old Faith' it could hardly expect entirely to escape the attentions of Henry VIII's Commissioners, who were so zealous in their liquidation of Oxford's friaries and monastic houses. But the king valued scholarship and did not let his men go too far. They kept well within their terms of reference, proceeding "with tenderness and admirable impartiality". Henry, a fierce and frightening man, let it be known that he would not "impaire the revenewes of anie one House by a single penie . . .".

All the same, colleges with monkish allegiances were not included in this declaration of good intent and every one of them was closed down. Furthermore, anything that smacked of 'popery' suffered spoiling or destruction. Statues, carvings, medieval stained glass, precious missals and manuscripts were broken up, burned or carted away. The priceless collection of rare books presented to the university by Humphrey, Duke of Gloucester in 1435, housed in a library over the Divinity School, disappeared completely and has never come to light.

The accession to the throne of 'Bloody Mary' marked a kind of counter-Reformation. For the five years of her reign, Protestants were in jeopardy and Roman Catholicism was once again the state religion. Academics who had expressed themselves too strongly for reform went in fear of their lives. The wise and discreet removed themselves to places of safety. Others were arrested and thrown into prison, where they received the harshest treatment. The ones with the courage of their convictions were done to death. In 1555, "in the Towne Ditch, over against Baliell Colledge", two Cambridge divines, Ridley and Latimer, were burnt as heretics. A few months later, kindly Archbishop Cranmer followed them to the stake. At Balliol, they still preserve a pair of ancient doors, blistered and blackened, it is said, by the heat of the fires in which the martyrs were roasted.

During this long and troubled period, the university had more money in its purse, although there was not much to show for it. Cash coming in went out again for a variety of purposes. A great deal was lent out to poor students free of interest. As security, they pledged any article of value they might possess: books, clothing, candlesticks and trinkets were favourite 'cautions'. Together with cash in hand, these were kept in chests under the guardianship of university officials. If the pledges were not redeemed within twelve months, the goods were sold off and the monies received paid into the common fund.

The university was thus engaged in a sort of academic pawn-broking business, a system which seems to have operated for at least 300 years. The endowment of a chest became a popular form of legacy in the wills of people wishing to help scholars. In the fourteenth and fifteenth centuries, no less than twenty-four were set up, representing charities of an annual value of some 2,000 marks. The very first was the famous St. Frideswide's Chest, established in 1240 by Grosseteste, by this time Bishop of Lincoln. At this period, Jewish moneylenders were charging students vicious rates of interest on loans, so the official chest must have come as a godsend to those in financial difficulties.

Until 1293, when the Countess of Warwick presented a gift of 120 marks, no other chest existed. For fifty years, all the worldly wealth of the university was contained in this one big iron-banded box kept for safety in St. Mary's Church. Into it came scholastic fees, fines paid by students and townsfolk for their various misdemeanours, occasional donations, a few jewels, books, papers, I.O.U.s, loan pledges and anything else of value. Out of it, all payments were made.

As with the founding of colleges, the great era of chest-endowment occurred during the Middle Ages. The system was crude and unsophisticated, but it worked and the number of chests steadily increased. After 1320, they were stacked in the Old Congregation House like coffins in a crypt: the Vaughan, Neale and Scapeia Chests; the Exeter and Chichele Chests; the New Chest; the Joanna Danvers Chest. Like parish chests, all had at least three locks, the keys for which were held separately by three custodians.

The fifteen century was a time of general reform. Under Gilbert Kymer, the only Chancellor ever to have been a Doctor of Medicine, there was a considerable revision of courses and lectures. New subjects were introduced and more stringent rules of behaviour laid down. Clearly, the university was beginning to feel its strength, but it was not satisfied merely to tighten up methods of administration and teaching. It wanted to build. The older colleges had already been in existence for nearly 200 years and some of them were housed in splendid buildings. Yet all that the university could show of itself at this period was the Congregation House, and even this was being mistaken for just another aisle of St. Mary's Church. "There was a desire which amounted almost to a passion", wrote Strickland Gibson, "to build schools of its own. . . ."

The little rooms rented from a variety of owners and scattered about the city were now considered too mean and inadequate for teaching purposes. In 1439 the Abbot of Osney provided a block of lecture-rooms in Schools Street, but he had already been anticipated by the university. As early as 1420, plans were made to provide the all-important Faculty of Theology with a suitable home of its own. Land was bought from the fellows of Balliol

College, appeals made for funds and the construction work started.

But the university still had no certain purse. Economies had to be made and the final building was smaller and less elaborate than originally intended. Nevertheless, the new Divinity School emerged as a glorious example of Tudor architecture. Before its completion, an upper storey was added to house the collection of books and manuscripts presented by Humphrey, Duke of Gloucester, brother of Henry V and the man who had fought by his side at the Battle of Agincourt.

'Humphrey', as this fine chamber is affectionately known, retains much of its original splendour and is nowadays one of the many reading rooms of the Bodleian Library. Together with the Divinity School down below, it was for sixty years the university's pride and joy, but after the visitation of the Royal Commissioners in 1550, was stripped bare of all its books and furnishings. For long, it lay dilapidated and derelict, and until the end of the sixteenth century no-one seemed very interested in its fate.

In 1598, however, the man who was to create one of the world's greatest libraries came to the rescue. The benefactions of Sir Thomas Bodley, one-time fellow of Merton, were so great that James I, a right royal cracker of corny jokes, commented that his name should have been Godly, not Bodley! But at this time, Sir Thomas was plain Master Bodley. After a busy political career as Queen Elizabeth's ambassador at various foreign courts, he returned home "to take his farewell of State employments and to set up his staff at the library door in Oxford . . .".

He soon announced his intention of restoring 'Duke Humphrey' and started the ball rolling with a very large personal donation. He had great influence at court, and was soon persuading some of his rich friends to make contributions. By the end of 1602, the building had been re-opened to scholars. Provided with some 2,000 books and manuscripts, it became the nucleus of the renowned Bodleian Library, of which this famous room still exists as the original and oldest part.

Within ten years, the number of books added to the collection was so great that the 'Humphrey' was bursting at the seams. The far-sighted Bodley had made a deal with the Stationers' Company by which his library was to be presented with a free copy of every new book published in England. Long since regularized by Act of

Parliament, the arrangement still stands and has been of great benefit not only to the Bodleian, but to the British Museum and the four other 'copyright libraries' entitled to share in the scheme.

Free books for all time may be fine, but they do create a continuous housing problem. Even in Bodley's day, when far fewer were published, his arrangement with the stationers and booksellers was creating difficulties. The need for extension became urgent and between 1610 and 1613, what is now called the 'Arts End' of the library was built, the whole cost being met by the good Sir Thomas.

Yet this was still only a beginning. While the extension was still under construction, he was already making inquiries about the ownership of a plot of ground next to the Divinity School. He wrote of the need for "better built schooles than those ruinous little roomes" then being used for lectures. The university itself had plans for a double-storey schools building on the same piece of land, so this indefatigable old gentleman sought to gain the best of both worlds by providing money in his will for the construction of a third storey as and when the schools project went ahead. Needless to say, this extra floor was to form a library!

This marked the start of the next university building, the Schools Quadrangle. Known today as the Old Schools, in spite of its main function as a part of the Bodleian Library, this fine square was the first real home of the various faculties of the university. The names of the subjects inscribed over its many doorways are a guide to the basically medieval curriculum still in use when these ranges of lecture rooms were built. Philosophy, logic, rhetoric, law, music, astronomy are all here, but the rooms in which they were taught have long been given over to Bodley's books. You may still enter the Bodleian through entrances marked *Schola Naturilis Philosophiae* or *Schola Medicinae* but many years have passed since any teaching took place inside.

Until the new Examination Schools were opened in 1882, however, undergraduates still came to the Old Schools to be put through their paces. Descriptions of their ordeals abound; some of them fact, some made into the most entertaining fiction. In *Tom Brown at Oxford*, the famous quadrangle is presented by Thomas Hughes as "for the most part, a most lonely place . . .".

The shuddering youth of Oxford still has to wear its dark 'subfusc' suit, its white bow tie, and its mortar board before presenting itself for "torture in the Schools". And even the female of the species must be suitably attired in dark skirt, white blouse and black tie. But nowadays, its agonizing and its celebrating takes place elsewhere. For the past ninety years, the New Examination Schools ("the only place in the world where the plough is used as an offensive weapon") have provided the setting.

This austere block, designed in the Elizabethan style and modelled upon Kirby Hall, is used mostly for university lectures, but for three weeks in June every year, some 3,000 candidates spend an average of six days each sweating it out in the question-and-answer mill of 'Final Schools'.

Decorated with carvings of happy scholars being examined by kindly professors, the encouraging main entrance is in the High Street. Round the corner, in Merton Lane, is a sort of superior back yard, until recently the traditional scene of wild shennanigans at the end of Finals. Here, it was always the custom for a man's friends to greet him with drinks and joyous cries at the close of his ordeal and the courtyard echoed with the popping of corks.

But all this came long after the time of Sir Thomas Bodley. He died in January 1613, before even the foundation stone of the Old Schools was laid. This last venture continued, however, and during the next few years, his executors paid out large sums in furtherance of the work. Finally completed in 1640 with the building of a west wing (the 'Selden End'), the whole scheme is a delightful essay in Jacobean Gothic with Renaissance trimmings.

Had Sir Thomas foreseen the day when his library would house two and a half million volumes, take over the Radcliffe Camera, have the huge New Bodleian Building as an annexe, possess subterranean bookstacks like catacombs and a maze of passages like the London Underground, he would no doubt have felt highly gratified.

The troubles of King and Parliament, the outbreak of the Civil War, the uncertainties of conflict and the unrestful days of the Commonwealth all brought university building to a temporary halt. Men had ideas, but these were expressed in regulation and statute, rather than in brick and stone. Construction began again only after the restoration of the monarchy, and as before, with no fixed income and little cash in hand, the university had to look round for benefactors.

The first to come along was Gilbert Sheldon, who had earlier been expelled from office as Warden of All Souls College by the Roundheads. In 1663, he was made Archbishop of Canterbury, but not before he had suggested the erection of "some public fabrick" in which university ceremonies of a secular nature might be celebrated more fittingly than in St. Mary's Church. A Convocation House had been provided under the 'Selden End' of the Bodleian complex some twenty years before, but this was basically a meeting room for business and hardly suitable for the splendiferous processionals on which the academics prided themselves.

The architect chosen for the scheme was Christopher Wren. He was then Savilian Professor of Astronomy and in between making calculations of the motions of the planets and observing the transit of Mercury through a telescope mounted on the tower of the Old Schools, he quickly produced a design. A scale model was knocked up by a local mason for £10, and after showing it to his fellow members of the Royal Society, he received official approval from the university and was told to proceed.

Although the Sheldonian Theatre is never used for the presentation of conventional plays, a theatre in the sense of being a setting for dramatic spectacles it always has been. It has also been much utilized for musical performances. In 1733, Handel played the organ here in the first performance of his oratorio *Athalia*, accompanied by "his lousy crew of German fiddlers . . .". That hard-bitten Jacobite, Thomas Hearne had much that was scurrilous to say about this "parcel of unconscionable scamps of musicians" and refused to pay for tickets at five shillings a time. In the end, however, the fame of Mr. Handel and the attraction of a brand-new work was too much and he and his anti-Hanoverian friends did attend "to try how a little fiddling would sit upon them". Every seat was sold.

When not required for academic promenadings, the Sheldonian is still used quite often for recitals and orchestral concerts. The acoustics are good and the surroundings frequently evocative of the period in which the music was written. To hear one of the 'Brandenburgs' under the painted ceiling of this fine classical interior can be a memorable experience.

Yet although the gods move around, all is on a very human scale. The component parts of the theatre—columns, doorways, balustrades and windows—are quite small for a public building, so that both inside and out the whole structure gives the impression of being domestic in scale. But there is at least one big feature: the great, plain doors, god-like in size, through which the processions enter. These are high enough and wide enough to admit giants, which was maybe the thought behind them.

The main interior space of the Sheldonian relies much upon the scene painter for its effects, the most famous of which is the ceiling, the work of Robert Streeter, 'Serjeant Painter to the Crown'. Wren wanted to give the impression of a typical Roman theatre, with its roof open to the warm Italian sky and asked Streeter "to provide the appearance of painted canvas strained over gilt cordage". This he did in dashing style ("better than Reubens", said Samuel Pepys) filling the blue vault of his theatrical heaven with some splendid figures representing Truth surrounded by a bevy of the Arts and Sciences, from whose lofty presence Envy, Rapine and Ignorance are being dashed down in disorder.

In its time, the Sheldonian has held as many as 3,000 people, but modern safety requirements now limit audiences to no more than half that number. Nevertheless, the big occasions see the open floor and tiers of seating packed to capacity. The 'Act of Commemoration', the Encaenia, is easily the biggest and best of the showpieces. Taking place at the end of the summer term, it is the high spot of the university's year. Originally held in St. Mary's, 'The Act' traditionally became an excuse for students to let off steam and poke fun at their academic elders. Sometimes, however, the rowdyism went too far and was not the sort of behaviour to be tolerated in a church.

Fortunately, the first Commemoration to be held in the new Theatre was notably free from interruption. On 7th July 1669 John Evelyn recorded in his diary that the ceremony of dedication was celebrated "with the greatest splendor and formalitie". To Oxford came "a worlde of strangers and other companie from all parts of the nation" and there were speeches and music making from eleven in the morning until seven at night. "A work of admirable Contrivance and Magnificence", the Theatre was Christopher Wren's "first publick performance" as an architect, in appreciation of which, Archbishop Sheldon presented him with a gold cup.

Since that first day, more than 300 'Acts' have taken place in the

Sheldonian and the ceremonies continue much as they have always done. Undergraduates, crowding the floor, persist in asserting their ancient right of interruption, alternately jeering and applauding the proceedings. In 1905, the novelist Henry James felt that the impressiveness of the Encaenia "was much diminished by the boisterous conduct of the students, who superabound in extravagant applause, in impertinent interrogation and in lively disparagement of the Orator's Latinity . . .". At the same time, he appreciated that this ill-mannered display was "only another expression of the venerable and historic side of Oxford . . . tolerated because it is traditional; possible because it is classical. . . ."

James was three generations away from the modern age of student protest. What he would have made of sit-ins, break-ins, demos, and almost daily explosions of violence is problematical. And whether he would still have regarded the goings-on of the nineteen-seventies as 'possible because they were classical' is very much to be doubted. At any rate, the Sheldonian, unlike some other university buildings, has not so far been violated. The reason may well be that on most days of the year it is a haunt of innocent sightseers rather than of those conniving reactionary/right-wing/ neo-fascist/academic jackals that the honest working/left-wing/ democratically-orientated student loves to hate.

X

CASH IN HAND

In 1957, embarking upon a fifteen-year building programme, Oxford University began a massive expansion of its facilities. This first great planned development, costing some £13 million, is nearing completion as this book is written. With the aid of huge government grants, new libraries, laboratories, lecture theatres and research centres have all been provided, together with a great deal of miscellaneous accommodation in which the various faculties were sadly lacking.

The sheer size and scale of this effort completely overshadows anything that has gone before. Previous university buildings have tended to come singly and in a comparatively haphazard fashion. But this is the age of the planner and of a modern technology that demands quick results. The processes of construction have been tremendously accelerated. Cathedrals are built in ten years, completely new colleges in less than five and a mere million-pound computer laboratory is run up in eighteen months. The face of Oxford, once hardly changing from one generation to the next, is almost transformed in a couple of summers. Tower cranes on the skyline compete for attention with the traditional spires and the dust and turmoil of half-a-dozen building sites reminds visitors—sometimes unpleasantly—that Oxford belongs to a modern age.

The work is by no means over. As one programme ends, another is to begin. The present undergraduate population of 10,000 or so may not begin to compare with the numbers of students in American State Universities, or the even greater numbers of the Moscow State University. Nevertheless, it is growing steadily. As a result of the policy adopted after the publication of the famous Robbins Report of 1963, Oxford plans to have 11,500 students by 1977 and five years later, the total should be reaching 13,000.

Perpendicular triumph—Magdalen Tower
A Morris monument—the tower, Nuffield College

An academic expansion of this order may be deplored by traditionalists, but once begun, there is no stopping it. The colleges extend to keep pace with the increasing flow of students. The university, under an obligation to provide them with the right facilities for study and research, has no alternative but to build and build and build. In May 1970, a report of the Sites and Development Committee again emphasized the need for still more of everything: for more faculty centres, more museums, more specialist libraries; for physics buildings in Keble Road, music buildings in Holywell, for a book repository at Nuneham Courtenay, the great classical mansion taken over by the university in 1950. There are schemes afoot for a vast new Pitt-Rivers Museum up the Banbury Road, and for extensions all over the place: to the Ashmolean Museum, to the Oriental Institute, to the Department of the History of Art and to a dozen other centres.

Apart from these, more accommodation is to be provided for even more sophisticated subjects. The computing sciences, chemistry, engineering, pharmacology, social medicine, metallurgy, bio-mathematics are all needing space and all must be taken care of. After 1972, when this new outburst of construction gets under way, the Grants Committee, which provides a great deal of the cash for all Britain's universities, will be faced with some staggering financial demands from Oxford.

Although its earlier buildings were nearly all in the nature of isolated exercises in architecture, the university has certainly been more active constructionally in certain periods than in others. After the appearance of the Congregation House, the Divinity School and the Old Bodleian group, further building took place in a series of definite waves. In the seventeenth century came the Physic Garden, the Sheldonian Theatre and the Old Ashmolean Museum; in the eighteenth the Clarendon Building, the Radcliffe Camera and the Radcliffe Observatory.

The first half of the nineteenth century saw the erection of the University Press, the Taylorian Institute and the New Ashmolean. After the great Victorian reforms began to take effect, there was a renewed energy. Ruskin's startling University Museum was completed in 1860, taking the first bite out of the green expanse of The Parks. It was followed by all kinds of laboratories and scientific departments, designed in a bewildering variety of styles The dream-scheme of Ruskin is in a sort of Venetian-Gothic, while the

9

New buildings, Somerville College
The 'Abbot's Kitchen,' Oxford's first chemistry laboratory

first Inorganic Chemistry Laboratory, finished soon afterwards is, of all things, "a sad replica of the octagonal Abbot's Kitchen at Glastonbury".

Away from the Parks, other buildings were soon rising above the scaffolding. The Union Society opened its new doors in 1864 and was soon to be re-decorated by those strenuous pre-Raphaelite gentlemen, Morris, Burne-Jones, D. G. Rossetti and Co. The New Examination Schools were in business by 1882. A few months later, the university was setting up the Indian Institute as a "centre of teaching and research on all subjects relative to the sub-Continent". By common consent and acclaim, this weird building on the corner of Holywell and Catte Street is reckoned as being easily the most ugly building in Oxford. Once described as "a pleasing mixture of Gothic and Oriental detail" it is eventually to be demolished to make way for something more worthy.

There was continuous development beyond the turn of the century and throughout the Edwardian era, until the outbreak of the First World War brought all work to a halt. Little was done in the nineteen-twenties, and few major projects were seriously considered, let alone started. Money was again hard to come by and it was acknowledged that far too many students were then being admitted to Oxford on the basis of their ability to pay the fees than on their intellectual attainments. Such buildings as were undertaken were designed with a strict regard for economy; a fact borne out by the utilitarian appearance of some of the structures in the 'Science Area' which had by now bitten very large chunks from the once-inviolable Parks. Natural stone, for centuries a *sine qua non* of Oxford architecture, was abandoned in favour of the much cheaper brick. Even the Rockefeller Foundation, which provided funds to build the Biochemical Laboratory in 1924 had to put up with "brick faced in aluminous cement to harmonize with the adjacent stone buildings". Which is a somewhat euphemistic way of saying that it was a cheap stucco job!

But in the last big building to go up in Oxford before the Second World War, there was a quite uncompromising use of masonry. Completed in 1940 at a cost of more than £1 million and designed to hold five million books, the New Bodleian Library rises like a cliff on the corner of Parks Road and The Broad. Nearly 375 years separate this huge block from Sir Thomas Bodley's modest beginnings, but the same questing spirit still seems to activate both places. They lie on opposite sides of the street, on opposite slopes of one of the ridges of history.

Upon the ridge, the Sheldonian Theatre faces two ways. In one direction, its windows look back towards the Middle Ages, saints and martyrs, friars, monasteries, the true faith, burnings, heretics, magic, fearful superstitions, the awful power of the Church. In the other its doors open to admit science, medicine, sanity, Newton, liberty of conscience, Jean Jacques Rousseau, Darwin, penicillin, the terrible power of the bomb.

When 'Oxford's faceless wonders'—those crumble-featured stone emperors which have just been given a face-lift, were being erected in front of the Theatre in 1669, religion still played a considerable part in the shaping of university thought and policy. But the Age of Reason was at hand and the old strength was noticeably weakening. Academic activities became increasingly secular and the need to provide for them in specially-designed buildings was obvious. In St. Mary's Church the official knee was still dutifully bent and religious observances harking back to medieval days were scrupulously maintained, but all other business was conducted elsewhere.

Even the venerable Old Congregation House was forsaken. Too small for the requirements of the time, it was considered both insufficiently impressive and too cheek-by-jowl with St. Mary's for a university that was now very much feeling its feet. The upper room, which Bishop Cobham turned into the first library in 1327, had long been made redundant by the development of 'Duke Humphrey' and the Bodleian. And with the provision of a House of Convocation in the Schools Quadrangle, the lower chamber also dropped out of use as the academic talking shop.

No one really seemed to know quite what to do with this first home of the university. After a long period of idleness, it was put to a variety of uses, some of them strange and most quite unconnected with learning. During the Civil War, the Royalists took over the place as a powder magazine. Under the Commonwealth administration, it became the *Domus Typographica* in which the university printers stored their founts of Greek and Oriental types. In Restoration days, it was utilized first as a bookseller's warehouse and then as a grammer school, but for most of the eighteenth century that followed, its two rooms were littered with rubbish and all was dilapidation and neglect.

The university seemed to be not only ashamed of its origins, but positively anxious to forget them. In the early nineteenth century, the fortunes of the House of Congregation sank to their lowest ebb when the ground floor was cleared out to make room for the official fire engine. Thereafter, there was some improvement. In the eighteen-sixties, the old place was turned into a chapel and lecture hall for non-collegiate students. This arrangement continued until 1923, when the upper floor was converted into a parish room and the space below made into "a repository for decayed sculptures" removed from the church.

This, in fact, is more or less the present usage, although the fine stone-vaulted lower room is now a crypt chapel. It is sad to think that while academic Oxford takes such pride in its centuries-old connection with St. Mary's (described in every guidebook as 'the University Church') the Old Congregation House is, by comparison, almost disowned. Every Sunday morning in term time, the traditional 'University Sermon' is preached in the pulpit from which men like Keble and Newman thundered, yet only a few yards away, "the very cradle of the University's being" stands silent and deserted, visited by tourists but neglected by those who ought to be its friends.

It all seems lacking in charity. Maybe there was something to be said for the old beadle who once remarked: "I have listened to University Sermons for fifty years but—thank God!—I still remain a Christian!"

Nevertheless, St. Mary's itself is a suitably splendid building. The great 200-foot spire makes a rich and magnificent focal point along the curving vistas of The High and is still, as Thomas Sharp pointed out, "the highest feature on Oxford's historical skyline". Oldest and finest of the dreaming spires, the wide-ranging views of city and countryside to be had from its tower are well worth the steps and the sixpence required to get to the top.

There are two ways of entering the church: either beneath the tower from the cobblestone calm of Radcliffe Square, or through the delightfully incongruous Baroque porch out of the roaring river of High Street traffic. Both lead into the serene beauty of a late-Gothic interior which, in spite of the racket outside, is surprisingly quiet. The whole place has a cool, dreamlike quality accentuated—on the right sort of day!—by rippling images of blue sky, soft white clouds and the noble curves of the Radcliffe Camera seen through watery glazing. At such times it is altogether *la cathedrale engloutie.*

But at no time is there anything subdued or submerged about that amazing Italian fairground-style portico which fronts onto The High. Theoretically, its twisted barley-sugar stick colums and broken pediment should be 1,000 miles away, and the fan vaulting and pointed arches of old St. Mary's might well scream blue murder at such an intruder. Yet in the Oxford context, where outrage can always become acceptable, they get on most happily together.

Built in 1637 to the order of Archbishop Laud, the porch was designed in the latest style by Nicholas Stone, the sculptor and master mason who had so much to do with Windsor Castle and worked with Inigo Jones on the new Banqueting House in Whitehall. Four years earlier, Stone had made such an impressive job of the big triple gateway to the university 'Physick Garden', laid out on the site of the old Jewish burial ground across the road from Magdalen College, that for many years it was regarded as the work of the great Inigo himself.

As late as 1809 an early guidebook was describing the Baroque extravaganza at St. Mary's as "being in the more modern taste". When first erected, the new porch made quite a stir, the sweet figures of the Virgin and Child over the top deeply offending Puritan sentiment. And when Laud was tried for high treason in 1645, these innocent enough carvings were put forward as damning evidence of the 'popish ways' that helped to send him to his execution on Tower Hill.

Unlike some churches in Oxford, St. Mary's has never been in any danger of being declared redundant. With an academic population of perhaps 20,000 to draw upon, its congregations remain large. But in recent years, redundancy has become a real threat to the continuing parochial existence of All Saints, the City Church. In 1896, when old St. Martin's at Carfax was pulled down for street widening, the Town officially transferred its allegiances to this handsome classical temple on the corner of Turl Street, whose title then became 'The City Church of St. Martin and All Saints'. To emphasize the point, stalls were provided for the mayor and corporation and this lofty building became the venue for civic services and other solemn municipal affairs.

By the beginning of 1970, however, attendances had fallen to disastrously low levels and the Archdeacon of Oxford was pointing out in the local press that it was "extremely rare for Sunday congregations to reach double figures". The rector and fellows of Lincoln College, next-door neighbours and patrons of the living, have plans to close All Saints and to turn its spacious Corinthian interior into their second library. As might have been expected, these proposals have created something of a storm, albeit in a tea-cup. The fight is on and may well develop into the very last of the battles between Town and Gown. Defenders of the faith may be thin on the ground nowadays, but the mutterings of older citizens have developed into a snorting indignation at this last imposition. But at least, there is little risk of the church being demolished, which in these days of mass re-development, is something to be thankful for.

The church is well named, since it looks for all the world like one of Wren's 'city churches' built after the Great Fire of 1666. Indeed, the designer of All Saints, Dean Aldrich of Christ Church, collaborated with Wren on several occasions. Completed in 1710, the new church replaced the ruins of a medieval predecessor, destroyed by the dramatic collapse of its tower in 1699. Nicholas Hawksmoor, a pupil of Wren and architect of the Clarendon Building, added the characteristic classical spire, and a beautiful piece of work it is, standing against the sky as delicately as the most filigree Gothic work. Free of columns, the interior is tall and cool and a fine example of the restrained English Baroque style. Of the ancient church, nothing is left.

The fourteenth-century font, elaborately carved, was brought from the old St. Martin's and is said to have been the one in which Shakespeare's godson, later Sir William Davenant, was baptized in 1606, with the bard standing by as his sponsor.

All Saints was in building while the Duke of Marlborough's vast classical Palace of Blenheim was rising in Woodstock Park. Oxford, which had clung tenaciously to the Gothic style, was by now almost fully converted to the fashionable English Renaissance architecture that was to come to its greatest flowering during the Georgian period. This new style was modern and had qualities of tranquillity and repose that appealed to minds versed in the Latin poets and knowledgeable about the lives of the noble Romans. Colleges like Queen's and Christ Church were soon showing what they could do in the new manner, and although some Gothic work was still going on in the eighteenth century (Oxford was one of the last homes of traditional medieval construction)—such things as hammer beam roofs, small mullioned windows and pointed arches were generally 'out'. Even pretty little St. Edmund Hall, an ancient gem of a college, turned from the old ways in 1682 and built itself a most delightful chapel in the formal classical style.

The university, too, adopted the new architecture. Although in some respects a strange exercise in classical forms, the Sheldonian Theatre had already pointed the way. In 1683, it acquired as a neighbour the building known today as the 'Old Ashmolean', originally provided as a repository for the collection of 'natural curiosities' donated by Elias Ashmole, antiquarian, astrologer and 'England's first great freemason'. The gift was made on condition that a suitable building would be provided, an obligation which the university fulfilled splendidly. The Old Ashmolean has been described as "a perfect piece of English Renaissance work" and the pedimented east doorway which faces the Sheldonian is without doubt a superb composition.

The original contents of the museum were indeed so curious that the place was commonly known as 'Ashmole's Nicknackatory'. Its fame spread abroad and visitors from many foreign countries came to inspect the exhibits. Von Uffenbach, the German traveller arrived full of anticipation in 1710, but went away very disappointed and wondering why everyone on the Continent made such a fuss about its excellence. The museum, he said, was very badly managed. The Chief Custodian, was usually absent, always "guzzling and lounging about in the inns". But Uffenbach did stay in Oxford long enough to compile quite a useful list of the main items in the collection, among which were: "A very beautiful stuff'd reindeer.... An extraordinarily large tortoise.... A tooth the length of a man's finger and 2 inches thick, supposed to have belonged to a giant from Pontefract.... An enormous cabbage stalk 6 feet long and the thickness of an arm.... A curious horn that had grown on the back of a woman's head and was $5\frac{1}{2}$ inches long...."

There were also "snales preserved in brandy" and "two fine chaines presented to Elias Ashmole".

Designed by Thomas Wood, a local mason and not, as long

supposed, by Sir Christopher Wren, the 'Musaeum Ash-moleanum' occupies an honoured place among the classical build-ings of Oxford. Traditionally connected with scientific subjects, the whole building has been used since 1939 as the Museum of the History of Science. Besides providing a home for that first 'curious collection' it also offered from the start certain teaching facilities. For many years, the lower floors were utilized as a school of natural history and one room in the basement with "a grand Apparatus for extensive lectures in Chemistry" became the university's very first laboratory.

By the beginning of the nineteenth century, however, "the twelve cart loads of rarities sent to Oxon by Mr. Ashmole" in 1682 had increased to such proportions that most of them had to be accommodated elsewhere. They were gradually dispersed, many finding their way to the stately New Ashmolean in Beau-mont Street. But until the time of the Napoleonic Wars, the original collection remained virtually intact and its main exhibits were still "the Bodies, Hornes, Bones &c of Animals, preserved dry or in spirits . . . together with numerous Specimens of Metals & Minerals and Dr. Lister's Collections of Shells, Ores & Fossils . . .".

There were some additional oddments, with the accent definitely on the odd. In 1810, "a large magnet of oval shape sup-porting 145 pounds", "a picture of our Saviour composed of the most beautiful lively feathers" and "an ancient piece of St. Cuth-bert" were thought to be "deserving of particular notice". To be fair, portraits by Vandyke and a religious picture by Breughel were also noted as "very good Paintings".

This group of university buildings between The Broad and The High, to which the Sheldonian and the Ashmolean were the newest additions, was now becoming an important part of academic Oxford. Professors delivered endless and often tedious lectures in the Schools; scholars happily buried themselves under mountains of dusty volumes in the carrels of the Bodleian; the hierarchy argued between themselves in Convocation House and formally forgave each other's trespasses in St. Mary's; and on state occasions, the whole lot of them contrived to pack the Sheldonian Theatre to suffocation.

More space was urgently required. The workings of the univer-sity had expanded and were becoming increasingly complex. As yet, there was no kind of central 'office', no bureau from which its affairs might be conducted. Its officials were mostly fellows of colleges who worked from their own chambers in various parts of the city. The set-up could hardly have been very efficient. Prestige buildings for pomp and circumstance were all very well and schools, lecture rooms and libraries might be fine for teachers and scholars. But as time went on, records accumulated, statutes and regulations had to be administered, rents demanded and collected, properties maintained, wages paid, trusts administered, finances kept in order. And not least important, as a profit-making concern, the University Press had to be looked after.

In fact, the printers were the next group of people to be provided for. Over a period of twenty-five years, their presses had thumped away in the cellars of the Sheldonian, sometimes literally shaking the Theatre on its foundations. The great weight of books and unbound sheets stored in the attics had caused Wren's ingeniously-engineered roof and ceiling to sag a good two inches in the middle and, to his great annoyance, anxious academics were urging major repairs. Always busy, the gentlemen of the press were swarming like ants in every spare corner. Compositors and proof correctors worked in little rooms built beneath the galleries and were soon spreading their activities across the main floor.

The position was serious and before the end of the seventeenth century, the workers had been moved out into empty houses along Catte Street. For once, the old habit of making one building serve several purposes had failed to pay off. The Sheldonian might have been designed by a genius, but its strange combination of printing works and public auditorium never quite worked out. By 1710, only a few stacks of paper and the smell of ink remained.

But events were moving in the printers' favour. The decision to erect a new 'printing office' had been taken ten years earlier but, as usual, shortage of money had held the scheme back. Fortunately, there were two unexpected windfalls. Firstly, the sons of Lord Clarendon made over the copyright of their father's *History of the Great Rebellion* to the university. Secondly, John Baskett, the King's Printer, offered £2,000 for the lease of one half of the official press.

Published posthumously between 1702 and 1704, Clarendon's book rapidly became an eighteenth-century best-seller. Large profits were made and sales produced a steady income. Indeed, it would be fair to say that the book largely paid for the building and even before work had begun, it was known to one and all as 'the new Clarendon Printing House'. The name is also perpetuated in the Clarendon Press, one of the university's well-known imprints.

The site chosen was on the corner of The Broad and Catte Street, close to the Sheldonian. A number of old properties, including St. Mary's Parish Room and Master Ball's Coffee House, had been purchased and demolished in readiness. By 1711 "the whole area of Ground next the Theatre" was cleared to "make a spacious Compass". On 22nd February of that year, Thomas Hearne, the diarist, watched the laying of the foundation stone. Baskett, the printer who was to be responsible for the production of Bibles and prayer books, gave the workmen four guineas. It seems to have been well earned, since they "dug 15 feet before they arriv'd at Gravel for a Foundation . . .".

The architect engaged for the job was Nicholas Hawksmoor. The one-time assistant of Christopher Wren, he had worked with Vanburgh at Blenheim and Castle Howard, was the designer of several fine churches in London, and at the time of the Clarendon commission was already busy in Oxford with schemes for the remodelling of Queen's College and All Souls. For the new 'Clarendon' he prepared a strong, simple, rectangular design and produced a building "of massive simplicity" that stands in beautiful contrast to the curving walls of the Sheldonian Theatre. The great portico with its Doric columns has something of the plain honesty of "the finest barn in Europe"—the church of St. Paul's, Covent Garden where Eliza Dolittle sold her flowers and which had been built by Inigo Jones nearly three-quarters of a century before.

The Clarendon is an even more impressive work, and one that clearly expresses its original function of accommodating the two distinct sides of the university's printing business. The building is both unified and divided by the central archway, through which one may wander freely into the mellow quadrangle of the Old Schools. The arch also makes of the Clarendon a kind of grand gatehouse, in which the magnificent wrought iron gates by Tijou form a glorious centre-piece.

When first built, there was equal provision for 'the Bible Press', solely concerned with the production of the Authorized

Version and the Book of Common Prayer, and 'the Learned Press', responsible for general printing and all other books. Now used as the main headquarters of the university, a fine panelled 'office' was provided right from the beginning for meetings of 'The Delegates of the Press' and is still used by them.

The printers made their next big move in 1829, when they transferred themselves to their present home in Walton Street. Hawksmoor's building was then "appropriated to the general business of the University" and adapted as a registry, police head-quarters and lecture rooms. The latter were soon used as offices, but the registrar and Proctors have been continuous tenants for the past 140 years. It is to the Clarendon that students who have sinned are summoned. It is here that the University's 'Cabinet'—the Hebdomadal Council—meets every week. It is here that those non-existent 'secret files' on the doings of undergraduates are supposedly kept. And as a prime symbol of the academic Estab-lishment, it is on the newly-cleaned walls of the Clarendon that protesters write rude words while hurling abuse at the remark-ably mild men within.

One further building was needed to complete the central com-plex. This, the Radcliffe Camera, was completed in 1749 and is considered by many to be the finest of all. Set plumb in the middle of Radcliffe Square, this superb circular reading room has been called "as grand and perfect a building as any in Oxford". Few would try to dispute the claim. A marvellous expression of the classicism of its time, it stands among quiet lawns in perpetual Olympian calm. For a sudden burst of splendour on a sunny day, one should try stepping out of the cool north porch of St. Mary's into the square. The immediate impact of the great drum and dome of the Camera, rising majestically towards its high lantern, is quite unforgettable, as massive and inevitable as the huge har-monies of a Handel oratorio. Yet for all its solid solemnity, this timeless building has about it a surprising grace, and a beauty that can hit the most untutored visitor for six.

It was known as early as 1711, when the Clarendon was still in building, that Dr. John Radcliffe, lately of Oxford, intended to bequeath money to the university for the provision of a new library. He had been a fellow of Lincoln College and a royal physician whose court connections brought him a fortune. On his death in 1714, the promise was made good. In his Will he left in the care of trustees: "forty thousand pounds . . . for the building a library in Oxford. . . . And when the said Library is built, I give One hundred and Fifty Pounds per annum for ever to the Keeper thereof . . . and One Hundred Pounds a year per annum for ever for buying books. . . ."

When the library was built, indeed! The legal complications took years to untangle. Part of the site was privately owned and some of the houses that had to be pulled down were a lawyer's delight of tenancies and sub-tenancies. Other properties belonged to colleges, some of which demanded compensation. The preliminaries went on for twenty years and the laying of the foundation stone did not take place until 1737.

Somewhat earlier, the Radcliffe trustees had been thinking about the appointment of an architect. All the leading men of the day were considered, among them Wren, Vanbrugh, Hawksmoor and James Gibbs. Death removed the two greatest from the scene, and the final choice lay between Hawksmoor and Gibbs. At first, the former seems to have been favourite for the job; his Clarendon Building had been much praised and he was well known for his work at the colleges. On the other hand, James Gibbs had not previously worked in Oxford, although as the architect for the great Senate House in Cambridge and fine churches like St. Martin-in-the-Fields, his reputation stood high.

In the event, both men were asked to submit designs and both produced beautiful scale models of their proposals. Now displayed in the Bodleian Library, the rejected 'toy' of Hawksmoor was used as a doll's house by several generations of Dillon children at Ditchley Park. The model of the approved scheme submitted by Gibbs has also found its way back to Oxford. In the garden of Number 18 St. Giles, a building that was in turn the Duke of Marlborough's town house, the official 'Judge's Lodging' at Assize time, and the boyhood home of William Morris's friend, Philip Webb, it forms the crowning feature of a pretty little pavilion.

The construction of the *Bibliotheca Radcliviana* went on for twelve years and this 'Physic Library' which consisted of "all Sorts of Books belonging to the Science of Physic as Anatomy, Botany, Surgery and Philosophy" was first opened to readers in 1749. Like many university buildings, the Camera was opened to the general public and remained so for the best part of 200 years.

Unfortunately, this concession was withdrawn at the beginning of the Second World War and has not been restored. Which, if understandable, is a pity, for with its superb staircase, the interior is hardly less splendid than the outside.

Since 1866, when the scientific collection was removed elsewhere, the 'Radcliffe' has been used as one of the reading rooms of the Bodleian, to which it is connected by an underground tunnel and conveyor belts for the delivery of volumes to readers. Beneath the north lawn, there is also a vast double-storey book stack, a mysterious cavern of knowledge which has provided a setting for a first-class 'whodunit' by J. I. M. Stewart, the Oxford don who writes so entertainingly as 'Michael Innes'.

But the Radcliffe Camera does not take lightly to levity. Books are a serious business and must be made to seem so. Of course, there have been lighter moments, in fact as well as fiction. In the year before Waterloo the Camera was cleared to provide the venue for a great banquet, a gastronomic party thrown by the Prince Regent in honour of the visit to Oxford of several European sovereigns. Even Oxford, well accustomed to royalty, was impressed; after all the King of Prussia and the Tsar of All the Russias did not visit the town every day.

Some years later, when Napoleon III was making threatening noises across the Channel, the Camera was put to more martial uses when members of the newly-formed University Rifle Corps used the basement as a drill hall. Initially, this paramilitary body had encountered difficulties in getting themselves organized. A deputation of enthusiastic undergraduates who asked the Vice-Chancellor for formal permission to form such an organization were politely reminded of an ancient statute that forebade any member of the university to carry weapons—other than bows and arrows!

The central university complex was now complete. To have attempted to crowd anything more into Radcliffe Square could have ruined what Thomas Sharp has called "the greatest architectural sequence in England". He chose the phrase carefully, emphasizing the fact that "although buildings stand still, their observers move". And as the visitor wanders down Catte Street towards the Bodleian, nowhere else in Oxford does a constantly changing viewpoint produce such visual excitement and sheer pleasure: ". . . first the rotunda, then the spire of St. Mary's, then

the dome of the Camera coming into view . . . with a result that
is architecturally speaking, sensational".

With the completion of the Radcliffe Camera, the academics of
the eighteenth century seemed instinctively to know when to
leave well alone and the university has long realized that this
masterly group is perfect as it stands. There has never been any
attempt, not even a suggestion that any other building should be
put up in the vicinity. Henceforward, the authorities looked elsewhere for development sites and there was no danger of Radcliffe
Square ever becoming a superior sort of Parks Road—so called,
said someone, because they "park buildings along there like
pantechnicons".

In any case, this great pure-classical wave of construction had
spent itself before the end of the eighteenth century. Dr. Radcliffe's apparently inexhaustible estate provided the money for his
observatory, a delightful Greek-Revival experiment in the
Woodstock Road, and for the infirmary next door, an institution
which benefited both Town and Gown. Until the building of the
new university press in 1830, however, there was virtually a sixty-
year pause, during which no new schemes were undertaken. Even
the colleges, with their own incomes and free to make their own
way, tended to mark time. Only Worcester, Oriel and Christ
Church embarked on anything in the nature of major projects.

The reasons for this slackening of effort were partly financial,
but the 'learned torpor' into which Oxford had sunk contributed a
great deal towards the lassitude and *laissez faire* which now existed.
People procrastinated and tomorrow and tomorrow were other
days. As Sir Charles Mallet pointed out: "Enthusiasm for study, if
not unknown, was rare; and except for violent politics, enthusiasm
of all kinds was out of fashion. . . ."

Intellectually, the place had become a 'stagnant backwater'
whose unpleasant odours became such a stink in the nostrils of men
like John Wesley. The atmosphere was not likely to encourage
noble benefactions. The Bodleys and the Sheldons and the Rad-
cliffes were long dead and such gifts as were made were used to
found chairs and lectureships rather than buildings.

Before the next architectural crop could be garnered, the university had to wait for the nineteenth century, and for a time when
it could seriously begin to put its other houses in order.

XI

COLLAGE

In Oxford, they still argue as to which college came first. To this apparently simple question there is no straightforward answer. Balliol was in being in 1263, although University College had received its first endowment more than a century earlier. On the other hand, Merton is generally recognized as being "certainly the oldest foundation to have true college form and stature".

University, Balliol, Merton: one, two, three; historians shuffle the order around and say that it all depends what you mean by foundation. . . . However, the niceties of official protocol have long given precedence to University College, which always holds pride of place in the annual *Calendar*. Its ancient claim to have been founded by Alfred the Great may be discreetly waived nowadays, but 'Univ' can point with satisfaction to the original legacy of 310 marks left in 1249 by William of Durham "for the maintenance at Oxenforde of ten needy Masters of Art studying Divinity . . .".

As stakeholders, the university made a mess of things. For more than thirty years, they juggled around with this first endowment and it was not until 1280 that the money was applied to its proper purpose and the *scolares Willelmi de Dunelmia* were established in their little college.

In the meantime, there had been other benefactions. As a house for poor scholars, Balliol was already calling itself "the moste auntient endow'd Colledg in Christendome". Its founder, the north-country baron John de Balliol, was in hot water for having "unjustly vexed and enormously damnified the Churches of Tyne-mouth and Durham". In penance, and for the good of his soul, he was scourged and then made to provide for the education of six-teen clerks at Oxford University. He did this on the cheap, allow-ing them only eightpence a week for victuals. Happily, John's wife showed more concern for the ultimate destination of his soul than did the man himself. When he died in 1269, she stepped up the weekly pittance and, in 1282, presented the scholars with a charter of incorporation as a college.

Other donors were also on the move. A few months before de Balliol was whipped for his sins, Walter de Merton, "sometime Chancellor of the illustrious lord Henry III, King of England" and a bishop to boot, made over the revenues of two of his Surrey manors "for the support of scholars studying at a university". Keeping the business in the family, he soon installed no less than eight of his nephews in one of the Oxford halls. Their numbers were steadily added to by more of Walter's numerous kith and kin, but he did admit a few outsiders. By 1274, detailed regulations governing courses of study and conduct had been drawn up. Still preserved in the college treasury, these beautifully inscribed statutes were to become "the model for nearly all subsequent collegiate foundations in Oxford and Cambridge". Certainly, they are largely responsible for the undisputed acceptance of Merton as "the first great permanent endowment of learning in England".

Walter de Merton wanted the best possible for his people. He intended them to be "better clothed, better housed, better fed than the average university student" of the time. His college was the first to have "scale and magnificence" and the emoluments paid to his scholars were at double the going rate in the rest of the university. It is not surprising to find that almost from the beginning, the fellows of Merton formed a rather exclusive set and were regarded as the academic aristocracy of Oxford.

Six colleges were founded during this first 100 years. University, Balliol and Merton were followed in the first half of the fourteenth century by Exeter, Oriel and Queen's. None were particularly well blessed with funds. In spite of its grand title of 'The House of the Blessed Mary the Virgin in Oxford, of the Foundation of Edward II of famous memory, sometime King of England', Oriel took in lodgers throughout the medieval period in order to make ends meet. The charter of Queen's College, dating from 1341, set out a grand and elaborate scheme for a corporation of Provost and twelve scholars, representing Christ and his twelve apostles. They were to live well, wear blood-red robes in hall in memory of the Passion, and be supported by seventy-two poor boys as 'disciples'. As an act of charity, thick pea-soup was to be

St. Catherine's College
The Blue Boar Buildings, Christ Church

dished out at the gatehouse every day and a select number of the blind, deaf and maimed treated to dinner.

All this was most laudable, but, as often happened, the money to implement the founder's intentions was not always forthcoming. Queen's, like Oriel, was forced to accept paying guests—John Wycliffe and Henry V were two of the most famous—and until the beginning of the sixteenth century it was rarely able to support more than three or four scholars and the same number of 'poor boys'. There is little doubt that until 1380, when William of Wykeham staggered the academic world with his splendid New College, Merton easily held first place, having more members than all others put together.

Indeed, the building of New College was the crowning achievement of medieval collegiate development. Thereafter, no other foundation came into being for fifty years. Meanwhile, Wykeham's creation which "in scale, in numbers, in endowment and in the size and splendour of its buildings far transcended all earlier colleges" not only consolidated and refined everything that had gone before, but looked ahead to a more modern world.

Built on a site "uninhabited, a place of gravel-pits and sand-pits where robbers lurked", this new 'St. Mary College of Winchester in Oxford' was a concept radically different from anything that had gone before. As Professor A. H. M. Jones wrote: "Its educational programme started a new era . . . being primarily designed to take *undergraduates* through their arts course." This was a big step forward. It should be remembered that all the earlier colleges had been close little communities admitting only *graduates* to membership. The vast majority of students stayed outside. They had neither college nor collegiate life but belonged to inns and halls, working somewhat haphazardly for a bachelor's degree. Their only allegiance was to the university. The fierce house loyalties and outpourings of the 'college spirit' were still a long way ahead.

For nearly 300 years the 'college student' was a comparatively rare bird. The private hall was still the predominant feature of Oxford's educational system. More than 120 such establishments are known to have existed during medieval times, when never less than eighty were licensed for teaching. Even at the beginning of the Tudor age, there were still fifty-six halls in Oxford as compared with a mere ten colleges. (Magdallen had come in 1458).

10

St. Aldate's
St. Ebbe's Baroque

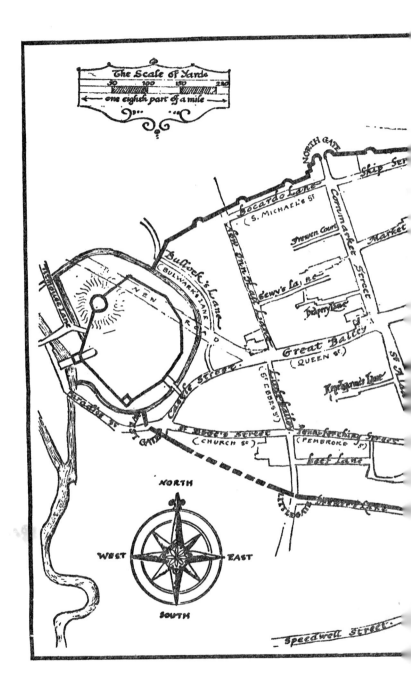

The Scale of Yards
50   100   150   200
one eighth part of a mile

NORTH GATE

Skip St.

Locardo Lane
(S. MICHAEL'S St.)

Cornmarket Street

Market

New Inn Hall Gate

Drewen Court

Bulbock's Lane
(BULWARK LANE)

Shew's lane

Ridmy Lane

Turrill Lane

NEW ROAD

Great Bailey
(QUEEN St.)

St. John

Castle Street

Littlegate
(ST. EBBE'S St.)

King Pigman's Lane

Town furlong Spires
(PEMBROKE St.)

Thames St GATE

St. Alegy's Street
(CHURCH St.)

Beef Lane

Brewery Lane

Littlegate

NORTH

WEST   EAST

SOUTH

Speedwell Street

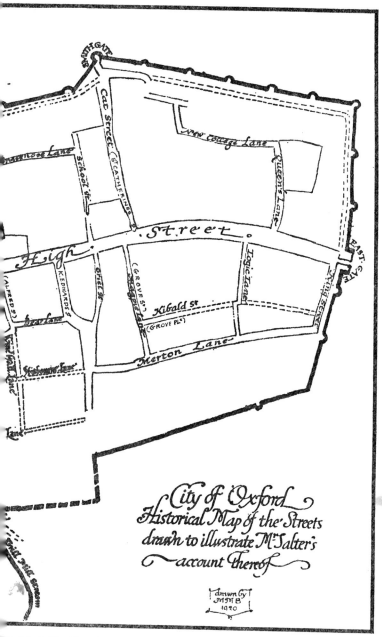

City of Oxford
Historical Map of the Streets
drawn to illustrate Mr Salter's
account thereof

drawn by
MMB
1920

E. Salter's The Historic Names of the Streets and Lanes of Oxford, *reproduced* *y* of the Clarendon Press, Oxford.

When Henry VIII came to the throne, however, the balance had already begun to swing over. There were fewer halls and more colleges, most of them richer and all of them much larger than their earlier counterparts. The Tudor period was a great time for new foundations. Brasenose, Corpus Christi, Christ Church; Trinity, St. John's and Jesus: all were established between 1512 and 1571, the first three within the remarkably short space of twelve years. Never had there been such a spate of college founding, nor was such an outburst of energy ever to come again.

Inevitably, the pace slowed down. The seventeenth century threw up only two colleges; Wadham, 'the youngest old foundation', and Pembroke, 'the nest of singing birds', formerly Broadgates Hall. In the eighteenth century, two more appeared, Worcester and Hertford, neither of them entirely new, but both developed out of ancient monastic or private halls. After the opening of Wadham in 1610, there was to be a great gap before Keble, the next completely new college, was founded in 1870.

Big, brick-built, striped, chequered and strident, Keble College is Victorian down to its foundations. The work of the *enfant terrible* of nineteenth-century Gothic architecture, William Butterfield, it is a monument to the spirit of an age: to piety, charity, unease of conscience and a general determination to do good, somehow. It offered "everything expected from an Oxford education, while ordering its corporate life in such a way that poorer men could live together within its walls without embarrassment". There was to be togetherness and apartheid at one and the same time! Nevertheless, long before State aid and student grants, Keble was indeed "making a university education possible to hundreds of men who would otherwise have been debarred for financial reasons . . .".

Two years earlier, and with much the same object in view, St. Catherine's Society for Unattached Students had come into existence. Its seventy-odd members used "a bare and uncomfortable apartment in the Clarendon Building" as a Junior Common Room and had converted the upper floor of the Old Congregation House as their 'Chapel of the Unattached'. Keeping much to themselves, this group of comparatively poor students developed a busy social and cultural life of their own with music, literary, rowing and athletics clubs. It was not until 1963, with the aid of large donations from the industrial and commercial world, that 'St. Cat's' became fully recognized as a college in its own right. Designed by the Danish master Arne Jacobsen, the sparkling group of buildings at the end of Manor Road are already accepted as one of the best examples of modern architecture in Oxford.

Victorian industriousness and a zeal for reform was much concerned with popular education and the under-privileged. The nineteenth century may have produced only one new Oxford college, but it also witnessed the small beginnings of St. Catherine's and several women's colleges, all of which originated in the years between the staid seventies and the naughty nineties. From this time onwards, the university's days as an exclusively male preserve were numbered. Ladies were looking beyond the circumference of their crinolines; indeed, they were discarding them altogether. Determined to shock the stuffing out of ponderous pedants, some of the hardier spirits had already taken to bloomers and bicycles.

The five women's colleges which exist today were all started within a period of fifteen years. Lady Margaret Hall, Somerville and St. Anne's (then The Society of Oxford Home Students) appeared in 1878-9, followed soon afterwards by St. Hugh's and, in 1893, by St. Hilda's. But girls had to wait for many years before the university was sufficiently gracious and enlightened to take official notice of their existence. The first degree ceremony for women did not take place until 1920 and it was 1926 before their thriving colleges received formal recognition.

Heavily chaperoned, the pioneers lived frugally in makeshift accommodation. For them, there was nothing of the romantic atmosphere of Magdalen or Merton, none of the majesty of Christ Church or the classical splendour of Queen's. Lady Margaret Hall began with nine young ladies in "a modest pseudo-Gothic family residence" at the end of Norham Gardens. The cost of fitting out this "ugly little villa" was £454 6s. 5d. and the founders were so hard up that one of the senior students offered to stain the bare floors and do the decorating herself.

Opening on the same day as 'L.M.H.', Somerville had twelve students, seven of whom were squeezed into a house in St. Giles rented from St. John's College. In spite of its nearness to the centre of the town, this had certain rural amenities, including two cows, a pig, a couple of talkative ravens and a pony called 'Nobby' who could be hired, complete with carriage, for country excursions. For a number of years, there was also a *closed* bath chair in which the Somerville girls could be "decorously conveyed to dinner parties . . .".

Humblest of the female foundations was St. Hugh's, which began life with four girls in a semi-detached house in Norham Road. Only St. Hilda's, founded by the formidable Miss Beale of Cheltenham Ladies College, was able to start off in really handsome quarters. For £5,000 she purchased Cowley House, a fine Georgian property originally built by an eighteenth-century professor of botany. In a beautiful riverside setting below Magdalen Bridge and with several acres of wooded meadow thrown in, the 'Old Hall', as it is now called, provided the perfect nucleus for a new foundation. The early years were very hard going. While the superior gentlemen of Oxford sat back and smiled, the first principal accepted a token salary and, helped only by her daughter, took on most of the domestic chores herself.

Almost imperceptibly, the five women's colleges settled down and became part of the academic scene, acquiring patrons, winning honours, turning out a succession of brilliant scholars and producing some good architecture. Their development has been quiet, orderly and conducted without undue fuss. The earlier buildings have had time to lose their high-school newness and are nicely mellowed. Quadrangles have a noticeable 'college atmosphere' and are already old enough to retain memories. Ninety years ago, there was little to offer but hope, great expectations and an unwavering faith in the future of the female undergraduate.

Not all colleges have had such tidy beginnings. The origins of some are at best a little hazy. Paradoxically, two of the most recent are also two of the most ancient. St. Peter's—the College of St. Peter-le-Bailey in New Inn Hall Street—was not fully recognized until 1961 although it existed in 1300 as Trilleck's Inn, just about the oldest known student 'hospice' of the Middle Ages. St. Edmund Hall, made into a full college in 1957, is even older, having had a continuous existence under this name for over 700 years.

The only one of 120 medieval 'halls' to survive into modern times, Oxford is properly proud of St. Edmund Hall, the smallest of its houses. Tucked away down Queen's Lane, 'Teddy Hall' continues to inspire affection. Representing everyman's idea of an Oxford college, the place is sheer delight. Every part is on such a small scale that James Morris was inevitably reminded of Lilliput.

A few steps away from the snarling High, you pass through a

little archway into a miniature world, complete and perfect. Like the set of a toy theatre, golden mellow buildings stand about a square of green velvet. In the middle is a medieval well and to one side an old wooden pump that might have come from a farmyard. Nothing is monumental but everything combines to give the impression of gentle domesticity. And against this background of mullioned windows flares a summer riot of colour: big pink-white stars of clematis, roses clambering over doorways, the scarlet blaze of geraniums and, leaning comfortably in one corner, a single friendly tree.

All has a happy air of undesign, almost of happening by accident. Even the chapel, a brave little classical piece that closes off one end of the tiny quad, has something of the small and home-spun about it. Built at the same time as the Old Ashmolean, which it vaguely resembles, it is the only bit of formal architecture to be seen. Balanced about a central pediment, the symmetrical façade speaks with a more genteel accent than the simple vernacular of the rest, but there is pleasant conversation between them.

The physical smallness of St. Edmund Hall is in some measure due to its cramped surroundings. Fronting hard onto Queen's Lane, it is hemmed in on one side by the church of St. Peter-in-the-East, soon to become its new library, and on the other by old houses, several of which it now owns. Lacking the broad acres of Merton or Christ Church, expansion is difficult. In the past, the only way of extending has been upwards, by building extra storeys here and there and making rooms in the roof spaces. The chapel itself does double duty, for upstairs is the original college library, "the first in Oxford to adopt wall shelving and the last to abandon the medieval tradition of chaining up the books . . .".

For a long time before its final recognition as an independent college, 'Teddy Hall' was constantly fighting off take-over bids by Queen's, its powerful neighbour across the street. After the Reformation, the whole property was acquired by the fellows of the larger college, who soon afterwards assumed control and were given the right to appoint the principal from among their own number. At frequent intervals, Big Brother made determined attempts to complete what appeared to be an inevitable process and it was not until 1913 that the game was finally abandoned as not being worth the candle.

The members of the little hall displayed a fierce independence of spirit and were not having any. Queen's might be old, but their house was even older and still had much to offer. In 1852 the University Commissioners had reported that "notwithstanding its lack of endowment, this hall is one of the cheapest places of education in Oxford". While students at other colleges were paying from £200 to £300 a year for their board and tuition, undergraduates at St. Edmund Hall were getting along nicely on a modest £60 to £80.

But in spite of this advantage, the Royal Commission of 1874 came out in favour of 'extinguishing' the few remaining Oxford halls. Three years later, legislation to achieve this end was brought in. The one exception was 'Teddy Hall', whose demise was, however, only to be deferred until such time as the principalship next became vacant. When that happened, the hall would be placed completely under the control of Queen's.

So for twenty-five years, the place led a nervous existence, living on borrowed time under the leadership of Edward Moore, a Dante scholar of world repute. In 1903, when he announced his intention of resigning, the way seemed clear for Queen's to make its final play. A statute which would have made the take-over final and absolute was put before Congregation for approval.

Fortunately, the university rallied to the support of the underdog. "Opinion was roused in defence of this last of the medieval halls and the statute was rejected by a decisive majority . . .". The decision of Dr. Moore to remain in office as principal consolidated the victory won in Congregation. By the beginning of the First World War, the future of the future smallest college was happily assured.

Between the initial appearance of St. Edmund Hall in the Middle Ages and the final emergence of St. Catherine's in 1963, there is a timespan of seven centuries. During this very long period, thirty-four full colleges were established in Oxford, of which five are exclusively for women and six cater for graduates only. In addition, there are five 'recognized private halls' maintained by religious interests such as the Jesuits, the Franciscans and the Benedictines. Although these are comparatively modern foundations, they are in some ways a throwback to the medieval system which operated before the coming of the colleges. Two, indeed,—Mansfield, sponsored by the Congregationalists and Regent's Park, sponsored by the Baptists—call themselves colleges; but in the eyes of the university, they are, as yet, no such thing.

To the uninitiated, all this seems very puzzling. And to add to the confusion, there are places like Manchester College—an imposing Victorian-Gothic pile run by the Unitarians that is officially neither a private hall nor a college, yet has been an established part of the Oxford academic scene for eighty years. In the same way, the even better known Ruskin College lies outside the official university pale. Founded in 1899 by an American couple and originally known as Ruskin Hall, it provides higher education for working-class men and women and many prominent trade unionists and socialist politicians have been among its students.

These 'colleges' are not listed in the *Oxford University Handbook*, which is at pains to point out that "no institution other than those stated . . . forms part of the University . . .". Yet strangely enough, one of Oxford's oldest and most respected colleges is not on the list either. All Souls, which has been flourishing since 1438, does not "have the right to present candidates to the University for matriculation" or to put them forward as members. In consequence, it gets hardly a mention in the official handbook, even though its scholars are generally reckoned to be some of the finest brains in the business!

The paradox is simply explained. From its very beginning, 'The College of All Souls of the Faithful Departed' has accepted only graduates for membership, preferring to leave the tutoring of students to other houses. In this, it has preserved a system common to all colleges in medieval times, and one which has been newly adopted by modern foundations such as Nuffield and St. Antony's. But only at All Souls has the old arrangement been carried on without a break for 500 years. Here, every member is a don who belongs to the university by virtue of his original graduation at another college. Membership is highly prized, and nowadays only men of the highest intellectual attainment can hope to be considered for a fellowship.

All Souls is a beautiful place and has been called "the greatest of all war memorials". Founded in the reign of Henry VI, it was especially dedicated to "the English captains and other subjects who drank the cup of bitter death" in the Hundred Years War against the French. At first sight, it appears to be remarkably small. Entered directly off the noisy High, the quiet front quad is no bigger than that of St. Edmund Hall and its buildings are on the same cosily domestic scale. Little has been altered since they were put up in 1441, and what one sees from the gatehouse is pretty much All Souls as it then existed. The sense of enclosure is complete and it is natural to assume that nothing much is to be seen beyond this pleasant green square.

Less adventurous visitors tend to take one turn around the lawn, admire the simple Tudor of the old living quarters, be suitably impressed by the splendours of the chapel in which the Fellows once kept a tooth of John the Baptist, and then, without penetrating further, they step back into the bustle outside. By doing so, they manage to miss one of Oxford's memorable experiences. To come suddenly out of the mini-world of the earlier college into its spectacular North Quadrangle is architectural magic of a rare kind. Although nothing like so vast as the Tom Quad at Christ Church, this fine square is nevertheless on a noble scale. It is also 'different', being neither medievally romantic like the ancient monks' houses at Worcester, nor cool and formal like the 'new' buildings of Magdalen. Because it is difficult to pin down its various component parts to any particular style the overall design has been criticized as 'impure', but modern critics find this 'Codrington Quad' quite a joy. There is a colonnade which vaguely anticipates something from the Brighton Pavilion and the two strange towers on the east side certainly do look as if they might at any moment collapse into themselves like the telescopes with which they have been compared. Without these spiky *tours de force*, the academic skyline would surely lose some of its richness.

Fortunately, the architect, Nicholas Hawksmoor, was a genius. In the hands of a lesser man, such an assemblage of Renaissance and Gothicky motifs could have been a complete mess. But even Horace Walpole, father of the Gothic Revival and dead against classicism was forced to admit that somehow, Hawksmoor had "blundered into a picturesque scenery not void of grandeur . . .". Certainly, no-one denies the magnificence of the huge Codrington Library, standing superbly across the whole of one end of the quadrangle and appropriately embellished with a great Christopher Wren sundial all blue and red and white and gold.

The library is centrepiece and masterpiece, but Hawksmoor extended his effects beyond the immediate confines of the square.

Knowing exactly what he wanted in the way of drama, he deliberately kept his colonnaded loggia on the west side long and low, thus providing a perfect horizontal foil to the lovely curves of Radcliffe Camera which rises so grandly on the other side of All Souls wall.

Its Fellows may be thus able to bask in and enjoy the reflected glory of classical Radcliffe Square as well as their own, but in contrast, the three nearest neighbours of All Souls butt up against the best bit of Gothic gloom in the whole of Oxford. This is New College Lane, which, taking in Hell Passage on the way, follows a tortured course from Catte Street, finally debouching into the broad river of The High as Queen's Lane. For twists and turns and kinks and bends, this ancient thoroughfare can have few rivals in Europe. A dog that possessed such a dreadful hind leg would surely have been destroyed at the whelping. But this ridiculous little street survives as the legal frontier between college properties, as the maimed evidence of 1,000 litigations, of 10,000 agreements, conveyances, writs and affidavits. Running like a canyon between prison-style walls, it was called "that grim ravine" by a shuddering Max Beerbohm. Its first section is grim indeed. Squeezed in by black masonry, the lane seems to peter out at New College gatehouse forming, as Sean Jennet says, "the meanest and most purely medieval approach to any college in Oxford...". To escape claustrophobia, you have to dive through a sudden archway on the right and hurry thankfully towards the slightly less oppressive length of Queen's Lane.

When it was built in the fourteenth century, no academic house in Oxford was so well able to defend itself as New College. Protected on two sides by the city wall, on the third by the blank backside of the cloister and on the fourth by an unbroken block of solid building, it could hold itself secure against most comers. Anyone approaching down New College Lane was unprotected and in full view. The gatehouse with the warden's lodgings over the top was for several centuries the one and only way in. Once the massive doors were shut, the world inside was a world on its own.

But after strolling past the colourful old houses of Holywell Street, many visitors now enter New College from the north. The gaunt Victorian buildings on this side are no great shakes and it is some compensation to find that they lie outside the original purlieus of the college. Designed by Sir Gilbert Scott, who among other things was also responsible for the Martyrs' Memorial and St. Pancras Station, they are looked at askance even today when nineteenth-century architecture is regarded with favour. The new library set at one end of this dull range is a much better job. Completed in 1939, it was the work of Sir Gilbert's grandson, Giles Scott and is remarkably similar in style to his much more massive New Bodleian Library, designed at about the same time.

Grandfather Scott's vast neo-Gothic barracks is better if kept at one's back. All the more worthwhile stuff lies ahead, notably the old city wall with its great bastions and garden walk known as 'The Slipe' forming the opposite long side of an immense rectangle. Here are flower beds and pleasaunces and smooth lawns laid where the town moat once ran and on which students may be seen concentrating with intense seriousness on that most bloody-minded of games, croquet. In his unrealized post-war plan for Oxford, Thomas Sharp was hopeful that New College might be persuaded to dedicate a public right of way along The Slipe, thus helping to open up a half-mile length of the walls to a population which had largely forgotten their very existence. Unfortunately, the scheme has never materialized and perambulations in New College gardens are still restricted to tourist hours. The old walls have been so attractively planted and maintained that they are nowadays far more beckoning than forbidding. Paths and focal points lead the eye through mysterious archways to the half-hidden splendours beyond. And there is no doubt that 'splendour' is the right word to describe some of the things that this college has to offer.

The Great Quadrangle, about which the whole life of the place revolves, was the first in Oxford and with the single exception of the much smaller 'Old Court' of Corpus Christi, Cambridge, the first quadrangle in England. Still remaining exactly as originally planned, it set the pattern for almost every college that followed. As they began to expand, even the older foundations such as Merton and Balliol adopted the new fashion. Quite soon, no house was without at least one quadrangle and by the eighteenth century, most had added a second. At Oriel, Brasenose and Christ Church, there were three, and if we count the tiny Patey's Quad, almost lost among its "undisciplined group of buildings", the total at Merton is now no less than five.

Although college life has changed considerably with the passing of time, colleges have not. Their basic elements are the same as they were five hundred years ago and the orderly arrangement of New College has never really been bettered. William of Wykeham's great concept remains as the archetype and basis of comparison. Nuffield College was completed only in 1958 but makes no bones about its antecedents. In layout and in feeling, it is entirely traditional. St. Catherine's, on the other hand, looks every inch a product of the technological age. It is all brick and glass and brand new and as different from Nuffield as chalk from cheese. Yet essentially, they are both colleges, serving the same basic purposes and preserving something of the old quad atmosphere.

Still a self-contained, self-governing and largely self-supporting unit, the physical form of the Oxford college clearly expresses its ancient function. To fulfil its purpose as a place of teaching and quiet study, certain requirements had to be satisfied right from the start. There had to be rooms in which scholars could work and sleep. There must be a common hall in which they could eat, drink and occasionally be merry. There must be a chapel for prayer and, not least important, a library for the safe keeping of books and manuscripts.

Without exception the colleges provide these things, but they offer more besides: an essential peace and quietness. That they still manage to achieve a near-silence in the heart of a brawling modern city is no small tribute to the skill of those early planners, and it is proof that quadrangular development is a very logical solution to the problems of collegiate design. The hollow square is an excellent plan form, being both insulator and integrator. Developing out of the monastic cloister (and for good measure, some colleges have cloisters too) the quadrangle not only turns the backs of its buildings on to the world outside, but provides at its centre a focal point and interchange for the multifarious activities of scholarship.

To spend a few minutes in an Oxford quad during term time is to witness its processes in action. A mere few yards from busy streets, the peak-hour traffic is muted to a faint humming of bees. Out-of-doors conversation is no effort and wrens make themselves heard in the cracks of garden walls. Gowned figures appear in archways and cross to mysterious doors with varying degrees of aimlessness or purpose. A telephone rings in the porter's lodge. The silver-haired and rather impressive custodian gestures meaningfully as he talks to someone who has failed to deliver the goods.

From the open windows of the hall, the after-lunch clatter of dishes gives way to tentative fiddles and a flute. Soon there is the bump-bump of feet in tennis shoes as the boys and girls of a Cecil Sharp set-up tread the elaborate measure of an English country dance. Across the lawn, the organist tries out a piece by Messiaen, making the chapel windows throb and rattle. A man with a sheaf of bills and a cheque book goes into the Bursar's Office. Discussing one of the college livings with a frustrated parson and thankful for the interruption, the Bursar waves the newcomer to a chair. On a bench outside, two undergraduates discuss Krishnamurti. With shorts and hairy legs and an armful of racquets, a third hurries past, his present flights of fancy confined to a game of badminton. A gardener prunes roses. Blossom drifts from a tree. There is a sense of available time, of a plethora of hours usable in many civilized ways.

Today, it is the middle-aged who are the hopeful and the young who are the cynics. The freshman may consider that tradition is eyewash, that the present is a bore and the past a dead loss, but not many undergraduates continue to look down upon everyone and everything but themselves as inferior. Even in retrospect, there are few real regrets for Oxford days. Membership of a society in which youth is always given a hearing is not to be sneered at. And one in which a young man can be ridiculous without being made to seem absurd is civilized indeed.

The privilege of belonging to such a society is nowhere epitomized so well as at New College, whose very form was aimed at producing a sense of common purpose and community. "A college", says James Morris, "likes to think of itself as a kind of family . . .", and in providing his scholars with such a well-ordered and splendidly appointed house, William of Wykeham must have had this very much in mind. They were part of his great experiment and he intended that they should be well looked after.

That New College has changed so little since its foundation in 1379 is due more than anything to his foresight and careful planning. The original buildings, ranged round the Great Quadrangle as they were in the fourteenth century, are not much altered. An extra storey was added to the Fellow's chambers in 1675 and in the Georgian period, sash windows replaced the crumbling stonework of the old traceried lights. The founder might have raised an eye-brow at these goings-on and the damage done to the chapel by the iconoclasts of the Reformation would certainly have distressed him. But he would still recognize the quad, the cloister in which so many scholars are buried and the gatehouse with its statues of the Virgin, St. Gabriel and himself.

We should be thankful that successive generations of New College men have resisted the temptation to 'go modern'. Unlike neighbouring Queen's, which in the eighteenth century tore down all its ancient buildings to make way for a brand-new set-up in the classical style, New College left well alone. It was fortunate in having land available for extension. The pleasant Garden Quad, dating from the 1680s, was added on without disturbance and its south wing cleverly masks that isolated but very necessary medieval structure known as the 'Longhouse' or more recently as the 'Long Room'. This was the scholars' 'house of easement', a two-storeyed latrine block, described by Robert Plot in 1677 as "a stupendous piece of building" in which rows of privies on the first floor discharged into a vast cesspit below "so large and deep that it has never been emptied since the foundation of the College, which was above 300 years ago, nor is ever likely to want it . . .".

Backing onto Queen's Lane, this Gargantua of a convenience is still in use, although the bottomless pit was filled in ninety years ago. The place was then 'modernized' by installing, of all things, primitive earth closets! By the time Queen Victoria died, how-ever, main drainage was available and the present bathrooms and water closets brought undergraduates greater comfort.

Another detached, but less noisome building is the fourteenth-century Warden's Barn, whose blank unbroken wall flanks New College Lane at its narrowest and grimmest part. Originally a medieval tithe-barn, it became the college brewery, last being used for ale-making in 1903. For centuries before, it had been utilized as stables and for the storage of produce from the orchards and gardens. It also took in payments in kind from the estates and farms which also provided the greater part of the college revenues. These were of vital importance, and in September each year it was the warden's duty to visit all the properties. Splendidly attired in velvet and ermine, mounted on the best of his six horses and attended by his bursary clerk and a senior Fellow as outrider, he went the rounds on rough roads and often in the roughest of weathers. Eventually, this semi-regal progress had to be abandoned, for by the beginning of the nineteenth century, the New College lands totalled 17,000 acres, spread over twelve counties!

Like most things at New College, the domestic arrangements were admirable and little was left to chance. The establishment was specified in great detail and, besides kitchens, butteries, launderies, larders, coal houses and beer cellars, there was accommodation for a considerable number of servants. The majority had a wage of 13s. 4d. a year plus clothing and keep and were under the control of three 'superiors', these being the butler (or 'manciple'), the cook and the porter. For 20 shillings per annum, the latter was something of a Figaro, for besides "making candels for the chappel" he was responsible for a variety of jobs, including shaving the Fellows and cutting their hair. There was a laundress living out, a gardener, a groom, two under-butlers, two assistant cooks and a general handyman rejoicing in the title of *Lator librorum* whose function was to carry heavy books between the college and the schools but who also wound the clock in the big bell tower and blew the organ in chapel.

The chapel played a very important part in the life of New College and is still notable for its fine music. The daily choral services were conducted by a large staff of ten chaplains, three clerks and sixteen choristers under the direction of an organist-choirmaster. The three clerks ranked as poor scholars, were given 20 shillings a year and keep, and had to wait at table. Below them were the choristers, all 'charity boys' who were fed on kitchen scraps and after-dinner leavings. Instructed in Latin and singing, they were expected to make beds and help with any odd menial tasks that happened to be going.

The Fellows lived rather well. They enjoyed two substantial meals a day and a regular diet made up of beef, mutton, veal, fish on fast days, pease pudden, home-baked bread, butter, figs, almonds, raisins, honey, fresh fruit and occasionally rice, all washed down with beer. Vegetables came from the gardens and the standard bill of fare was varied by the "curious spiced delicacies" served up on the statutory 'gaudie nights' held twenty-one times each year. On these special occasions, a fire was lit in the Great Hall and the Fellows sat round the table "seriouslie discussing poems, chronicles of kingship and the wonders of this

Commemoration Day in Catte Street

worlde . . .". As an extra treat, "there was an allowance of chease to bee eaten after the ffellowes had sung derges . . .".

But on most nights, they had to be more circumspect. "Songs and other honest solaces" were forbidden as were dice, chequers, chess and wrestling and dancing. Latin had to be spoken, and during dinner a strict silence was maintained while one of the clerks read passages from the Bible. Afterwards, everyone had to quietly disperse to their studies or go to bed, which, considering that their working day commonly began at five in the morning, was a sensible habit.

Facing onto the Great Quadrangle, their quarters were as sensibly planned as everything else. 'Sets' of rooms arranged round 'staircases' are now so traditional a feature of Oxford that it is sometimes forgotten they were once a novelty. A few of the monastic schools had a roughly similar arrangement—the sweet little *mansione* cottages at Worcester College are a surviving example —but New College was the first to adopt such a regularized layout.

A 'staircase' approached directly from the quad serves four 'sets', two on the ground floor and two above. The original 'set' consisted of a large communal bedroom, off which opened three or four little studies, and was occupied by the same number of Fellows. Although very much standardized units of accommodation, these chambers soon acquired an individual reputation for comfort or the opposite. Some were better placed than others and received more daylight. Until 1536, the four-man 'sets' downstairs had floors of beaten earth and tended to be damp. In consequence, there was constant intriguing for better places whenever a vacancy occurred. Invariably, the four most junior Fellows came off worst, being relegated to the worst set under the western end of the hall. Dark and gloomy and without a fireplace, this was known as The Cock and was far from popular. The staircase sets on the opposite side of the quad had prettier names: The Crane and Dart, The Christopher, The Rose, The Vine, The Green Post, The Vale —it all sounds rather like a suburban street.

But as living became less rough and habits more refined, the rooms at New College and elsewhere were gradually remodelled and made more comfortable. Open roofs and ceilings were plastered over, windows glazed and in the Elizabethan period, a good deal of fine panelling was introduced. Eventually 'my rooms

High Street and the "City Church" of All Saints

at Oxford' could be a phrase synonymous with charm, elegance
and comfort in all departments except sanitation. Even today, college plumbing leans towards the archaic and seems to base its
standards on pre-classical, if not actually prehistoric models.

In 1868, as a don of Christ Church, Lewis Carroll took over a
set of "spacious and unusually imposing apartments" from the
young Lord Bute. Splendid quarters they may have been, but for
the next thirty years, he still had to perform his morning ablutions
"in a japanned tin sponge-bath full of tepid water" placed in a
corner of the spare bedroom. Such baths were a familiar part of
life in college for over a century and they finally disappeared only
in the 1920s. Most people rejoiced in their passing but, inevitably,
a few diehards regretted the change. They were the last of those
appallingly hearty muscular Christians, one of whom as late as
1900 was advising the freshman to: "Rise briskly when you are
called, and into your cold bath, you young dog! No shilly-shally,
but into it! Don't splash the water about in a miserable attempt to
deceive your scout, but take an Honest British Cold Bath like a
man!" How awfully jolly!

The cult of the cold bath seems to have been a form of sado-
masochism, believed in by many but enjoyed by none. Victorian
scouts were well accustomed to hearing the anguished shudders of
their young gentlemen as they took the morning plunge.

Fortunately, good hot baths could be had in the town for a
shilling a time and were generally appreciated. Finding it both
difficult and expensive to instal individual bathrooms in their old
buildings, some colleges erected communal bath-houses, often at a
considerable distance from undergraduates' rooms. A Keble man
remembered that after the First World War: he was comparatively fortunate, ". . . only having about fifty yards to go in the
open to reach the bath-house. Today, Keble undergraduates live
in luxury and no longer have to trudge through snow in their
dressing gowns. . . ."

Cleanliness has not always been equated with godliness and for
quite a long period, an excess of washing was considered positively harmful. Such a sentiment accorded well with the Oxford
tradition of not pampering its students. Nowadays, it may seem
that the old policy has been reversed. Nevertheless, some colleges
still seem a little reluctant to put money into plumbing.

For, although they sometimes tend to plead poverty, the

financial position of the colleges as a whole is not exactly bleak. Their total income is very considerable and until the advent of government subsidies, far surpassed the revenues of the university. In 1871, for example, college endowments and income from properties brought in no less than £366,000 a year, as compared with the university's modest £47,000. The disproportion between the two is a fair indication of their relative importance at a time when the colleges owned nearly 185,000 acres of land and Christ Church alone had an annual income of £57,000.

The balance has since swung strongly in favour of the university, which now takes the lion's share of an annual budget of some £7 million. To this, the colleges contribute about 6 per cent of their income as a sort of levy for teaching and other services provided by the various Faculties. Fifty years ago, the equivalent budget figure was £824,710, of which nearly half went to the colleges. They were then just about at the height of their power in Oxford. The influence and prestige of the university was at a low ebb, and to say that the colleges were self-important to the point of arrogance would not be over-stating the case.

To many academics, their 'house' was the be-all and end-all of life. Some took delight in opposing the slightest changes or improvements proposed by the nominally greater body. Described by Vice-Chancellor Farnell as "someone who acted as if he was in no way a member of the larger organism of the University, but belonged to a rival and potentially hostile institution", the typical 'college man' did all he could to keep the two apart. It took another official inquiry, followed by strong legislation, to put an end to separatist nonsense and bring the two together.

As early as 1907, attempts were being made to remedy this sad situation. At a time when 'universal education' already meant rather more than secondary schools for working-class boys, both Oxford and Cambridge were under attack as being "mere playgrounds for the sons of the wealthier classes". Reform was once more in the air, but further action was delayed by the onset of the First World War. It was not until 1919, after the university had approached the government of the day for financial assistance, that the long-promised Royal Commission was appointed.

Published in 1922, its report recommended changes which were not at all to the liking of the colleges. Their accounts, previously wrapped in mystery, were now to be freely published for all to see. A common university entrance examination was to be established, the idea being that colleges would eventually be forced to kick out undergraduates "who were not making a reasonable minimum of intellectual progress". But more controversial was the proposal to make every university professor a fellow of one or other of the colleges. The advocates of this saw it as a bold move towards "creating a sense of fellowship between the representatives of Oxford's dual system of teaching; the college tutors and the University professoriate". The new professor-fellows would automatically become part of the governing bodies of their colleges and therefore able to "present broader University interests".

Incensed by the mere thought of such outside interference, the 'college men' dug in and tried all kinds of obstructionist tactics. At one stage, the President of Corpus Christi staggered everyone by trying to prove that it had never been legally a part of the university and was therefore not subject to its statutes.

But much bigger issues were involved. Even in the twenties the urgent need for more scientific research was apparent, and it was even more obvious that a great expansion of higher education was in the offing. Neither the colleges nor the university had the kind of money needed to finance large-scale development. To help Oxford on its way into the twentieth century, it was known that the State was ready to offer a big golden handshake and that large annual grants would ultimately be made available from public funds.

The old-style academics were thoroughly frightened. To them, it seemed that the university was about to lose its long-cherished independence. The Royal Commission was seen "simply as a device to bring Oxford and Cambridge under the authority of the Board of Education". One eminent Professor of Divinity said that the situation "reminds me of the proverbial mouse tempted into a trap by the prospect of subsidies of cheese . . .".

Things all round turned out better than expected. It was a triumph for the men concerned that state intervention did not result in state control. Unlike some continental institutions, Oxford remained a national university and did not become a National one. Moreover, the worst fears of the colleges proved groundless. Their autonomy was preserved and their continuing existence as corporate societies assured. While reluctant to admit that they had rightly been put in their place as component parts of

a much greater whole, they were happy to find that their importance had not been under-rated. No-one ever tried to run down
their unique method of teaching, nor to alter it. The weekly
'tutorial' with its free and individual discussion between don and
undergraduate stayed as the key feature of collegiate education.
Supplemented by lectures provided by the university, it was still
recognized as a vital part of the dual system traditionally associated
with Oxford.

Most important, a serious breach had been healed. In the words
of one of the commissioners: "We turned the faces of the colleges
towards the University. . . ."

XII

GRADUATES AD PARNASSUM

Oxford's two stock characters are the Undergraduate and the Don.

The first has been appearing in *Charley's Aunt* for eighty years and both have been the butts of *Punch* for considerably longer. Sunk in sublime cerebration, the Don is gowned, profound, a bit of a bore, a bit of a fool, a bit of a boor. In contrast, your Undergraduate is callow, conceited, busting out all over with the brave brashness of youth—and utterly charming. He spends half his time rowing on the river. The remainder is spent in consuming cucumber sandwiches and vast quantities of champagne.

Fiction adds colour to untruth and these figures of fun are larger than life and twice as unnatural. Even the known facts are at variance. Admittedly, there are still dons who look like Mr. Barrett of Wimpole Street and student sharp-dressers with the sartorial elegance of Regency bucks. On the other hand, the erudite college fellow is just as likely to be a tweedy type whose diction is bucolic and whose weather-beaten face speaks more of swedes than Swedenborg. Or a telly person with a Brummagen accent and a delivery that would add lustre to any shop-floor slanging match at Cowley Works.

You never can tell. Beer does more than champagne can to justify dons' ways to man. Both for economic and other reasons, it is now the preferred drink of the chicken 'n chips generation. Oxford, as James Morris says, is "a notoriously bibulous city" in which nothing washes down the carbohydrates quite so well as a pint of keg bitter. Some colleges are reputed to spend £10,000 a year on maintaining their stocks of great wines. In the town, however, the popular pubs do a roaring trade in more proletarian tipple. At Merton's high table, they may sniff delicately at the *Batard–Montrachet '59*, but jolly good ale and old is the stuff they

mainly knock back in the boozers. Beer, glorious beer, is the stuff
to give the troops of Town and Gown alike.

As a general rule, academics and townsfolk tend to stick to their
own drinking spots. In common law, neither is debarred from the
haunts of the other, but in practice—and certainly during term—
the two prefer to keep their own counsels in their own favourite
houses. Pubs like the 'Turf', the 'Turl', the 'White Horse', 'Bear',
'Royal Oak', 'King's Arms', near to the colleges and in some
cases actually owned by them, are the natural haunts of the undergraduate. The only outsiders to be seen are tourists in search of
atmosphere, rather than townsmen in search of trouble.

But trouble can be found. The prudent student knows that certain 'locals' are better avoided, particularly in the evening. Even
at lunchtime, the noonday dominoes-players will eye him with
hostility, the barman will be brusque and mine host far from
genial. Down St. Ebbe's and Jericho, wild words at closing time
lead too easily too late-night punch-ups.

Yet, of necessity, modern Oxford provides places in which
Town and Gown needs must meet on neutral ground. Cinemas,
supermarkets, Woolworths, Marks and Spencer, washeterias,
cafeterias, snack bars; Chinese, Indian, Italian, French, even
English restaurants: here you see them both, pushing, shoving,
noshing, queueing. Even a few of the pubs now contrive to serve
and make the most of two worlds. Hidden behind the more
famous Mitre Hotel, a typical example of split personality is the
Turl Tavern with its two separate bars. Each caters almost exclusively for its own special clientele. Into the long Turl Room troop
dons and undergraduates from nearby Lincoln, Jesus and Exeter.
The *hoi polloi* and others make instinctively for the Tudor Lounge.
The twain meet in the yard and the gents, but not too often.

Meanwhile, the venerable 'Mitre' still presents its coaching inn
frontage to The High, although it has now become a multi-
roomed steak house. Half-way across the street and deep below
the traffic are its original thirteenth-century cellars, splendidly
vaulted and absolutely right for *A Cask of Amontillado*. The
'Mitre' was already 200 years old when Lincoln College, its current owners, acquired the property as far back as 1475. But in
Oxford, such long-term landlordships raise few eyebrows. There
are older ones.

Another hotel known to all undergraduates is the 'Randolph', a stiff Victorian pile on the corner of St. Giles and Beaumont Street. In spite of its gloomy Gothic appearance, the 'Randolph' always claimed to be smarter and more superior than its rivals, advertising itself at the turn of the century as "The only *modern-built* hotel in Oxford, with Ladies' Coffee Room, Night Porter and *American Elevator*". A few years before, good accommodation was harder to come by. In 1860, Murray's merciless *Oxford Guide* had described the city's inns and boarding houses as "bad, comfortless, dirty and high in charges . . .".

Nevertheless, some were considered good enough to receive royalty. The Clarendon Hotel, which was pulled down in 1950 to make way for the new Woolworths, was celebrated for the crowned heads which regularly rested on its pillows.

The Oxford hotels used to offer some strange attractions as an inducement to visitors. In 1902, the Eastgate Hotel had just been rebuilt and was proudly announcing that its superior accommodation was now "lighted by the new electricity", the manager drawing attention to the fact that "Our New System of Sanitary Arrangements has been passed by the University Sanitary Surveyor . . .". On the other hand, 'The Roebuck' claimed to be "most conveniently situated for Commercial Gentlemen, Tourists and Boating Parties". Its special glory was a fully-equipped dark room for the use of amateur photographers.

But by Oxford's historic standards, these were modern innovations. A product of the railway age, the hotel industry was entirely a creation of the Victorian era. Tourism, as distinct from the individual tourist, was a new phenomenon. It is interesting to note, however, that the curious traveller was being catered for at quite an early date. The earliest guidebooks appeared in the eighteenth century and people were doing the rounds long before this. In the summer of 1668, Samuel Pepys 'did' the university and colleges in less than a day, rushing round the sights at a speed that would have done credit to the most determined American visitor. He found it all "very sweet", had a hair-do and shave for half-a-crown, tipped porters, potboys and college butlers lavishly, ate strawberries, sniffed at the preserved hand of John Middleton, the court giant, in the cellar of Brasenose and after spending a total of £3 9s. 8d., went on to Abingdon, "where had been a fair of custard", well pleased that "Oxford was a mighty fine place, well seated and good entertainment. . . ."

Like most visitors of his time, Pepys 'lay' at an inn, of which there were very many. The main business of such hostelries was still the provision of drink and simple food. Luxury was neither offered nor expected, although several had already built up a reputation for cleanliness and solid comfort. One of these was the Crown Tavern, the remains of which still exist in Cornmarket. As well known in its day as 'The Mitre' and almost as old, 'The Crown' thrived for 500 years until the greater part of it was demolished to make way for shopping developments. The few bits that are left are scarcely recognizable, but over the top of Lyons teashop can be found the Painted Room, now the headquarters of the Oxford Preservation Trust. It was in such quarters as these that the fashionable and famous stayed. "Wm. Shakspere did commonlie lye at this house in Oxon, where he was exceedinglie respected ..." gossiped old John Aubrey of Trinity, only a few years after the poet's death. And it was at 'The Crown', in 1675, that six dons who should have known better inflicted dishonourable defeat upon Admiral van Tromp by getting him stupified on a mixture of wine and brandy.

Almost unknown in England before the seventeenth century, brandy was soon to become quite a killer. Not a few dons died from alcoholic poisoning and a succession of undergraduates followed their example. In 1704 a gentleman-commoner of Magdalen went on an all-night drinking jag, ending up in his chambers with three companions. Having started on strong ale, they moved onto brandy and made short work of ten bottles before dropping senseless. They were found next morning by a terrified servant. Inett, the commoner, was stark and dead and his three cronies "raving and half mad".

On the other hand, that veteran warrior, Field-Marshal Blücher, could hold his liquor like a superman. During his official visit to the city in 1814, it was his daily habit to knock back a bottle of cognac on waking, eat a hearty breakfast and then take a brisk walk round one of the quadrangles. He considered it was all very good for the digestion.

It may well be that drink is one of the shorter cuts to Parnassus or Elysium. Or, for those who need escape, to oblivion. Happiness and unhappiness can both lead to the bottle and in Oxford there is no shortage of either. There is also the age-old desire of youth to show off its prowess and to go one better than the next man. Together, these things sometimes open the door to more than beer and skittles. As in most towns, drugs have made their appearance in Oxford in recent years and are still a growing problem to those in authority. Pot parties no longer make the headlines. Reefers and pills change hands in the oddest places and people are prosecuted for being in possession of cannabis.

Fortunately, Oxford in general continues to prefer cakes and ale of the older fashioned sort and the demand for stimulation is still largely met by the pubs. In the seventeenth century, there were at least 370 alehouses in the city. Inevitably, such proliferation led to wild behaviour. From medieval times onwards, Oxford history abounds with stories of brawls, bawdiness, violence, rapings and occasional murders. In these matters, there seems to have been little to choose between Town and Gown. Both had their moments of madness and the behaviour of academics ranged from the merely bad-mannered to the downright beastly. There were drunken undergraduates at St. John's who fought each other in the common room and then "came drunk into chapell and vomitted into their hats". New College, too was "much given to drinking and gaming and vayne brutish pleasure". But the most severe strictures were reserved for Balliol, whose students frequented 'The Katherine Wheel', a tavern most happily situated right outside the main gate. It was: "A dingy, horrid, scandalous alehouse, fit for none but draymen and tinkers, where the Balliol men continually lye and by perpetual bubbing, add art to their natural stupidity to make of themselves perfect sottes. . . ."

Their conduct became so bad that the Master called members of the college together and solemnly warned them of the dangers of "drinking that hellish liquor called ale". He forebore to mention his own custom of carousing at 'The Split Crow' up the road in the company of the Vice-Chancellor and his friends. In the circumstances, it is not surprising that the men of Balliol—known as 'the Sons of Belial'—carried on as before.

It should be remembered, however, that for the first 500 years of the university's existence, taverns were the only places in which scholars could relax. The majority of colleges provided cold comfort. Discipline was strict, the regimen near-monastic and, even after the Reformation, the daily demands of religious observance onerous. There was not even the privacy of a monk's cell. Until the end of the seventeenth century, it was still the common practice for several men to share one room. Compatible and incompatible alike were forced into close and intimate contact with little chance of escape. Dinnertime was the only general social occasion, but for at least half the year, most college halls were cold and cheerless places, full of howling draughts and shivering students looking at an empty hearth. Wrapped in their gowns, they were forbidden to talk but were supposed to enjoy the toneless reading of the Bible clerk as he plodded through page after page of the Old Testament. Merriment was out; but who would want to laugh in such conditions?

No wonder Oxford had so many alehouses! And no wonder they were so popular! Then, as now, a cosy room with a roaring fire, a bawdy ballad and a bosomy serving wench, had much to commend it. The stern asceticism of the colleges and the uninhibited vitality of the town were scarcely comparable. Fellows and students alike escaped into the streets like children let out of school, eager to live it up and enjoy whatever life happened to be going.

Only the development of the college common room did something to lessen the sharp contrast. Before 1661, when the first Senior Common Room was set up at Merton, the one place in Oxford where academics could sit and talk and be warm was the nearest inn. "Common rooms", wrote Rice-Oxley, "where there is warmth and comfort; where wine and conversation can flow freely, and where social amenities are obtained, are comparatively modern institutions. . . ."

Merton's lead was soon followed by the other colleges, but the early common rooms were for Fellows only. The first Junior Common Room was opened in the Garden Quad of New College in 1678, thus establishing the now-traditional pattern by which every house has its 'S.C.R.'—Senior Common Room—for the dons and its 'J.C.R.' for undergraduates. In surroundings which nowadays range from the grand and club-like to the fun parlour or discotheque, both can work hard at taking it easy. Here, academics indulge in the niceties, kick the wit around, take sherry and biscuits, knock back a beer, become bitchy, complimentary or bloody rude to one another, carry on intrigues, take the universe apart, practise their verbal swordplay, enjoy good conversation, imagine themselves as *vainqueurs des vainqueurs de la terre*, be boring, boorish or brilliant, talk history, make history

and occasionally come very close to being 'the complete man' of
Renaissance idealism. Sometimes, they also make complete asses
of themselves, for in vino is twaddle as well as truth.

Like their occupants, common rooms have changed with the
years. The current impression is that they are places buzzing with
brainpower; elegant oases of civilization in an otherwise arid
world; rooms 'dark with oaken wainscot' in which timeless
intellectual square dances are endlessly undertaken. At best, this
may not be far off the mark, although it must be said that the
general reality tends to be more workaday and the atmosphere a
little less rarified. The elegant, even beautiful common rooms por-
trayed in novels, films and more lately on television do exist, but
what goes on inside them lends itself to exaggeration.

Certainly, it was quite a long time before their pleasures and
comforts ousted those of the tavern. In the hard-drinking eighteenth century, the alehouses of Oxford were still at their peak as
centres of extra-mural merriment. "At the *Mitre*," wrote a
German traveller in 1782, "there was hardly a minute in which
some students or other did not call, either to drink or to amuse
themselves with the landlord's daughter. . . ."

This so-called Age of Elegance was also the age of Hogarth's
"Rake's Progress" and "Gin Lane". When aristocrats besotted
with brandy could slide under the table without causing surprise
and when ordinary folk "drunk for a penny or dead drunk for
tuppence" lay undisturbed in the gutter, it is small wonder that
the drinking habits of Oxford should arouse little more than mild
amusement. Even the great Doctor Johnson boasted of his ability
to guzzle three bottles of port at a sitting, and in 1780 a much
respected Doctor of Divinity was so far gone in drink that, reaching Catte Street on his way home, all sense of direction failed and
he spent the night making countless circumnavigations of the
Radcliffe Camera on his hands and knees.

Reverend gentlemen, no less than laymen, took to their tipple
as readily as ducks to water. For them, 'The Mitre' was a favourite
meeting place. Towards the end of the century, Moritz, a Swiss
pastor, found himself among a covey of cursing clergymen in the
back room, all drinking steadily and arguing among themselves as
to whether the Bible proved that God was "a drunkard and a
wine-bibber". At cock-crow they were still at it and the party
broke up only when the chaplain of Corpus Christi lurched to the

door shouting loudly: "Damn me! I have to read prayers at All Souls this morning!"

Slowly, the common rooms began to provide rival and more comfortable facilities and aristos like Lord Lovelace, who "was never sober but 12 hours and used every morning to drink a quart of brandy" were able to get themselves sozzled without setting a foot outside college precincts.

Long after the world in general had learned to play them down, Oxford carefully preserved the social distinctions. For centuries 'birth and breeding' counted above most things and there were periods in which they mattered more than mental ability. As late as 1911 someone was writing seriously of "the three main divisions of the *genus undergrad*", these being the scholars, the commoners and the 'toshers'. This latter term covered those who were classed as 'non-collegiate' and did not properly belong to the university at all. Altogether outside the pale were the working-class students of Ruskin College, as far removed from major and minor nobilities as the poles.

Often enough, the term 'gentleman' was something of a misnomer when applied to students. Dressed in rich clothes, wearing special gowns and gold-tasselled caps, and entitled to purchase their degrees as 'Grand Compounders', the arrogance of some of the richer undergraduates knew no bounds, frequently leading them into dreadful exhibitions of loutishness. "Rich men's sons", wrote Harrison the historian in the reign of Elizabeth I "often bring the University into much slander...."

When they were not either living it up, whooping it up or taking the lead in provocative excursions against the despised townees, the upper crust tended to keep themselves to themselves. Faintly amused, they stood above and apart from all around them. They belonged to exclusive Oxford clubs and societies like the Bullingdon, kept dogs, gambled heavily, rode to hounds, treated Vice-Chancellors with familiarity and tutors with contempt, found examinations hilarious and generally did not give a damn. Some were immensely rich. Lord Dalmeny came into an income of £30,000 a year while still an undergraduate of Christ Church.

This was in 1866, when the Victorian sun was approaching its zenith, income tax was minimal and the pound sterling had perhaps nine times its present purchasing power. The middle classes were on the move and making their presence felt, but the top people were still the envied aristocrats who lived like princes and saw no trace of writing on their walls. A few years before, the University Commission had "recommended the abolition of all distinctions between Noblemen, Gentleman-Commoners and Commoners" but to no real purpose. The categories officially disappeared but the differences remained. Ostentatious displays of wealth and high birth might be frowned upon, but no serious attempts were made to restrict them. The colleges regarded these notions of equality with abhorrence. Private wealth had made them what they were and it was natural that most houses should favour their richer and well-born members. It was argued that class distinction was "merely a reflection of one of the most unalterable aspects of human society" and if the son of a nobleman "wanted a better table, better rooms, more servants and horses" than the rest, then let him have them.

Thus, Dalmeny, later fifth Earl of Rosebery, "lived in some state and saw regrettably little of the rest of the University". He went racing, threw frequent and lavish breakfast parties in his rooms, took time off during term to visit Italy and Russia and enjoyed himself hugely at country house-parties. As a freshman of 19 he refused point-blank to attend compulsory morning chapel and stayed in bed. "The Dean", he wrote, "was very amiable about it."

This future Foreign Secretary left Oxford without taking a degree. He was eventually sent down, not from lack of intellect or dislike for hard work: indeed, he did very well in his earlier examinations and was confidently expected to get a First in 'Greats'. His removal from the scene was due entirely to the fact that he owned Ladas, a racehorse which was confidently expected to come first in the 1869 Derby.

But the Dean and Fellows of Christ Church felt that this was going a bit too far. Young Rosebery, as he had now become, was given the option: "either his horse went, or he did". To everyone's surprise and to "the astonishment of his tutor, the admiration of the Bullingdon set, and the horror of his family", he chose to leave. For an undergraduate to own horses was no crime, but to own racehorses was definitely not the thing to do!

Even in modern times, belted earls have been thick upon the Oxford ground, tending to grace with their presence only the more 'socially prestigious' colleges. Magdalen and Christ Church are traditionally aristocratic in their membership, and in his memoirs, Cecil King, a nephew of the newspaper barons North-cliffe and Rothermere, recalled that Christ Church in particular was "an extraordinarily snobbish institution".

The attitude of the university as a whole towards the occasional royal undergraduate seems to have varied both with the time and the nationality of the princelings concerned. They have ranged from the youngest sons of African chiefs to the heirs-apparent of European monarchs. In 1924, two greatly different 'royals' were in residence: Crown Prince Olav of Norway and the diminutive Prince Chichibu of Japan. Chichibu spent two years at Magdalen and, with an eye to protocol, the President politely inquired what he would like to be called. "Not Chichibu, if you please," said the little prince, "It means 'The Son of God'." The President nodded, and replied, "That's all right. *We've had the sons of many famous people here!*"

One cannot imagine this being said in 1859, when the first member of the British royal house to study at Oxford arrived. This was no less a personage than the highly-repressed, over-protected and fun-loving Albert Edward, Prince of Wales, who was later to become King Edward VII. Almost as a matter of course, he was entered at Christ Church. 'The House', after all, had in the past lodged if not educated some of his illustrious and notorious ancestors, notably the two Charlies and within living memory, 'Prinny', afterwards George IV.

But Edward did not have rooms in college. His prudent parents decided that whatever else might happen, their young prince was not to risk "possible contamination from too intimate an association with ordinary undergraduates". In consequence, he was given the whole run of Frewin Hall in New Inn Hall Street, where a very large household catered for his every need. There, in complete privacy, he was tutored in matters of religion by a deferent Dean Stanley and in history by Professor Godwin Smith. The few open lectures attended by 'Teddy' called for a consider-able ritual. As soon as he entered the lecture room in his specially-designed gown, all present had to rise respectfully and seem suitably impressed.

The high-minded Prince Consort had previously warned his son against casual social calls and the consequent dangers of mix-ing with other young men. Forbidden to smoke, drink, or do any of the things normal to most students, Albert Edward nevertheless managed to enjoy his heavily-guarded year.

In contrast, his grandson, the Duke of Windsor, had a rather better time of it. His two years at Oxford were, by comparison, both free and easy. At the age of 18, this new Prince of Wales was already showing himself to be a more modern sort of man, confessing that he found such things as state visits "rot and a waste of time, money and energy". In his memoirs, he admits that "the easy conditions under which I took up residence ... were a vast improvement over those laid down for my grandfather ...". He played roulette, enjoyed "the more sophisticated pleasures of carousing" and made the most of any excuse for a celebration. Wanting so much to be an ordinary young man, he mixed it at 'bump suppers' at the end of Eights Week, danced round bonfires in the quad and thoroughly enjoyed twenty-first birthday parties which "by custom called for the carrying out of those who could no longer walk by those who thought they could ...".

H.R.H. was in residence at Magdalen from 1912 to 1914 and was frequently driven out and about in a huge Daimler limousine. The freedom with which he appeared to come and go was acclaimed by the newspapers as irrefutable evidence of the way democracy could work within the framework of a constitutional monarchy. But he was under no illusions as to his real status. He might well agree with "the socialist son of a miner" who sat next to him at lectures that they did not exactly share the common lot. The royal Daimler marked him for its own. He was excused Responsions, the university's entrance examination. His set of rooms under the Founder's Tower in 'Cloisters' were specially redecorated and provided with the first private undergraduate bathroom in Oxford. There was to be no cold douche in a tin tub, no shivering walk to the morning showers, even for this wanting-to-be-one-of-the-boys prince. Downstairs was the bedroom of his private tutor, Hansell, and his valet Finch stayed always within earshot. "And all around me", he wrote "were young men united in friendships formed at public schools." For H.R.H., no such friendships were possible and he confessed to feeling terribly lonely. Perhaps the nearest he was able to come to the true camaraderie of college were those Sunday evening sessions after dinner in Hall when "everybody who counted for something repaired to Gunners—a musty little taproom at the foot

Georgian elegance in The High
Blackwell's Bookshop from the Sheldonian

of the stairs leading to the Junior Common Room". Here, in pub fashion, Gunstone, the steward, "dispensed beer and other drinks . . .".

The prince's days in Oxford were brought to an end by the onset of the First World War. The four years of slaughter which followed emptied the colleges of most of their students and a majority of their Fellows. By the summer of 1915 the number of undergraduates still in residence had dropped from 3,000 to 1,000. At the end of 1917 the student population was reduced to an all-time low of 350, a figure which even the Black Death and successive plagues had failed to achieve. A year later, the academic body consisted largely of the totally unfit, a few medical students, some refugees from France and Belgium, a handful of friendly neutrals, a score or so of very old men and a group of grey-faced dons in their fifties and sixties who, for various reasons, could not be placed into government or other official work.

Colleges, halls of residence and lodgings were put to a variety of usages, all of them connected with the prosecution of the war. Officers under training clattered up and down staircases and strolled self-consciously round the quadrangles in unaccustomed khaki. Companies of soldiers drilled endlessly on The Parks, charging at straw dummies with hoarse screams and bayonets fixed. In fields and open spaces everywhere, they were instructed in the noble art of gas warfare, taught, in a rudimentary sort of way, how to survive, and laughed inordinately just to keep their peckers up. The green slopes of Wytham Hill became a wet maze of practice trenches and the first time that many a young Englishman went 'over the top' was under an Oxfordshire sky.

At first, the realities of war were no more than the brave music of distant drums. Smartly-dressed soldiers appeared. The colleges were transformed into genteel barracks. Exeter provided quarters for the Oxfordshire Light Infantry and for the horsy men of the artillery batteries. Dons and their ladies provided concerts and comforts for the troops.

But this was still playing at war. While knitting circles were bothering themselves with mittens and Balaclava helmets, England's lost generation was being made into mincemeat on the Somme. Rupert Brooke was dead and buried, not in the stinking morass of Ypres but on the sunlit slopes of a Greek island. The splendidly patriotic selflessness of "The Soldier," forgotten by all

12

St. Ebbe's, "the walk to the Paradise Garden"

except old gentlemen in England still abed, was giving way to the stark and bloody truth of Siegfried Sassoon and Wilfred Owen. An "Anthem for Doomed Youth" accurately summed-up the inner feelings of the cattle sent to the slaughterhouse of the Western Front.

Oxford began to realize what war really meant. German prisoners were seen around Hinksey, human beings like Englishmen, penned behind barbed wire or working freely on the farms. In the city, people looked with embarrassment on men without arms, legs, eyes and sometimes without faces to speak of. Places had to be found for the wreckage. Being conveniently close to the Radcliffe Infirmary, Somerville, a women's college, was soon converted into a military hospital. Having accepted the gallant offer of temporary accommodation in the St. Mary Hall Quad of Oriel, its few remaining girls moved out and moved in. To prevent illicit fraternization between the sexes, the passageway leading to the men's quarters was bricked up, the Provost of Oriel making it clear that he wanted "none of your Pyramus and Thisbe business". But in spite of his warnings, the dividing wall was quickly breached and half its bricks removed while the mortar was still wet. For several nights, the college enjoyed the not unromantic spectacle of the gap being guarded by Doctor Phelps of Oriel on one side and Miss Penrose, Principal of Somerville, on the other.

Coming to University College as a freshman in 1917, C. S. Lewis found to his astonishment that only five other undergraduates were in residence. The number eventually rose to a round dozen, the dons rarely putting in an appearance. "Hall is in possession of the blue-coated wounded", wrote Lewis shortly before he was sent off to fight in France. The gassed and maimed and blinded occupied the whole of one quad and its quarters, and, like the Apostles, the twelve young men dined in a small side room.

The man who was to write *Out of the Silent Planet* and *The Screwtape Letters* counted himself lucky to return to Oxford alive, and more or less in one piece. For too many, it was but a short step from Parnassus to death in Armageddon. Some were killed or shattered on their first day in the trenches. The men in hospital blue were seen everywhere, taking over not only whole colleges, but such unsuitable havens as the Examination Schools and the town hall. More than 6,000 men from the city never came home. The university lost 2,700 of its members, and this when the total academic population never exceeded 3,000. Individual colleges suffered terribly. Christ Church had 256 of its men killed in action, New College 263 and Keble—a much smaller foundation—163. It is not to be wondered at that in the sheer relief of Armistice Night, "certain persons unknown" started to paint the town red by daubing the faces of the statues outside the Sheldonian bright crimson.

Of course, this was by no means the first time that Oxford had lived through war. In 1900 patriotic citizens and students out for adventure served in South Africa, and fifty years earlier a few Oxonians fought against the Russians in the Crimea. Under the threat of invasion by Napoleon at the beginning of the century, they had put on remarkable uniforms, banged drums, waved flags and generally marched about to show how brave they were. But by and large, war was considered a matter for the professionals and a few devil-may-care amateurs. Only during the Civil War had the man in the street been more directly involved. In 1642, after the Battle of Edgehill 30 miles away: "The University bellman went about the city, warning all privileged persons that were householders to send some of their family to dig at the defensive works through the New Park. . . ."

The ordinary townsfolk hated these 'privileged persons'. The term covered everyone employed by the colleges and university, from the Vice-Chancellor at one end of the scale to kitchen boys at the other. Many could neither read nor write, yet they were all formally matriculated as members of the university, after which they were able to enjoy its full protection. For all except the most serious offences against the law, the ordinary courts could not touch them. Willy-nilly, they supported their masters in all disputes and when academic Oxford sided with the King against Parliament, the privileged persons did the same, helping the scholars to dig entrenchments and throw up earthworks round the city.

Anticipating some amelioration of their unhappy lot in the event of a Roundhead victory, the townsmen sided with Parliament. Although they too were enlisted for the business of fortification, they worked with a marked lack of enthusiasm. When Charles I rode round to inspect progress, he found only twelve grumpy citizens leaning on their spades, instead of the 400 who had been summoned. By contrast, the colleges did their best to keep the King solvent, supplying him with large sums of money from their treasuries. And when actual cash was running out, most of their splendid gold and silver plate was carted to the royal mint in New Inn Hall and melted down for coinage.

After it was all over and the King executed, the cold days of the Commonwealth began. It was not a happy time. The mildest excesses were frowned upon. Frivolity was a sin. Reaction to repression, which came with the restoration of the monarchy, was vicious. The madly gay whirl of the nineteen-twenties did not begin to compare with the vice and bawdiness and amoral attitudes of the sixteen-sixties. Drunkenness increased. In Oxford, as elsewhere, venereal diseases were rife. Dons and undergraduates fathered scores of bastard children, the unfortunate mothers being, more often than not, bedmakers, laundresses and servant girls. Inevitably, there were tragedies. Some drowned themselves for shame. One, "a handsome mayde living in Catte Street" fell in love with a Junior Fellow of New College, found herself with child, and in despair, poisoned herself with ratsbane.

At the end of the Civil War, Ann Green, a kitchen maid in the great house of Duns Tew was sentenced to death for the murder of her newly-born illegitimate child. After she was hanged at Oxford Castle, her body was cut down and carried away for dissection by the anatomy students of Christ Church. An hour or two later, they were amazed to find that she was still alive. The two doctors present "for humanity as well as their Profession's sake" managed to revive her. She was granted a free pardon, became quite a local celebrity, married a man from her home village of Steeple Barton, had three more children and died there in peace ten years later. A full account of her miraculous deliverance is given in a contemporary pamphlet "News from the Dead" which also included poems on the subject by Christopher Wren and a group of his friends.

Another girl who suffered a similar fate was not so fortunate. In 1658, she too killed her bastard baby and was executed before a large and not very sympathetic crowd. "Her body was ordered for anatomizing; but after it was taken from the gallows, Coniers, a young physician of St. John's College, discovered life, which was speedily restored . . .". They took her to an inn near Magdalen Bridge, where she began to recover: "But the bailiffs of the towne hearing of it, they went between 12 & 1 o'clock of the night to the house where she layed, and putting her into a coffin, carried her to Broken Hayes, and by a halter about her neck drew her out of it and hung her on a tree. She was then so sensible of what they were about to do that she said: 'Lord, have mercy on me. . . .' "

It was thought that the man concerned came from one of the colleges, but he escaped both detection and punishment. But remorse sometimes drove scholars to make an end of themselves. Thomas Ashwell "a popish undergraduate" hung himself quietly from a beam in his room, "being in want and in love". Always with an eye for grisly detail, Anthony Wood noted that "he hung there till the stink of his bodie betray'd him, and he was taken down all blacke a week after . . .".

In this seventeenth century, the punishment of crime could still be a brutal business and there was not much tempering of justice with mercy. Offenders were flogged, mutilated or put to death while the world at large shrugged its shoulders. A Jacobite sympathizer wandered into the common room at Brasenose, and for raising his glass to the deposed Stuarts, was cruelly whipped at the cart's tail all the way from Carfax to East Gate. The crowds cackled, just as they did at executions, by long custom a public spectacle. In 1680 a man accused of the murder of a Balliol undergraduate was strung up and slowly strangled outside the college gates. The body was left on show for a while, but beginning to smell, it was cut down and taken to the gibbet on Bullingdon Green, under Shotover Hill. There it hung in chains for the best part of six years.

In spite of the considerable protection given them as members of the university, it was not always possible for undergraduates to escape the death penalty for serious offences. The amazing Doctor Routh, born in 1755, President of Magdalen for sixty-three years and a man who lived to be 100, recalled seeing two students hanged for highway robbery on the 'Gownsman's Gallows' which stood at the junction of Holywell Street and Longwall. A few years before, a servitor of Christ Church had gone to the scaffold in the yard of the castle for stealing plate and other valuables from various colleges. Some offenders had better luck. In 1677 John Bradshaw, a Corpus Christi man, was sentenced to hang for robbery with violence, having broken into the room of one of the fellows and savagely attacked him with a hammer. At the eleventh hour he was reprieved, sent to jail for a year and expelled, ending his career as a much-respected schoolmaster in Kent.

Each age likes to think of itself as being both more informed and rather more civilized than those that have gone before. People are no longer burned at the stake, stretched on the rack or even hanged by the neck until they are dead, the last bit of Christian barbarism to survive into the twentieth century. But what, one wonders, would men of these past ages have made of the madness of a modern war in which 20 million human beings were killed or maimed?

XIII

PARNASSUS

This 'war to end war' failed in its avowed purpose, but did achieve other things. Sadder, wiser, those who came back found that the old Oxford of medieval dreamings, Victorian leisure, Edwardian spaciousness, was no more. Freshers who had been mere schoolchildren during the carnage, came up to a changed and changing world. The mood everywhere was one of eat, drink and be merry. Tomorrow did not matter. Yet for all their wildness and apparent superficiality, the new young people were no fools. Emerging out of the maelstrom, their generation was tougher, more cynical and less given to sentimentalizing than the one that had plunged into the deep end five years before. Youngsters who had lost fathers, friends and brothers had few illusions about the facts of life and death. The wise, foolish old men had failed them. Dons might deplore their morals, their irreverence, their jazz, their feverish parties, their endless chatter; nevertheless, escapism was a necessary anodyne and ultimately the only -ism that mattered.

Oxford was rapidly becoming a different place. At Cowley William Morris had stopped making Stokes bombs, hand grenades and sinkers for naval mines and was getting into full production with his first post-war motor-cars. After working on munitions for four years, some college servants realized that they were much better off working for Mr. Morris than being civil to undergraduates. Industry was expanding and presenting them with new opportunities. They did not return to their traditional employment. In the ancient streets, the noise of traffic increased. Town became less and less dependent on Gown. And if the university did not exactly play second fiddle, then the academics at least began to sing a somewhat quieter tune.

Many purely Victorian characters were still around, regretting the past, at cross-purposes with the present, refusing to face the future. The new generation thought they were funny old things. Now in his eighties, but still Warden of New College, Dr. Spooner pottered about dodging absent-minded clergymen on bicycles, telling a freshman to get himself "a well-boiled icicle".

Equating women with cats, a don who disliked both species was Canon Jenkins. Stacked from floor to ceiling with ramparts of books, his lodgings were permanently fumigated by the smoke of a foul pipe, an implement which sometimes shot out blue flames because of his habit of stuffing in sleeping pills as well as tobacco.

No less a personality was the aged Canon Carlyle, last of Charles Kingsley's original Christian Socialists and a cleric who had enjoyed the worldly delights of Paris in its genuine *La Bohème* days. As absent-minded as the best of them, he once announced his text for a sermon as "Suffer the little children to come unto Me" and then proceeded to deliver a lecture on the more earthy novels of Emile Zola.

These were men who struck no attitudes, followed no fashion, made no play for popularity. They were natural eccentrics. Such people are not so often seen nowadays. It may be that on average, dons are younger than they used to be; or perhaps they fear that to cultivate eccentricity might imply that they were poseurs. Mad behaviour is no longer the thing. And for all their sound and fury, even the undergraduates are a quieter, less spectacular lot. Fewer chamber pots are hung on the dreaming spires than formerly and today, one rarely sees ladies' knickers fluttering bravely from inaccessible pinnacles.

But these once-popular mad or illegal sports are not what they were. The general easing of discipline has taken the spice out of things. How tasteless are unforbidden fruits! Surreptitious entry in the small hours is now lacking in its old excitement. When late passes and keys are freely available, when modern colleges like St. Catherine's seem wide open to comings and goings, what is the point of being mutilated on horrid spikes and broken glass? Some still take the risk, but, even so, climbing into college has become almost an academic exercise. People do it merely to say that they have done it. Sometimes, they have to take the consequences. Not long ago, one unfortunate undergraduate "clambering over the gate" hung cruelly impaled through the leg for half an hour before his moanings brought friends and an ambulance to his rescue.

During the twenties, however, these things were still for real. The old rules remained onerous and were therefore to be broken or circumvented. Chapel stayed highly obligatory, especially in religious foundations like Keble, where, if you did not put in an appearance at chapel three times a week and a fourth—in surplice —on Sundays, you were up before the Warden for a wigging. The spikes still meant something in the days before Trinity quietly smoothed away their terrors (and their challenge) with little rubber balls. When John Betjeman was up at Magdalen, certain colleges—among them Wadham, Oriel and Hertford—were considered impregnable after hours. Undergraduates whose windows faced the street were considered lucky, since rope ladders were an easy means of access and egress. To stand on the saddle of a bicycle leaning against certain convenient lamp-posts was considered equally effective, if a little more precarious.

This inter-war period, uncertain, evanescent, slightly frenetic was the age of the last big spenders in Oxford. As always, there were some poor scholars, scratching along on a pittance and many students had to nurse their allowances carefully in order to make ends meet. But most undergraduates had quite enough for their needs, while not a few were far richer than was good for them. "For financial reasons", wrote Sir Maurice Bowra, "colleges accepted candidates whose intellectual claims were painfully slender. . . ."

These were the years of Oxford bags, Balkan Sobranies, the Sunflowers of Van Gogh "blooming in reproduction on every wall" and clever young men like Evelyn Waugh and Louis Macniece. And as Osbert Lancaster recalls, they were also "a period of conspicuous consumption—the last, perhaps, that under-graduates were ever to know . . .". Parties were big, wild, frequent and very expensive. For his twenty-first birthday, one wealthy undergraduate hired a river steamer "complete with brass band and loaded down to the Plimsoll line with champagne . . .".

Champagne, of course, was the *de rigeur* drink on almost every celebratory occasion. Hosts wishing to cut a particular dash indulged in magnums and at many a breakfast table Virginia ham was washed down with half-a-dozen bottles of Bollinger as the favoured few discussed Socialism and the fate of the Welsh miners. Oxford accents were in the ascendent and a strangely brittle brilliance of conversation the order of the day. Lesser lights rowed up to the 'Vicky Arms'—the 'Victoria' at Marston Ferry—or argued over tea and buns in the local cafés.

For those wishing to idle away an hour or two on the cheap, the teashops were always popular resorts. The storm of protest that arose when Vice-Chancellor Farnell tried to put them out of bounds led to a hurried retreat by authority. Before the war, the café trade had been developing remarkably to cope with the growing need for 'somewhere to go'. In Cornmarket was a whole string of tearooms and restaurants, ranging from the Japanese Café—in 1904 offering as one of its features 'cool rooms'—to the Queen's Restaurant, which for two bob a time did a splendid five-course meal. Even sixty years ago, a lunch consisting of soup, fish, roast beef and vegetables, puddings, cheese and coffee was, for a mere couple of shillings, a remarkable bargain. 'The Queen's' proudly advertised its French chef, but was careful to point out that "No Foreign Meat is used in this Establishment". At the high point of their empire-building, the English were still mighty insular in outlook.

Nevertheless, restaurateurs and others assiduously wooed the Oxford clientele with a variety of peculiar attractions. Lloyd's Oriental Café catered for all tastes, providing a "Splendid Smoking Gallery" for the gentlemen and a "Tea Room Especially Reserved for Ladies". Moreover, its special luncheons and famed afternoon teas were "daintily served with despatch". Nearby, the Restaurant Buol boasted of a Swiss proprietor and Parisian chef and the same combination of talents was responsible for an "exquisite selection of Continental pastries" to be purchased at the Swiss Café in Broad Street. Back in Cornmarket Street, the Cadena lured its patrons inside with the promise of "American Soda-Fountain Drinks", while the adjoining Creamery Café pursued a more cerebral line with "Chess Men and Boards for the Use of Customers".

To sit round a table and talk was, and still is, one of the essential undergraduate pleasures. English licensing laws still militate against those endless café-cognacs which loosen the minds and tongues of students in other parts of Europe. Entry into the Common Market may well lead to a relaxation of the present anomalies whereby Englishmen get drunk in public at their peril and in private at their pleasure. In the meantime, and outside official licensing hours, they must contrive to enjoy the "days of buns and coffee" described by C. S. Lewis. As long ago as the nineteen-twenties, he was looking back to erudite talk in Oxford cafés as something golden, something longed for, something never to be recaptured. As a don, the gap between generations was recognizable but quite unbridgeable. "The young men from school", he said, "think that we have only come to clean the windows."

In spite of their name, the cafés dispensed far more tea than coffee. Tea drinking may be something of a tribute to Dr. Johnson, whose giant teapot is preserved at Pembroke College, and certainly something of a homage to the commonest riches of an Indian empire. Yet before the palmy days of the East India Company, the Englishman's great non-alcoholic social drink was undoubtedly coffee. And in this habit Oxford paralleled and even anticipated London. In the capital, the first coffee house seems to have been 'The Rainbow', in Fleet Street, whose owner was admonished in 1657 for "making and selling a drink called coffey ... whereby he annoied his neybors by evil smells". At this time, however, the more fashionable Oxonians had already been enjoying the stimulus of the new drink for several years. In his diary for 1638, John Evelyn refers to one Nathaniel Conopios, sent as a student to Balliol by the Patriarch of Constantinople. This Greek, later Bishop of Symrna, was according to Evelyn "the first that I ever saw drink coffey, which custom came not into England until thirty years after ...".

In fact, Oxford's first coffee house had been opened by 'Jacob the Jew' in 1650. As early as 1621, in his *Anatomy of Melancholy*, Robert Burton had written of "coffey that helpeth digestion and procureth alacrity". A few years later, the learned Edward Pocock, of Corpus Christi, published his thoughtful *Nature of the drink Kahui, or Coffee*. Against this at least quasi-intellectual background, Oxford's coffee houses began to flourish. Long before 'tay' became popular—and well before the end of the seventeenth century—'caffee' was the up-and-coming drink among the *cognoscenti*, dons and undergraduates alike. Caffeine was a stimulant, alcohol a depressant. The facts might not be recognized scientifically, but they were appreciated practically. The entrepreneurs moved in. Cirques Jackson, one of Jacob's brethren, was selling coffee "in a house between Edmund Hall and Queen's

College Corner" in 1654. Ten years later, the apothecary Arthur Tillyard "sold coffey publickly in his house against All Soul's Colledge" and did very well out of people such as Christopher Wren who "esteem'd themselves either virtuosi or great wittes".

There can be little doubt that for many years, the Oxford coffee houses were extremely popular. Colleges had their favourite coffee shops, as they had their favourite taverns. Men from Merton, Corpus, All Souls and Oriel drank their brew at 'Horseman's', in The High. Magdalen, Queen's and St. Edmund Hall patronized 'Harper's', a house on the corner of Queen's Lane. In Holywell Street, 'Bagg's', a stone house built of surplus materials left over from Blenheim Palace, enjoyed the custom of Hertford, Wadham and New College. 'Malbone's', a dark little basement dive under Turl Street, was the favourite talking shop for dons and undergraduates from Trinity. But the fashionable men of all colleges spent their afternoons in Tom's Coffee House, "a gay and expensive place" not far from the site of today's covered market.

Down the years, those in authority made many attempts to put an end to the supposedly effete habit of coffee drinking. Anthony Wood asked: "Why doth solid and serious learning decline, and few or none now follow it in the University . . .?" He provided his own answer: "Because of coffee houses, where they spend all their time; and in entertainments in their chambers, where studies are become places for victualers; also great drinking at taverns and alehouses, spending their time in the common chambers for whole afternoons together, and thence to the coffee houses. . . ."

Wood's attitude was an early manifestation of the new puritanism later to be encouraged by John Wesley, the moral force behind the ethos of the middle class of mid-Victorian England. If drinking and drunkenness did not die out in Oxford, in the nineteenth century they did generally confine themselves to common rooms and dark corners.

It is a little difficult to understand why such drinks as tea, coffee and chocolate aroused official opposition. As early as 1675, Charles II published a decree requiring coffee shops to close down altogether. Fortunately, a storm of protest forced the King to withdraw this unreasonable demand. Coffee houses had already become far more than mere places in which to pass an idle hour. Both Whigs and Tories found them convenient for meeting and talking. Customers were supplied with newspapers and handwritten newsletters and as in the coffee houses of the City, both business and intrigue flourished "over the steaming bowl".

All attempts at prohibition were howled down and did not last for long. Both tea and coffee soon established themselves as the 'in' drinks of the seventeenth century, vying for popularity with chocolate. The influence of the East was quite remarkable and the exotic triumphed over the philosophic. New drinks imported from distant lands were part of the changing social scene and the scorn of moralists and topers counted for little. Henry Savill might sneer at the tea and coffee drinkers as namby-pambies "whose buttery hatch is no longer open and who call for *Tea* instead of pipes and bottles after dinner—a base and unworthy *Indian* practice" but the habit persisted and spread.

By this time, coffee houses had become the acknowledged centres of wit, learning, local gossip and serious discussion. Some provided not only newspapers, but also possessed considerable collections of books. Thomas Warton, a Fellow of Trinity for most of his life and towards the end Poet Laureate, was writing in 1780 of "the many libraries founded in our coffee houses for the benefit of such as have neglected or lost their Latin and Greek . . .". With jellies and whipped syllabubs to eat and endless coffees laced with rum and arrack to drink, it is not surprising to learn that "in these libraries, instruction and pleasure go hand in hand, and we may pronounce . . . that learning no longer remains a dry subject".

Not that Oxford has ever been entirely dry. Even those kill-joys, the Puritans, could not stop the flow of liquor and to this day some of the colleges are justly proud of their noble vintages. It seems that Parnassus is always best approached glass in hand and with learning in tow. One feels that if Britain had followed America through an era of prohibition, the students of the twenties would soon have set their hands to distillation and made the slopes of Shotover Hill fairly bubble with moonshine.

Happily, maybe, those days never came to pass. The Establishment failed even to put down coffee drinking. Undergraduates were able to pursue the old uneven tenor of the old undergraduate ways. Yesterday; today; tomorrow: one has the impression that all are the same, will be the same. Indeed, as far as Oxford students are concerned, *plus cela change, plus cela est la meme chose* seems to sum up modern opinion. People keep on saying this and writing this and lead us to the inescapable conclusion that there must be something in this. The sophisticated fresher reared on Bartók, the Beatles, Vietnam and *Hair* may think himself 800 years, twenty-seven planets and a couple of galaxies away from the youngster who jogged from Lincoln to Oxford on a spare-ribbed hack in the year that Thomas à Becket was murdered. But is he so different? Basically, they are the same boy: scared to death, bursting with life, a whole world before them both.

The more one delves into Oxford history, the more one has the feeling that it has all happened before: the anguish, the love, the application, the glory; the lot. A sense of *deja vu* is never far away. "Men vanish," wrote Max Beerbohm, "and their places are filled by others. . . ."

Beards are at present in again but will no doubt go out again. For the moment, long hair floats free but will in time be eschewed for closer crops. In the seventeenth century, Dr. Kettle of Trinity detested both so much that inside his winter muff, he kept a large pair of scissors especially for the purpose of clipping the curls of his undergraduates while they were at dinner. He firmly believed that the then-fashionable periwigs were "the tanned scalps of men, cut off after they were hanged" and once, having mislaid his famous scissors, he "chopped young Mr. Radford's hair with the knife that chips the bread on the buttery table". This thing about long hair has gone on and on through the generations. In 1836 even John Ruskin had to take a solemn oath "never to cut or comb my hair fantastically".

Changes in Oxford tend to be shifts of emphasis rather than revolutions. Human desires and human nature do not change, and if not exactly satisfied in the same old ways, are pretty well satisfied by variations of the same old ways. Drink, women, a platform, the need to be heard—all are still there. The young are young and this truism is at the root of everything. Dons give superior smiles but sigh secretly for their lost youth. In middle age they comfort themselves with the knowledge that they too were once twenty years old, while the prancing youngsters have disillusion still to come. It is a hollow triumph. Many a don, Faust-like, would swap his indigestion for a few youthful joys.

For all its comings and goings, the heart and core of academic Oxford stays much the same. The seasons do not alter, nor do terms. Three times a year, students come up and go down. Once it was on foot, with ragged young men begging alms along the way. Once it was on horseback, struggling through deep snow. Once it was by week-long journey at fivepence a day on the carrier's cart. Later they came by rumbling stagecoach and later still by the chuffing iron horse. Nowadays, slick and soulless diesels bring them by the thousand into a rebuilt Oxford Station and the independent minority arrive by motor-scooter or drive up The High in secondhand cars stuffed to overflowing with luggage.

The business of coming up gets under way towards the end of each vacation. Once the colleges have got rid of their conference delegates—who may be dentists or sanitary engineers or sixth-formers doing a course on current affairs—they prepare to receive their proper residents. A few days before the influx begins, there is a pause, although much is going on behind the scenes. Tourists find that visiting hours are more restricted. They tend to get in the way. People with jobs to do dash in and out of doorways. In the background, a subdued bustle faintly implies that the casual visitor sauntering round the lawns is *persona non grata*. In the gatehouse, the porter's traditional cloak of benign authority wears a little thin and, like his nerves, is a bit frayed round the edges.

Things begin to happen. Outside the lodge, trunks, cases, boxes, golf bags, guitars, small mountains of luggage are piled high. Vans from British Rail arrive with still more. "Where d'you want this, then?" a driver demands, dumping a tea-chest full of books perilously close to the porter's foot. "For cryin' out loud!" he groans, "You tryin' to wall me in or summink?" A thin youth appears, pushing a little handcart. Nervously, he gives his name and asks if his possessions have arrived. The porter consults a list and nods. "Come this morning," he says, and indicates the largest mountain, "Somewhere under that lot." Silently, the youth begins to burrow and eventually turns up two suitcases, a canvas holdall, an iron-bound box from the Army Surplus Stores, three badminton rackets and a shapeless parcel that would make a good Exhibit A in a murder trial. Relieved, he loads them onto the cart and trundles off towards one of the staircases. His name is already posted up on a board at the bottom of the stone steps. This is his first day at Oxford. He tries to be casual, but when someone speaks to him he can only blush with pride.

The days are long since gone when freshmen came up to

Oxford knowing that rooms in college would be theirs as of right for the whole of their three years. The university now has more than 10,000 students and residentially, the colleges just cannot cope with such numbers. They do their best, of course; since the Second World War, every one of them has built new blocks and tried to fit extra accommodation into every odd corner. There are, however, physical limitations on expansion. Some of the older foundations are tightly constricted on small sites and are left with no elbow room at all—one very good reason for Lincoln College wishing to take over the city church of All Saints as a library, and for little St. Edmund Hall doing the same with the splendid little church of St. Peter-in-the-East. The upshot of this serious lack of space is that undergraduates can hope actually to live in college for at most a couple of years. Some manage only one year in residence. For the rest of their time in Oxford, they must make do in 'digs'.

Digs are an eternal problem. Not long ago, an article on the subject in the magazine *Isis* was illustrated by pictures of a wretched room in North Oxford which had been occupied by two second-year students. The four-letter word 'slum' sufficiently describes it and it was about as far a cry as is possible from the mellow oak panelling and gracious surroundings traditionally associated with the academic life. "The more sophisticated items", ran the report, "include a broken electric fire and a cracked light fitting which dangles perilously from the broken plaster. ... Everything was damp, even to the daily newspapers and abandoned essays on moral philosophy and the photos on the walls. The cold and the damp, the stench and the draught, must have been intolerable. ... Why were students living there?"

Why, indeed? Landlords blame the students, the students blame the landlords, and both turn to the Delegates of Lodgings for answer, justification and help. No-one denies that there is an accommodation crisis in the city. Everyone knows it and the Delegacy—the body responsible for the registration and official approval of digs—admits it. Like so many things in Oxford, the problem is by no means new. Rather the reverse; from the time of Thomas à Becket onwards, students and landladies have been locked together in an intermittent war. One Victorian writer said that "really good lodgings in this city can be numbered on your fingers, and the really bad multiply".

At work in Peckwater Quad, Christ Church
College defence works

Until quite recently, students not living in hall had to "reside and keep term in lodgings situated within three miles of Carfax". Because accommodation is in such short supply, the radius has now been extended to 6 miles. A great many undergraduates have become commuters, almost strangers in their own colleges. This is one inevitable side effect of university expansion. The old order changeth and the old sense of community becomes weaker. But the complaints grow in number and become more vociferous. "Moving into digs for the first time", wrote one student, "is a shock. . . . Living in college becomes a nostalgic memory. . . . Only when you have been pushed out into the cold of Iffley Road or North Oxford do you begin to appreciate the vast living space, the room service, and the almost complete non-interference from authority which college life offers. . . ."

Said another: "The landlady may expect you to tailor your life to *her* convenience. After a free and easy college life in which one's sole obligation was to placate a benevolent and usually absent scout, it is hard to get used to the petty domestic tyranny of digs. . . ."

The college scout is not so much in evidence as he used to be, although he is still as familiar a figure in collegiate life as the don and the undergraduate. In various forms, he has certainly existed for quite as long. A sort of father-big brother figure, the typical scout looks after a 'stair' and will attend to the miscellaneous needs of the occupants of the various 'sets' of rooms opening off it. He may have eight or ten men to look after or, more probably in these days of staff shortages, perhaps as many as sixteen on two staircases. In the *Oxford University Handbook*, P. C. Bayley reckons that "the scouts do more to maintain the spirit, discipline and good feeling of a college than the dons". Even in these non-trad days, because of the long and unbroken traditional relationship between servants and students, there is a rather special affinity between them. The best scouts are tyrants, but friendly ones, and their paternal instincts tend to come to the surface on awkward occasions. It is still another sign of changing times that the 'old-type scouts' are slowly becoming extinct. Because of their history and reputation, the more famous colleges have managed to maintain the succession. But in others, the scouts "are more like hotel servants and far less concerned with the college as an institution . . .".

At University College C. S. Lewis's first servant fussed over

13

The Golden Cross Hotel, an inn for 800 years
"The Bullnose Morris" at Cowley

him and always made him change his socks when they were wet. He had already served the college for forty-six years, but this was no record. In 1968, Trinity threw a champagne party in honour of Dick Cadman, a tremendous old character who had scouted there for sixty-seven years and retired on his ninety-fourth birthday!

The old-style scouts may impose their subtle but friendly discipline upon the 'gentlemen' within the college, but the overall exercise of authority is still the job of the Proctors. Once a year, they issue their "Proctors' Memorandum", a guide and gentle warning to freshers and to the more junior members of the university. This annual memo is a digest of the many rules and regulations governing the conduct of undergraduates. A copy is handed out to everyone when they matriculate and the underlying theme is that students shall not do anything which is likely to bring the good name of Oxford into disrepute.

Thus, in their first year, students are officially forbidden to own a motor-car. Afterwards, cars have to be registered and an appropriate windscreen sticker affixed. Before six o'clock in the evening, parking in central Oxford is prohibited; in practice, however, unregistered cars are thick on the ground. The proctors do their best to bring offenders to book, but with thousands of cars coming in and out of the city every day, they do not have an easy task. The comparatively few offenders who are caught are duly fined by the proctorial body, but many more get away with it. Nevertheless, this official ruling, together with the practical difficulties of finding a place to park, is undoubtedly responsible for the survival of the bicycle as a popular means of student transport. Plans are afoot for a gigantic multi-storey car park close to the bus station at Gloucester Green; a proposal which is being opposed at every step by Nuffield and Worcester Colleges nearby. In Oxford, as in many other traffic-choked cities, things with four wheels and an engine seem to be taking precedence over things with two legs and a heart.

Within the colleges, discipline is a domestic matter and both Proctors and Delegates of Lodgings give way to the Deans, those benevolent underlords who deal mainly with intra-mural transgressions. Most colleges have a roughly similar set of rules and these are broadly and liberally interpreted. Poor work invokes a mild wrath; a complete failure to work results in considerable sternness; sexual indiscretions bring a remarkably gentle tut-

tutting, while climbing into college after hours may result in a prolonged oh dear, oh dear, oh dear. An undergraduate has to do something very bad before he is kicked out. The modern academic establishment is surprisingly tolerant—even anxious—to come to terms with its younger generation. Even in the eighteenth century, Walter Savage Landor, living up to his middle name, fired pistols at a political opponent and yet was given the chance of apologizing before the reluctant authorities expelled him. And not many years later, the poet Shelley (whose frontal nudity statue in University College still occasionally shocks lady visitors) had to profess out-and-out atheism before he was sent down. Today, atheism is a mere nothing and physical violence must be carried to extremes before the authorities consider expulsion. In general, both college and university discipline has been greatly eased. All has happened before, and will eventually happen again. In 1850, the University Commission was setting down the most obvious evils in Oxford as: "sensual vice, gambling in all its forms, and extravagant expenditure . . .".

The commissioners found that within the city itself, "external decency" was well preserved, but regretted that in the villages around—"and in places still more remote from the Proctor's jurisdiction"—vice was abundant. London itself (and what wickedness was conjured up in those days by the mere name of the metropolis!) was "not beyond the reach of ill-disposed or weak young men . . . who might often have the whole day at their command". The railway, they said, would tempt half the student population to gallop hot-foot and goat-foot into the sensual delights of the capital.

But this was only one of the dangers threatening Victorian Oxford. Dons were still nominally celibate, women were supposed not to exist, and from time to time even tobacco caused a throwing up of hands. Some considered that smoking was a great evil. One doctor claimed that "many Oxford and Cambridge men are tenants of lunatic asylums", which he attributed to the fact that "so many Oxonians and Cantabs have a cigar or pipe between their lips all day, and the greater part of the night . . .". The Royal Commission of 1850 took up the same theme, saying that "the excessive habit of smoking is totally ruinous in many colleges, tobacco bills of up to £40 a year being all to common . . .".

Victorian rules lived on for a long time. A freshman of the nineteen-twenties recalled:

> If you lived in college, the gates closed at 9.05 p.m. After that time, you had to knock to get in. If you came in after 10.0 p.m., you were fined a small sum; if after 11.0 o'clock, a larger amount. If after midnight, you had to see the Dean, and then might be gated or fined. . . . Unless exempted on religious grounds, you had to attend Chapel at least 3 times a week. Only 2nd or 3rd year men could keep a car. For this privilege, you had to get a University licence at 10 shillings a year. In town, after a certain hour in the evening, you had to carry or wear a gown. It was quite forbidden to enter a public house, or to take the cheaper seats in cinemas. . . .

What would modern militants have made of such restrictions?

One of the few features of old-time undergraduate living that has survived is the running up of debts. Quite recently, students appearing on a television programme openly admitted stealing books from Blackwells and other Oxford bookshops, some because they could not live within their student grants, and others because they saw nothing wrong in thieving from a society which clothed, fed and provided them with a first-class education.

Fortunately, such attitudes are not common. Most students are as mild and law-abiding as the next citizen. Oxford traders who suffer much from shoplifting and petty pilfering, do not lay all the blame at the door of the university. They do business in a city of 110,000 people, of which only one-fifth belong to the academic fraternity. The proportion of Town to Gown has altered considerably over the years, and dramatically so within living memory. In 1914, about 54,000 people lived within the city boundaries and of these, only 4,000 were undergraduates. By 1939, the student numbers were still only 5,000, although the overall population had by now almost doubled. 'Morris Oxford', as we shall see in a later chapter, had come into being.

Far different were the comparative figures for earlier years. In 1801, the university population was more than 3,000 out of a total of 11,000 odd—over a quarter. Eighty years later, the academics were still only 3,500 against a city population of 35,000—a proportion of one-tenth. These figures confirm the story already told; in spite of its numerical decline, the intellectual elite with its built-in privileges still dominated the life of the city. Aided by long tradition, Gown still dominated Town. For too long, too many townsfolk of Oxford were entirely dependent upon the university for their livelihood.

It is good that the balance has swung in the opposite direction. Shopkeepers no longer rely almost entirely on university custom for their survival, fearing the lean days of the long vacation, longing for the start of each new term and its crop of freshers.

There are still some shops in central Oxford which cater mainly for undergraduates and for those vicarious undergraduates, the tourists—the ones who for an hour or two imagine how pleasant it must be to be in college at Oxford. Even in 1939, many shops still relied almost entirely on the colleges for their trade. Colin Lunn advertised himself as an importer of cigars and high-grade tobaccos, and also as "a specialist in Persian and Oriental Rugs and real amber . . .". He offered clay, briar and Meerschaum pipes—"including the famous Brasenose pipe"—carved with a representation of the notorious knocker. In The High, Rowells sold "silver pendants, spoons, brooches and bookmarks" all embellished with enamelled crests and, not far away, Cooke's ("by appointment to H.R.H. the Prince of Wales") supplied "the genuine *Yenidjch* Turkish Cigarettes" at 8s. 6d. the hundred. They also ran 'The Gentlemen's Toilet Saloon' in opposition to the better-known 'Martyrs' on the corner of Cornmarket and The Broad. In 1904, 'Martyrs' provided "Antiseptic Hair Cutting Rooms for Ladies and Gentlemen" but wishing to make the tonsurial art seem less of a surgical operation, soon changed its description to "Martyrs' Hygienic Hair Dressing Rooms (with Facial and Scalp Vibro-Massage)".

Because students are students, Oxford has never been short of tailors, tobacconists and wine-sellers. But above all, bookshops have abounded. The three best known—Blackwells, Parkers and Maxwells—do a roaring trade. Blackwells is so much a part of academic life that its subterranean Norrington Room has been constructed beneath the main quad of Trinity College. Down beyond Magdalen Bridge, Maxwell's is housed in the Waynflete Building extension of Magdalen College. Back in The Broad, Parker's—established in 1731 as Joseph Fletcher's Bookshop—occupies a very modern, very split-level building on the corner of The Turl. All allow you to browse freely and no-one proffers the 'can-I-help-you' of the modern departmental store.

Oxford traders have traditionally offered long-term credit,

although in recent years their patience is not quite so inexhaustible as it used to be. As late as the nineteen-thirties, the older shops were accustomed to waiting as long as ten years for the final settlement of accounts outstanding.

In the nineteenth century, student debts were a very serious problem. Way back in 1837, the committee engaged on the revision of the university statutes came up with a scheme for restricting undergraduate credit to no more than one term. Proposals were made for copies of unpaid bills to be delivered to tutors, but the new system never really got under way. 'Gentlemen' had always worked on the basis of credit. The university had some control over the tradespeople of Oxford, but could do nothing about shopkeepers in London and other cities. When they ran into trouble locally, the big spenders of the university merely transferred their custom elsewhere. Still considerably protected by privilege, the sons of the major and minor gentry were not easily brought to book. In 1847, Edward Napleton Jennings was hauled before the debtors' court as a bankrupt. In two years, he had run up bills in Oxford to the tune of nearly £1,700. Being pressed for payment, his custom was shifted to London, where he incurred further debts amounting to £600. The son of a Yorkshire clergyman, Jennings was both clever and unscrupulous. Knowing that so long as any single debt did not exceed £20, he could not be touched, his custom was spread between no less than seventy-six different shopkeepers.

The Jennings affair caused great excitement in the city. For once in a while, the Town was confident that it would triumph over Gown. But far from condemning the frauds, the commissioner who heard the case made it clear that he had little sympathy for the unhappy tradesmen. Indeed, they were soundly castigated for "subscribing to a credit system which allowed such calamities". The long-suffering Oxford Tradesmen's Association pleaded in vain with the university for some redress. Their suggestion that the authorities should let them know when student debtors were about to graduate went unheeded; although it was admitted that once a man finally 'went down' he was lost to the Oxford scene. All too many undergraduates, and more notably graduates, cleared off, leaving unpaid debts behind them.

In 1851, however, a group of undergraduates ill-advisedly brought a private prosecution against a moneylender named

Caudwell. Surprisingly, this was not for financial reasons, but for common assault. Angry because they had got themselves deeply in hock, the gang thought to frighten the man off by creeping to his house in the middle of the night and smashing in the windows. But Caudwell was a man of spirit and retaliated with a couple of barrels of buckshot, forcing them to retreat in disorder. One student, wounded both in pride and backside, was left for dead on the field of battle. The moneylender duly appeared at the Assizes, in a court packed with undergraduates, insolent, arrogant and confident that he would soon be sentenced to a long stretch in gaol. These 'gentlemen' behaved so badly, however, that on the judge's direction, the jury returned a verdict of Not Guilty. Outside the courtroom, a waiting crowd of townsmen went wild, cheering Caudwell and yelling blue murder at the totally discomfited students. All the makings of an old-style Town and Gown riot were in the air, but fortunately no one was hurt.

Students can still be violent, as the window-smashing at the Garden House Hotel in Cambridge in July 1970 shows. Yet the same unhappy affair also indicates that the objectives of violence in the universities are nowadays different. The motives for savage behaviour are mostly political rather than individual. Personal cruelty has slowly declined down the centuries. The need to work off physical exuberance has long been recognized; before the Victorians began to worship the great god Sport, the passions of youth frequently expressed themselves in very unfortunate ways. Bullying and vicious ragging were all too common and many an apparently good-natured lark ended in grief and distress. Juvenal's *mens sana in corpore sano* may be a bit of a giggle for the modern generation, but the nineteenth-century doctrine based upon it did produce some useful results. And as games and athletics became organized rituals, life in the colleges became slowly more endurable for the shy, the timid and the awkward who at one time could expect to be persecuted without mercy.

For some reason, Oxford colleges have never indulged in the elaborate and sometimes bloody initiation ceremonies common in European and American universities. The nearest thing to an initiation was the 'salting and tucking' of freshers, a practice which died out 200 years ago. After his first dinner in hall, the freshman had to stand on a bench before the fire and make a speech. If this was to the taste of his seniors, he was given a flagon of beer or sack; if, on the other hand, they disapproved, the victim had to swallow down a gallon or so of heavily salted water, otherwise known as 'cawdel'. In some colleges, salting was followed by 'tucking', a more barbarous business. In 1638, Ashley Cooper was instrumental in "causing that ill custom of tucking to be left off at Exeter College . . .".

"One of the seniors in the evening called the freshmen to the fire and made them hold out their chin. A senior with the nail of the right thumb left long for that purpose then grated off all the skin, from the lip to the chin, and then caused them to drink a beer glass of water and salt. . . ." Cooper was not having any. When his turn came, he gave the torturer—a son of Lord Pembroke—a smart clip on the ear and urged the other freshers to turn and fight. This they did to some purpose, clearing the hall and buttery in quick time. The seniors were so badly beaten up that "old Dr. Prideaux, the Rector, arranged terms that led to an utter abolition of this foolish custom . . .".

Less liturgical forms of ragging do survive. Sheer devilment often bursts out as a form of spontaneous combustion. People are pitched head-first into fountains, bathtubs and the sluggish Isis itself. Periodically, someone is drowned in the process, and when this happens, it is not very funny. Afterwards, everyone is full of regret and remorse and those who know their Oxford history shake their heads, because it has all happened before. High spirits are expected, but the dividing line between a harmless bit of horse-play and real tragedy can be very tenuous indeed.

When the Exeter crew rowed Head of the River for the third year in succession in 1884, all hell and happiness was let loose at the end of Eights Week. A "Bacchanalian mob", wrote Lewis Farnell, "felt that they had every right to paint the universe red". A great opponent of what he called 'the games-cult', he reluctantly accepted the fact that this was a rather special occasion, and for once did not try to put the damper on things. As Subrector of the college, his main concern was "to save life and prevent serious destruction". He succeeded in doing both—but only just. An enormous bonfire had been built in the main quad and when this got going, it threatened not only to consume Exeter, but half Oxford as well. A fantastic quantity of furniture, including an out-of-tune grand piano, served as fuel for the flames, and drunk and delirious undergraduates danced a wild corroboree for hours on end, leaping through the fire with scorched clothing and smoke-blackened faces. Outside, high above the Turl, a tin bath was hung on wires stretched across the street, "filled with fireworks and terrifying combustibles" which rained down upon a crowd of townsfolk below. They were not pleased and retaliated by breaking nearly every window in the college. The Oxford City Police stood benevolently by, claiming that unless someone read out the Riot Act, they were powerless to do anything. Inside, tragedy was narrowly averted. One student took a running jump at the bonfire and, quite unobserved, fell into the middle of it. Fortunately, Farnell spotted a pair of boots sticking out of the blaze and "the half-singed form of a man, apparently dead" was pulled out in the nick of time. Anticipating the later days of fire-watching and incendiary bombs, the keepers at the nearby Bodleian maintained an all-night vigil, fearful for their books as scores of spent rockets clattered onto the roofs.

All this was fairly innocent stuff and generally tolerated by the authorities. What worried them far more were the occasional instances of sadistic bullying. Not long after the Head of the River celebrations, Farnell discovered that a second-year student was the victim of systematic persecution by a group of the college bloods. For more than a year, this unfortunate youth had been dragged from his bed in the small hours, two or three times a week and "chased ignominiously round the quad", half-naked and terrified. He was close to a nervous breakdown when Farnell got to hear of the business and tackled the boy about his troubles. But in the good old public school tradition, he would give nothing away, least of all the names of his tormentors. To his credit, the Subrector sat up for nights on end, trying to catch them at their little game. Eventually he did so, confronting them in the victim's rooms after making an entrance "which might be called spectacular". There was no further trouble. The six were sent home—'rusticated'—for the rest of the term and the persecuted man went on to take a very good degree.

It could have ended differently. Farnell considered that his intervention prevented "disastrous results"—a euphemistic way of saying suicide. Self-destruction is not unknown at Oxford and the accounts of some undergraduate deaths make melancholy reading.

The strains and diversions of undergraduate life are many and inevitably, there are those who cannot stand the pace. For most, to be twenty is marvellous, but for the few it can be murderous. Illusion and disillusion walk hand in hand and some grow tired of life before it has properly begun. Happily, the majority make the grade. Contemporary cant is forever knocking the student; he is the popular cock-shy for the popular press; he is effete, lazy, truculent, ill-mannered and ungrateful. Amazingly enough, people were saying much the same things 100 years ago, when Oxford was very much more of a playground for the aristocracy and the sons of rich men. Yet even then, far from all under-graduates cut lectures, reduced tutors to despair, lived nothing but the gay life, were brainless imbeciles who went down without a degree. The same is true today, but far more so. The work is there if you really want to do it. Many do so; some grudgingly, a few brilliantly and most sufficiently. In between times, they enjoy life, and this is one of the good reasons for going to Oxford.

"The trouble about an Oxford education", said a graduate of St. Hugh's College recently, "is that no-one—but *no-one*—pressures you into working." She had had a good Oxford, and was neither clever nor cynical, nor sentimental about it. The pleasures and satisfactions she got from her three years seemed directly pro-portional to what she had put into the place. As a fresher, her first tutorials were "terribly frightening" and her tutors "absolutely terrifying". Soon enough, however, she realized that even the most intimidating were as "soft as butter underneath—and rather sweet". The breakthrough came when one fierce little don gave her afternoon tea with huge slices of chocolate log. This, together with the sight of Penguin whodunits half-hidden among learned texts, finally persuaded her that such men are not gods, but human beings.

She was in no doubt at all about the tutorial system, "ultimately the most satisfactory form of teaching ever devised". This is a big claim, but one that has never been seriously challenged. College tutors have existed for a very long time and the present combina-tion of private tutorials and public university lectures seems to work pretty well. The early halls and foundations appointed their own teachers almost from the beginning. The system was regularized by Archbishop Laud's statutes of 1634, fell into dis-repute during that unhappy "period of learned torpor" in the eighteenth century, and was finally organized into something like its present form during the Victorian era.

Traditionally, the tutor is supposed to be guide, philosopher and friend to his charges. In the last century, this was often their relationship. There were 'reading parties' during the vacations, walking and climbing holidays in Switzerland, classical expeditions to Italy and Greece. Such thing are no longer common. Life moves at a less leisurely pace and the number of students in a college may be three or four times what it used to be. In the days of 'Lewis Carroll' a tutor was responsible for only a handful of undergraduates. Even ten was considered to be more than enough, and at Christ Church, Carroll felt himself to be very hard pressed when he had to cope with fourteen would-be mathematicians. Today, a don sometimes has twenty-five or thirty assorted hopefuls under his wing. Moreover, the typical tutor does not live in college, as his celibate, bachelor predecessors used to do. More often than not, he is a married man, with a house in the suburbs and a wife and family waiting for him when work is over for the day. For all the comforts of college, he prefers to get away from its responsibilities and put his feet up on the domestic hearth.

In general, undergraduate life can be as hard, or as pleasant, as the individual chooses to make it. This is not to say that people can take fate by the throat or shape their own destinies. Life deals the odd knock-out blow to a student, as much as to anyone else. But given the reasonable level of intelligence now required as a prerequisite for entry to Oxford, and a fair amount of work, he will collect a degree and, in front of his admiring parents, take part in one of those splendiferous ceremonies in the Sheldonian. Unless he is among the superbrains, it is unlikely that the degree will be a First. 'Firsts' are comparatively rare birds and most do not fly so high. But an 'upper Two' is still something to be proud of and a 'lower Two' not to be sniffed at. A 'Third' or less and— well—you got through.

It has often been stressed that the basic reason for going to university is to receive a first-class education. Years ago, this did not necessarily mean taking a degree, desirable though this might be. 'Education' meant everything that Oxford or Cambridge had to offer (or nearly all!). Even in Victorian times, when the basis of the present-day examination system had been firmly established and a surprising number of men worked very hard, the 'feverish exam-cult' was deplored by many. Students with good brains, whose will to work had been sapped by over-indulgence in the pleasures, continually woke up to the fact that 'Schools' were in the offing and finals not far away. Panic-stricken and long since given up as a bad job by their official tutors, they went for crash courses to the 'pass coaches'—men outside the regular tutorial system who, for a considerable fee, were prepared to act as 'crammers'. They achieved no small success, their best customers being "fashionable undergraduates who at best might manage a poor pass-degree . . . derelicts of the lecture rooms who went for coaching in gangs".

It is too easy to condemn those who fail as drones and layabouts. The diversions of Oxford are too many, all the time clamouring for attention. You like the river: it is there. You like theatre, music, ballet: they are there. You like wine, good food, modern jazz, fencing, rugby, cricket, country dancing, archery, athletics, rowing, polo, poetry, cinema, photography: you name it and Oxford has it. There is Pinter at the Playhouse, *Traviata* at the New Theatre, voyeurism at the Scala and up at Headington, yet another generation of undergraduates goes to see the umpteenth re-run of *Jules et Jim* at the little Moulin Rouge. Once a term, the local National Union of Students publishes its *Vade Mecum*, a fifty-page guide to eight hectic weeks of what's on in the colleges, the university and the city as a whole. Apart from the many more general attractions aimed at culture-vultures and others, at any given moment, there are something like 200 separate academic clubs and societies, some of them highly esoteric in approach and some definitely unacademic in outlook. At the beginning of Michaelmas Term, dozens of eager hon. secs. go the rounds of colleges, seeking out freshers who seem likely candidates for membership of the Baha'i Group, the Cecil Sharp Club, the Contract Bridge Association or the Nietzsche Society (which casually announces its aims as "to study the Universe").

Every society is supposed to register its existence with the Proctors, who must also be notified of all activities and receive copies of notices and publications. Most do their best to conform, but clandestine clubs do exist. Certainly, Oxford memoirs are full of stories of strange little organizations which suddenly appeared, had their little day and vanished. Some were more widely known and a few quite notorious. The oldest social club on record was the Phoenix Common Room, later called the Hell-Fire Club. Founded at Brasenose in 1786, it flourished for nearly fifty years as the meeting place of the very smartest set. One President attended a meeting rigged out "in white Turkish trousers and flowered black velvet waistcoat" and although sharp dressing was encouraged, this was thought to be going too far. "Noted with disapproval," said the minutes. The Hell-Fire was wound up abruptly in 1834 when the last President died in *delirium tremens*. There had been earlier troubles; a few years before, in Brasenose Lane, a townswoman dropped dead after being plied with brandy from a window of the rooms in which the club met.

The Hell-Fire had a more learned and less alcoholic predecessor in The Martlets, a select literary group at University College. Founded in the 1600s, it was still in existence when C. S. Lewis came back from the Great War in 1919. There were never more than a dozen members, and when he later became a Fellow of Magdalen, a somewhat despairing Lewis tried to get a similar group organized there. For a time during the twenties, all college societies had been forbidden at Magdalen, "because of the savagely exclusive clubs of rich dipsomaniacs who really dominated the whole life of the place". He wrote to a friend: "I found that any Magdalen undergraduate who had interests beyond rowing, drinking, motoring and fornication sought his friends outside College and indeed, kept out of the place as much as he could. . . ."

There have always been snob clubs at Oxford. In the thirties, John Betjeman described the famous Bullingdon as "still the biggest non-intellectual and social influence, consisting of the well-born and the very rich". Originally dedicated to steeplechasing, membership was largely confined to old Etonians who also happened to be up at Christ Church and Magdalen.

The Bullingdon Club has lasted, but the names of a thousand others are lost among the ephemeral litter of college histories and recollections; names dimly remembered and purposes forgotten. Slightly precious set-ups have always proliferated. There was the Uffizi Society founded by a very young and aesthetic Anthony Eden; or The Myrmydons, "a small and very select dining club drawn from the gilded youth of Merton". Max Beerbohm was once a member and remembered the splendid purple evening coats, specially made, in which he and his friends dressed for club dinners. Less exclusive was the S.C.S.—otherwise the Septem Contra Somnum or Seven against Sleep, whose sole object was to hold riotous drinking parties as often as possible. In contrast, the

Merton Essay Society, whose members read interminable essays to each other on such subjects as 'Totemism' and 'The Ideals of Mazzini' was "very serious—and very short-lived".

Many more recent and still-existing college societies are equally serious and give people the chance to meet and argue—which, after all, is largely what Oxford is all about. On the other hand, some more recent clubs put forward very tongue-in-cheek aims, largely as an excuse for merrymaking. The Charon Club, for example, exists "to defend the noble and ancient art of punting and to clear the Cherwell of transistor radios and undesirable characters". To qualify for membership, you must have at some time "entered the Cherwell fully clad from a punt". The Luddite Society was ostensibly formed "to resist scientific and techno-logical innovation" and meets fortnightly in a local pub under the chairmanship of 'The Supreme Wielder of the Golden Axe'. Less devious in its announcement of intentions is the Wodehouse Society (Hon. President—P. G. Wodehouse), which simply "exists to entertain its members". Rumour has it that unlimited quantities of free vintage claret are served at all meetings.

Other organizations are frighteningly fierce and serious. What they profess to be, what they talk about and occasionally what they do, pays inadvertent tribute to the overall toleration of Oxford. Thus, The Anarchist Group "promotes the Revolution"; the Marxist Society is "devoted to the building of a new revolu-tionary leadership for the Working Class"; the Labour Club has numbered among its Vice-Presidents Che Guavara, Fidel Castro, Ho Chi Minh and Jean-Paul Sartre; while the Communist Club says nothing and is content to let its name speak for itself. All, one feels, are likely to be taken over at any moment by the under-ground Phataphysical Society, which aims to "terrorize the rational, destroy the established, create the unborn, bury the nihilistic, emotionalize the intellectual and love the unloved . . . ".

Some tongue, some cheek! Thank God, one thinks, for the Oxford University Tiddlywinks Society, whose Grand Master of the Winks and his devoted followers do nothing but "spread the gospel of Tiddlywinks and try to beat the Cambridge threat".

XIV

THE TWO MORRIS OXFORDS

There have been two Morris Oxfords. Now there is only one. The first was Victorian, "a vision of grey-roofed houses and a long winding street, and the sound of many bells". The second is the harsh reality of the modern city: a place of car parks and ring roads and Woolworths and factories and the unceasing racket of twentieth-century life.

These are the two Oxfords: the one of William Morris—the poet, artist, dreamer, printer, socialist and maker of wallpapers; the other of William Richard Morris—tycoon, philanthropist, philistine, multi-millionaire and maker of motor-cars. Possessing the same name and, for a short time, inhabiting the same world, they were nevertheless worlds apart. If Morris of motor-car fame ever heard of his namesake who wrote *The Earthly Paradise* and *The Dream of John Ball*, he would probably have sniffed and dismissed this combination of medievalism and the new Utopia as so much guff. And if Morris the artist had lived on to see the uncontrolled spread of present-day Oxford, its streets choked with men and machines pursuing the frenetic ends of a materialistic society, and the total industrialization of a town which, for him, "had breathed from its towers the last enchantments of the Middle Ages", he would have been appalled.

The two never met. When Morris of the wallpapers and the Pre-Raphaelite connections died in 1896, Morris the future Viscount Nuffield was little more than a boy of 19. For three years, however, he had already been running his own little cycle repair business from a shed at Cowley. In the later years of the nineteenth century, cycling had become an absolute craze. Mad on cycle racing, the future Lord Nuffield was already outright champion of three counties. He did well out of his youthful enthusiasm. Loving the sport, he soon built up a reputation, selling and servicing machines to enthusiasts from Town and Gown alike. It was not long before he began to build them for himself, and in 1897 his name was already appearing in local business directories as "William Richard Morris—Cycle Maker". Four years later, with a shop in the High Street, he was advertising himself as "Sole Maker of the celebrated Morris Cycles".

But bicycles were only a beginning for this enigmatical little man, who, through his own efforts and ambitions, pulled a protesting Oxford into the twentieth century. He was a good engineer and a first-class mechanic, who by 1900 had already built with his own hands a single-cylinder engine which he then fitted into a modified bicycle frame. This was the prototype motor-cycle which was put on show a couple of years later and went into production as the Morris Motor Cycle.

At this time, the total work force was made up of four men and two apprentices, including Morris himself and his father, who acted as bookkeeper. Half a century ahead was the British Motor Corporation with 50,000 employees, but even for W. R. Morris this was a dream beyond a dream. In 1903, his sights were not ranged so distantly, even though the firm had by now broken into the motor business proper with the setting up of 'The Oxford Automobile and Cycle Agency'.

Pushbikes and motorcycles became more and more of a sideline. Like Henry Ford, he saw the world of the future as the world of the motor vehicle and he set about staking his claim. The more well-to-do undergraduates were already driving about in their own cars, and at the old stables in Longwall Street he was soon providing garage accommodation and servicing. The business thrived and the Longwall premises were known to locals as 'The Oxford Motor Palace'. Hire-cars, with or without be-goggled chauffeurs, were available; driving lessons were given; there was a Morris Taxi Service, and all the time more and more cars were being sold.

But these were cars made by other people—Humbers, Hupmobiles, Singers, Standards and Wolseleys. Morris was still an agent and not a manufacturer. Yet, diverse as they were, all his activities centred on the ultimate dream: the Morris Motor-Car, incorporating Morris ideas and built in Morris workshops. He realized that motoring was already more than a rich man's hobby, He foresaw the day when the car would be as common a possession

The Isis, punts and barges
Head of the River—the triumph of the intellect

as the kitchen stove. It was increasingly obvious that the days of the horse and carriage were numbered. For cheap and speedy travel, the car was the coming thing and Morris's great ambition was to make and sell in large numbers to a large public a good, reliable, and low-priced runabout.

Superbly confident of his own abilities, he pushed ahead with designs. Production of the 'Morris-Oxford Light Car' was announced at the 1912 Motor Show. A few months later, the first model appeared, a compact little two-seater with the familiar 'bullnose Morris' radiator, selling at £165. Components came mainly from specialist firms in Coventry and Birmingham; bodies were supplied by an Oxford coach builder who was already suffering from the final recession in the carriage trade; chassis were made and the cars assembled in Morris's own shops. A London agent had ordered 400 'Oxfords' in advance and, using the old Military College at Cowley as his first real factory, Morris was soon turning out fifty cars a week.

His initial programme was for 1,500 'Oxfords'. Inevitably, the onset of the Great War slowed down and eventually halted production, but not before 1,300 cars had been made and Morris was established as a man to be reckoned with. He was now a considerable employer. The Military College buildings had been extended several times, and when war was declared the old parade ground was being covered over with a very large assembly shop of 100,000 square feet. If the civic authorities were impressed, they did not show it. They had already clashed with Morris on a major public issue, and Morris had won.

In 1913 the big story locally was 'The Great Oxford Tram Controversy', a matter that brought Morris into prominence in a big way. The city's public transport system, started thirty years before, consisted of a few lumbering horse-drawn trams which rumbled along at little more than walking pace. Archaic from the word go, these antediluvian conveyances had long been a joke but were now a source of public irritation and annoyance. For ten years, the city council had argued the pros and cons of replacing them with electric trams, but nothing was done.

To Morris, electrification, with its ugly overhead wires and inflexible routes, was no answer to the problem. What an expanding Oxford needed, he said, was the motor omnibus, which could go anywhere and be re-routed without difficulty as circumstances

14

The "dreaming spires" from Godstow Lock

demanded. Moreover, he was prepared to provide such a service, and forthwith applied to the council for an operator's licence. His letter went conveniently unanswered. The tram proprietors did some powerful lobbying and Morris was ignored. Exasperated by the double-talk he lost all patience and, at the risk of prosecution, went ahead with his plans. Knowing that it was quite illegal for his buses to ply for fares in the normal way, he overcame the difficulty by operating his services on a sort of credit basis. Shops along the routes sold coupons in advance and no money changed hands in the vehicles themselves. The system worked; crowds turned out to cheer as the first buses roared past, and within hours the new Oxford Motor Omnibus Company was doing a roaring trade. To the accompaniment of jeers, the trams crawled along empty.

Badly nettled, the city fathers did their best to stop this presumptuous little man. A deputation of councillors went off to London to take counsel's opinion. They were told that if Morris was taken to court, he might well end up in prison. The moderates on the council were all for caution and compromise, aware that the townsfolk were solidly behind this plain-speaking local man who had given them their long-awaited bus service. Two mass meetings called by Morris showed clearly which way the wind was blowing. Common sense prevailed. There was no more talk of prosecution and jail sentences. After a short but salutary lesson in public relations, the council climbed down. The affair ended when the corporation bought Morris out and ran the bus service themselves.

He was amused, but it all left a nasty taste in his mouth. Harsh things had been said about him and some of the officially-inspired whisperings that questioned his motives were downright slanderous. It was a long time before he was on friendly terms with the Oxford authorities. Twice he refused the freedom of the city, and it was only in 1951, at the third time of asking, that he finally accepted the honour. For its part, the university had made him an Honorary Doctor of Civil Laws twenty years earlier, following this up in 1937 with a Master of Arts degree. And no wonder! Between 1926 and 1951 he had given nearly £4 million to the university and its colleges.

Even with the war in its second year, Morris continued to make ars at Cowley. Britain was still not fully geared up to intensive armaments production and most people were convinced that victory was just around the corner. As yet there was no conscription. Men and women went about their pre-war jobs, grumbling about shortages, cheering newly trained volunteers as they marched down Queen Street to the stations, but generally regarding 'war' as a detached and somewhat distant business. It was not until the middle of 1915 that Morris turned his attention to munitions production. But even then on a very modest scale. He was still far more interested in the development of his second motor-car, the famous Morris-Cowley, than in turning out hand-grenades and mortar bombs. Determined to put on the market the cheapest and most efficient car yet seen, he ordered 3,000 engines from the Continental Motor Manufacturing Company of Detroit at the fantastically low price of £17 9s. 3d. each! Half of them were sent to the bottom of the Atlantic by German submarines, but the rest arrived safely at Oxford, enabling him to make and sell 1,300 wartime 'Cowleys' at 158 guineas a time.

This was still a far cry to the early mass-production days of 1923, when, after a disastrous slump in the motor industry, the Cowley Works produced and sold 20,000 vehicles, a figure which by 1925 had risen to 50,000.

But we must hark back to the days of 'that other William Morris'—'Wallpaper Morris', he is sometimes unkindly called, for it was during his time at Oxford that the patterns of the future were being shaped in more ways than one. Beginning in the cheerless North, the Industrial Revolution had moved southward, flowing through the Black Country and the Midlands and eventually reaching the rather surprised Home Counties. Understandably, the mechanized wave washed past and beyond most of the old agricultural centres, lacking as they were in coal, iron ore, communications and the basic necessities of the new way of life. Out of the mainstream of progress, Cambridge was by-passed and remained largely agricultural. Oxford, in the way of it, stood as a rock and cast out progressive ideas as an old clergyman casts out devils. Oxford did not want to know.

The railway came to the city in 1844, yet ten years later the venerable Dr. Routh of Magdalen went about saying: "Railways, sir! I know nothing of railways!" and refused to acknowledge their existence. A man who had spoken to Dr. Johnson was quite content with stage-coaches, the last of which was still running between Oxford and Cheltenham in the eighties.

Oxford, as always, fought for the old images and never-never lands. Socialist and visionary though he was, the first William Morris's New Utopia was no more than a world of up-dated medievalism. In *News from Nowhere* this protégé of the Pre-Raphaelites dreamed of a small commonwealth in which all would be simple joy through honest labour. Essentially this was to be a world of the childhood story, of the innocence of youth, of simple forms, clear colours and no dark undertones. It could never come to pass. Morris was the crusader, a gentle knight seeking his grail. In splendidly purple poetry he re-created legends, campaigned for the preservation of ancient buildings, set out to be a latter-day Caxton and, at the Kelmscott Press, printed gorgeous books in his own neo-medieval tradition. He had a vision of the future, but basically it was a future of the past. In some tiny country beyond the rainbow's end, it might have worked out, but in a brash, mucky-mouthed, increasingly materialistic society, it was something of a laugh. The common man did not understand such dreams, but he could have respect for the second Morris, a chap who could build a bike, or turn a part on a lathe, and, after starting life at a village school, provide good jobs for thousands of ordinary folk.

People did not want to tread a measure to pipes and tabors, or weave things on hand looms, or play at Merrie England. They were mostly honest philistines who preferred to follow one of their own kind. The man for their money was Morris the Second. Let his namesake talk of white-armed maidens and a pastoral world of handicrafts and hay-making if he liked; it was all too arts 'n crafts and evening classy for the workers in St. Ebbe's and Jericho. Over the years, they had put up with more than enough from overbearing academics. Unconsciously, they were seeking for a new freedom and the man who was to offer it to them already lived in Cowley.

If 'Wallpaper Morris' ever saw a motor-car, he never made a note of the fact. His Oxford was still rural and medieval. Cattle were driven across Carfax and down The High, mooing their way over Magdalen Bridge to the water meadows beyond. 'Topsy' Morris loved it all and for him the place was timeless and changeless. He sat at the feet of Ruskin, went on brass-rubbing expeditions, had thoughts of founding a monastery, rowed on the Isis, sang and shouted mightily, wrote his first poem, read aloud to Burne-Jones and "to work off his superabundant energy" spent hours in Maclaren's Gymnasium in Oriel Lane, boxing, fencing and bashing about with singlesticks.

In 1853 sport was still far from being the organized cult which it became later in the century. In Oxford, the first outdoor activity to be ritualized was rowing, a sport which for generations had been little more than pleasure boating. Eight-oared racing seems to have originated at Eton, whence it came naturally to the university. The earliest 'eights' race between colleges took place in 1815 and, the first Oxford and Cambridge Boat Race was held at Henley fourteen years later. In 1856 it became an annual event and was soon transferred to the now traditional course between Putney and Mortlake, where half-a-million people watch the two crews fight it out each spring.

The windings of the Thames at Oxford and the narrowness of some of its reaches also gave birth to that peculiar form of inter-collegiate rowing known as 'Bumps'. During the week of 'Summer Eights', a long series of daily 'bumping races' takes place. The college boats set off at equal intervals, one after the other, and the object of every crew is to catch up with the boat immediately in front and bump it in the stern. Successful bumpers are awarded a place in the next race until eventually, by a kind of climbing-the-ladder process, one 'eight' finishes as top dog and its college becomes Head of the River. Eights Week is a great time for merrymaking and Bumps suppers figure prominently in Victorian reminiscences. A college that goes Head of the River is expected to go mad, and usually succeeds in doing so.

Oxford rowing is for ever associated with Folly Bridge. Here are boatyards and barges and Salters' river steamers, trim vessels that will take you "through ninety miles of glorious Thames scenery" down to Windsor and Kingston. Here are canoes and punts and launches and odd craft for messing about in; but the oddest craft of all are the old college barges, some decrepit, some smart, one looking for all the world like a Mississippi steamboat, another that could have carried Cleopatra and still others, high-pooped, classic-columned, white-painted and out of this world; so much more characterful than the squat and ugly boathouses which have all but replaced them and which look, as someone wrote recently, "like a lot of blessed boot-boxes".

Nearly everyone regards the barges with affection, yet until a fund was opened to preserve the best of them a year or two ago, most were slowly rotting away. The last one to be specially built was commissioned by Keble in 1899. Others were variously acquired and converted for use as changing rooms and social clubs. During Eights Weeks and regattas they become floating grandstands and are loaded down to the gunwales with spectators.

Rowing was always the great sport, but as the century progressed, rugby football and cricket began to come into their own. Even so, it was a long time before "the University went forth en masse to watch a football match or colleges celebrated victory on the field by a midnight orgy". Nevertheless, the Bumps suppers of the rowing men were "already helping to inaugurate a new religion".

"The first symptom of the new sports mania", wrote Lewis Farnell, "was the taking over of games by the clergy as a proper theme for the pulpit." One chaplain, indeed, preached an admonitory sermon on the total failure of his college's oarsmen during the Eights. This, he intimated, was displeasing both to God and to himself; for the good of their souls, his listeners were exhorted to make greater efforts in the future.

John Ruskin, on the other hand, denounced games and athletics as an unproductive waste of energy. He suggested that as an alternative, undergraduates might like to use their muscles in a bit of useful Christian hard labour. In 1876, he persuaded several of them—including Arnold Toynbee and Oscar Wilde—to have a go at paving a 2-mile stretch of a wretched farm lane at North Hinksey. Hopeful of being invited to breakfast by the great man, they "shovelled away mud under the prophet's eye for the whole of a long afternoon". The breakfast did not take place and the road was never finished.

Oscar Wilde was one of Oxford's more notorious aesthetes. There have always been 'fops and swots' at the university, but it was in Victorian times that the diametrically opposed cliques of 'aesthetes and hearties' emerged. The aesthetes were the precious people, the ones who were supposed to spend their languid lives sighing over lilies and old legends. The hearties were rough, tough and red-faced. As the nineteenth century, with its growing idolatory of sport, wore on, the division between the two extreme types became more marked. The games men, the rowing men, the rugby men and the athletic men became more muscular and less Christian. The pale poets became more and more precious and were mercilessly pursued. In their heyday, the beefy, thick-skinned, thick-skulled hearties were kings of the colleges. They tyrannized the timid aesthetes, whose only real weapon was wit. But of what use were words against giants who thought that to half-drown some embryo poet in the Cherwell was one big laugh?

It took men like Oscar Wilde and Max Beerbohm to stop them in their tracks with the flickering blade of repartee, and even this did not always work. The majority of the underdogs either kept out of the way or scuttled for shelter. Or, like Ethelred the Unready, they bought off the loud-mouthed sportsmen with Danegeld. As late as the nineteen-twenties, a friend of John Betjeman confessed that he had "bribed the Boat Club with a cask of beer" when its more unruly members were threatening to break up an arty-party.

The hearties did not always have it all their own way. Osbert Lancaster recalled that when they tried to wreck one memorable literary evening in 1927, the bully-boys "fell like ninepins before a barrage of champagne bottles . . . flung from the top of a stair-case with a force and precision that radically altered the pattern of Oxford rowing for the rest of Term . . .". But, as James Morris points out: "there have been periods when the elite of the under-graduate body was formed entirely of its notable athletes . . . and even now, a 'Blue' is often more admired than a First".

Mercifully, the situation today is more balanced. It is right that the great sporting triumphs should be recorded and remembered in Oxford's annals; that Olympic stars should drop casually into Vincent's for beefsteak and kidney pie; that down at the Iffley Road track, a plaque records the fact that Roger Bannister was the first man in the world to run a four-minute mile. On the other hand, it is right to remember that Oxford is not just a sportsman's paradise, an eternal practice ground for the next Olympic Games. At times, it has seemed so. At the height of the competitive games cult, and to their shame, one or two colleges "came perilously close to the American system of awarding scholarships to very able sportsmen" without the slightest regard to their I.Qs. Looking back on the more recent history of the university, one cannot help wondering how many good minds have been excluded from Oxford because of the over-riding claims of men who could run faster than most, or captained their school fifteen, or seemed probables for the inter-varsity match, or took five wickets for Eton against Harrow.

In the earlier days of the university, physical exercise was far more of an individual matter, and 'sport' included some rather doubtful pastimes. Poaching was always popular, adding to the excitement of the chase the thrill of taking stolen fruits. In the same year that young Will Shakespeare was taken up for killing deer in Charlecote Park, students were being let off far more lightly for committing the same offence in the woods around Oxford. Hunting and hawking were proscribed for a time by Archbishop Laud but his ban had little effect. Undergraduates still ride to hounds, and in 1920 C. S. Lewis was thrilled to see a member of his college stroll casually by with a hooded falcon on his wrist.

Cricket, one of the original team games, was first played on Bullingdon Green in the middle of the eighteenth century. Football, of a primitive, fighting kind, was much older. Its origins shrouded in medieval mists, it was not considered as a game fit for gentlemen and those who took part risked banishment from the university. The game as we know it was very much an invention of the mid-Victorian era, when, apart from rowing, the greatest exercise of all was walking. Gladstone, a double-First of Christ Church in 1831, did his 10 miles a day without thinking twice about it. Casual four or five-hour strolls were common and Sunday walks of 20 or 30 miles far from rare.

Little of this was 'competitive' in the modern sense, and certainly none of it was conceived as spectator sport. Men swam at Parson's Pleasure for the fun of it. They took part in the water-steeplechases organized by the Hare and Hounds Club not for the greater glory of their college, but for sheer pleasure, wading through flooded winter meadows in the sheer satisfaction of being young. To them, and to men like Gladstone, hard physical exercise was no more than the necessary adjunct to hard mental exercise— a means to an end and not, as it was later to become, an end in itself.

Against this background of hopes for the future and despair

with the present, the Town was getting on with the business of being a town in its own right. Final reconciliation with the Gown was far from easy and still far ahead. Nevertheless, a start had been made as early as 1771, when, by the first Mileways Act, the town regained some control over its own market, a privilege which had been surrendered after the St. Scholastica's Day Riot of 1355! A series of such Acts set up the new Covered Market, made provision for the lighting, maintenance and widening of streets and bridges and took cognisance of the fact that a city of 30,000 inhabitants needed a more efficient form of administration than the one it had endured for so long. Needless to say, the university still had a very large say in municipal affairs and was not to give up its 'ancient rights' without a struggle. Little by little, however, the Town edged its way in. The Oxford Police Act of 1868 established "one Constabulary Force for the Whole District" and was managed by a committee on which the mayor and eight councillors were in the majority. Moreover, the town bore the greater part of the cost and in due course was able to call the tune. The new police force was generally welcomed, since it was now possible, for the first time in centuries, for citizens to walk the streets at night without risking questioning and being packed off home to bed like naughty children.

The last of the university's 'privileged persons' had disappeared in 1835, and henceforth, academics and townsfolk alike stood equal in the eyes of the law. In 1858, the humiliating oath of fealty which had for hundreds of years been the unhappy lot of each new mayor was finally discarded. The city, whose population quadrupled between 1801 and 1901, was beginning—however timidly at first—to have a hand in its own affairs.

And almost without realizing it, some dons were becoming townsmen. When the first Reform Act was passed, the university had been described as "a society of celibates with little or no leaven of family life". Much earlier, the *Monthly Review* had denounced academic celibacy as "an absurd relic of popery" and it was generally accepted that the pseudo-monkish way of life forced upon college Fellows led inevitably to some unfortunate extra-mural as well as intra-mural relationships. Until the final lifting of the so-called 'celibacy rule' in 1877, most dons were bachelors in holy orders who lived within the wholly male establishment of a college. Lewis Carroll was a typical example of the species: shy, retiring, brilliant in his way, yet with a liking for little girls that caused the Dean of Christ Church great concern. If such a man wished to marry, there was only one way out: "he first took a college living, and then a wife . . . after which, Oxford knew him no more". The only married men, and the only women allowed within college precincts were the Heads of Houses and their wives and families.

Surprisingly, the reforming University Commissioners of 1852 were all for keeping the colleges celibate. They argued that if Fellows were allowed to marry, they would move out into the town in droves, to the great detriment of their young charges. After 1877, this is exactly what happened. Dons sought the connubial bed with almost indecent haste, rushing into matrimony and out to North Oxford, building their Gothic villas and "living their blameless lives in little red houses with a perambulator and a bicycle on either side of the front door". They became suburbanites and commuters and suddenly found that they were citizens as well as academics.

Although one or two colleges held out against it, the university took this drastic change remarkably quietly. St. John's, for example, had no married Fellow on its roll until 1898, by which time the feminine influence in Oxford was very strong indeed. There can be little doubt that the end of celibacy marked the beginning of academic emancipation for women. The female of the species was soon to infiltrate into all parts of the Establishment, first as unattached and officially unrecognized students and finally as undergraduates, dons and professors; the equal of men in most things and not least in brain power.

As we saw in an earlier chapter, the first women students had a difficult time. Most of the men pooh-poohed their intellectual ambitions and authority frowned heavily upon them. In no small measure, it was due to the sympathetic attitude of the new race of dons' wives that intelligent girls were finally able to break into the still largely male preserve of Oxford. The novelist, Mrs. Humphry Ward, a niece of Matthew Arnold, was leader of an informal ladies' group "on fire for women's education". She and her husband, a Fellow of Brasenose, lived in a small house in Bradmore Road, "furnished with antique chests, Morris wallpapers and blue pottery", which became "a centre of modern ideas where the daring new ideas for women were discussed".

These young wives were youthful, up-to-date and outrageously outspoken. They organized lectures, nagged their husbands and helped to bring about a situation in which girls, though heavily chaperoned, were at last allowed to attend lectures. This was a very big step forward. Professor Ruskin might thunder that he "would not let the bonnets into his lectures on any account" but they came all the same.

Full recognition did not come for fifty years, and even then it was grudgingly given. Although five women's colleges had been set up before the turn of the century and although their students had over and over again produced the most brilliant examination results, it was not until 1920, with universal female suffrage an accepted fact, that the first women graduates of Oxford received their degrees at a moving ceremony at the Sheldonian.

The end of the nineteenth century marked the end of the first Morris Oxford. It had been a century of struggle and reform for both Town and Gown. The university had been forced to come to terms with modern and progressive ideas. In both camps the diehards were having to realize that the immediate future was likely to be very different from the immediate past—which in the case of Oxford also meant the more distant past. Outside the walls of the colleges, ordinary men and ordinary women busied themselves with ordinary, humdrum tasks, and what they did had less and less to do with the learned men within. The town was growing and a new century was beginning; its people were beginning to believe that, after all, they might be citizens of no mean city. Released from centuries of second-fiddling and university domination, they dimly perceived a better future.

XV

MORRIS COWLEY

Of Oxford in the mid-nineteenth century, John Richard Green was able to write, with some degree of truth: "The town has no manufacture or trade. . . ."

Admittedly, this was a historian's generalization. There was some trade and there was some manufacture, but most of it was on quite a small scale. Such factories as existed were not much more than overgrown workshops. Out at Cowley, agricultural machinery was made by hand; there were paper mills at Sandford and Wolvercote; gloves were produced at Woodstock and in the city itself was a little ironworks, together with malthouses and several breweries. By Folly Bridge, Salters had a reputation for their boats; there was an organ works at St. Clement's, and in 1874 Frank Cooper's wife was boiling up her first pans of that chunky Oxford Marmalade known to later generations of undergraduates as 'squish'. Builders and stone-masons prospered, but their work was largely geared to the needs of the colleges and to the considerable development of the university. Few firms employed more than a score or so of people and most consisted of less than ten men. Without the patronage of the academic world, half the tradesmen in the district would have gone out of business.

As well as being the largest indirect employer of labour in and around Oxford, the most important single undertaking was also owned by the university. This was the Oxford University Press, which by 1900 was employing more than 300 workers in its printing house in Walton Street. No other firm could approach such numbers, and in an age of unparalleled industrial expansion the city fathers saw all too clearly that, like it or not, the local economy was still based upon the continuing existence of their academic cuckoo in the nest. Through no fault of its own, the town's eggs were all in the one basket.

More than once attempts had been made to remedy the situation, and a splendid opportunity came in 1865, when the Great Western Railway wanted to set up its main carriage works at Oxford. Delighted and enthusiastic, the council offered the company a big meadow behind the station as a site. Townspeople marched up and down with placards bearing encouraging slogans. Buildings were plastered with posters painting a grim picture of the plight of local tradesmen during the long vacation, "when pockets are empty and streets deserted for nearly half the year".

As might be expected, the university squashed the railway scheme flat. Horrified at the thought of the town being "flooded with mere mechanics" a deputation led by the Vice-Chancellor was despatched to London for a meeting with the directors of the company. Discussions dragged on for nearly three years, but in the end the project was abandoned and the G.W.R. built its carriage works at Swindon. Once again, the town had been humiliated and shown quite clearly who was really the boss.

During the negotiations there had been much talk of the dangers of "disfiguring an ancient and beautiful city" and "damaging the interests of a national university". They were valid points, but underlying all the arguments was an almost pathological desire to preserve the status quo at all costs. In spite of the reformers within its ranks, the university did not want change; the quiet, dreamy life of a sleepy town suited its members very well. And railways, in any case were anathema to most academics. The civilized mode of transport was the stage-coach: when the branch line from Didcot reached the city in 1844, there were still seventy-three coaches a day in and out of Oxford.

Rail travel and transport not only sounded the death knell of coaches and canals, but "made of Oxford an open city". Previously, communications had not been good; they were sure, but slow. Heavy bulk loads such as coal were brought by barge up the Thames, or down from the Midlands by the Oxford Canal, opened in 1778. Yet in less than ten years, the situation was completely changed: by 1854 there were rail links to Banbury and Birmingham and by way of Worcester to Wolverhampton; there were two stations and there was even to be a direct service—the 'Varsity Line'—to Cambridge, a facility which was not withdrawn until 1968, when one undergraduate wrote sadly: "No more commuting from Magdalen Commem. to King's Ball, throwing empty *Louis Kremer* bottles onto the track. . . ."

By 1900, with excellent communications, a central position, good services and roads that seemed ready to receive the first fruits of the internal combustion engine, Oxford was ripe for development and expansion. As Professor E. W. Gilbert put it: ". . . the city's natural nodality awaited man's exploitation". Yet at this time, everyone—with the exception of Motor-car Morris —accepted that "Oxford is prevented, as if by fate, from ever attaining to the position of a great industrial or commercial centre."

Within twenty-five years, this one man was to make nonsense of such statements. True, the place remained primarily a university city until the end of the First World War, but after that its emergence as a major industrial centre was little short of spectacular. The amazing transformation of a rather old-fashioned market town into a bustling modern city was due almost entirely to the energy and enterprise of Morris. And as Ruth Fasnacht points out: "the transition was so rapid that it was a *fait accompli* before anyone realized what was happening". Had the university, or the city council, known what was in Morris's mind as he built his first motor-cars, they must surely have had misgivings. It has even been suggested that they would have put the brake on his ideas. As things turned out, the development of his factories was encouraged, rather than impeded, and by the time their sheer size was giving cause for concern and the authorities discovered that they "had a monster on their doorstep", it was too late.

A man who in 1923 produced 20,000 cars, who was soon to build a second factory in the Woodstock Road, and who single-handed had solved Oxford's perennial problem of unemployment was a major force, and one to be treated with respect. By 1926, with production at 50,000 vehicles a year, Morris had absorbed every bit of surplus labour in the area and "unemployment and poverty had virtually disappeared from the Oxford scene". The critics might sneer about "pale-faced mechanics in Oxford bags walking down the Cornmarket" and complain that he was ruining the dear old city; the fact remained that he was providing security and a higher standard of living for thousands—something which no-one else had ever done, or had even bothered to think about.

With the setting up at Cowley of the Pressed Steel Company, there was no longer any pool of local labour to meet the demand for workers and in the later twenties, the great immigration into Oxford began, a process that was to continue for many years. Between the wars, 10,000 new houses were built; money flowed freely; shopkeepers prospered, and for once the university had to stand on the sidelines, secretly appalled at what was going on, but quite unable to do much about it.

The population statistics for the first half of the century tell their own story. By 1920, when the figures for neighbouring towns had remained more or less static, those for Oxford had increased by 7,000. But the really dramatic increase came between 1919 and 1939. In this second twenty-year period, the number of people living within the city boundaries leapt by another 30,000. By the outbreak of the Second World War, the various companies in and around the city making up the Morris empire were employing nearly 10,000 people—more than one in ten of the whole population and almost 40 per cent of all insured workers.

Statistics are dull, but these were exciting. No other organization for miles around could offer the wages or continuity of employment provided by Morris. The University Press, with 800 employees, and the Eagle Iron Works, with 500, were small fry by comparison and found it very difficult to compete in the labour market. There was no stopping the development of Cowley. In the artificial conditions of wartime, the numbers working there rose to 17,000, dropped back temporarily to 12,000 in the immediate post-war years and have since climbed steadily to their present peak of 25,000. In 1951, the two-millionth Morris car rolled off the assembly line and soon afterwards, the great merger with Austin Motors gave birth to 'B.M.C.'—the British Motor Corporation.

The works at Cowley now covered 350 acres, to which not only an army of 'the new Oxonians' came every day, but which drew workers by the bus load from places as far away as Witney and Banbury. There was scarcely a parish in Oxfordshire that did not send someone on the daily journey to Cowley and, ultimately, Morris not only changed the pattern of life in Oxford itself, but helped to bring prosperity to towns and villages over a very wide area. The city boundaries were extended and extended again. Separate villages like Headington and Iffley, Wolvercote and Water Eaton became suburbs, largely occupied by car workers. Vast pink rashes of housing broke out, spreading north beyond Summertown, south to Hinksey and Littlemore, east to Barton and Risinghurst. Only to the west, where the winter river still floods the fields and the roaring by-pass runs like a causeway across some inland sea, has the sprawl of the city been contained.

B.M.C. has become in its turn B.L.M.C.—the British Leyland Motor Corporation. With its 25,000 workers, Cowley is periodically beset by labour troubles: there are strikes and walk-outs and pickets parade up and down, occasionally supported by rather self-conscious student 'sympathizers'. Management grumbles and rumbles, and even hints that if things don't improve the plants may have to close down for good. To which the militant unionists say Ha!—not believing a word of it. They now turn out as many vehicles in a single week as 'the Old Man' used to produce in a year and they see the bonanza years going on for ever.

The wheel has turned. With nearly a quarter of the city's population engaged in the motor industry, the economic importance of the university is now quite small. Yet, as in the old days, Oxford is still firmly tied to one major employer. It has often been pointed out that a slump in this one industry could spell disaster for the whole area.

The danger was brought out in the first year of the 1939–45 War. During the thirties, Oxford was one of the three most prosperous towns in Britain. Unemployment was all but unknown, wages were high and the days all golden. With the outbreak of war, however, the situation changed rapidly. Both Morris Motors and Pressed Steel took longer than expected to switch their activities from motor-cars to munitions. Eventually, the organization got into its stride, building tanks and midget submarines, making Bofors guns and repairing aircraft. But this was not before half the jobs had gone and thousands were thrown out of work. It was a new and salutary experience. There were long dole queues and applications for relief and the town knew once again the meaning of hardship. During the Great Depression, through clever planning and, as in 1920, by cutting profit margins, Morris had kept his factories running and his people at work. In 1939–40, he was not able to do this. People left the district in droves and the town seemed half empty.

After the war, the experience was not forgotten. In his famous post-war plan for Oxford, Thomas Sharp attacked the popular concept of "the twin cities of Oxford and Cowley", calmly suggested that "the great Nuffield and Pressed Steel works should be removed to some other part of the country" and recommended industrial diversification, with the setting up of trading estates and many small factory units to offer a greater range of employment. It was an impossible dream, and seems likely to remain so. Oxford is stuck with its motor industry and its university and neither is likely to depart. There has been some movement of other industries into the locality, but compared with B.L.M.C. and Pressed Steel Fisher, the new firms are very small.

The story of the Nuffield benefactions is too well known to need repeating in much detail. During his lifetime, he made a vast amount of money, worked hard, lived simply and did his best to give most of it away. At the time of his death in 1963 he had donated nearly £30 million to hospitals, colleges, distressed areas, the disabled, his own employees, the Red Cross and a host of worthy causes. He had an amused contempt for academics, yet handed over £4 million to the university. He had no time for socialists and reckoned he had agreed against his better judgement to found Nuffield College as "a meeting ground for politicians and trade unionists". He once referred to it as "that bloody Kremlin where Left-wingers study at my expense". Nevertheless, the residue of his estate, another £3 million, went to Nuffield College when he died.

In Oxford, his epitaph could well be that of Christopher Wren, for truly, *Si monumentum requiris, circumspice*. Directly and indirectly, the work and influence of William Richard Morris is everywhere to be seen. The vaguely neo-Cotswold college in New Road is obvious and a better piece of architecture than many critics would have us believe. The Cowley complex, vaster and in its way even more impressive, is more deserving of the crack that "*C'est magnifique—mais ce n'est pas l'architecture!*" On the other hand, the university itself has much to answer for in the depressing dullness of some of its own buildings. There are one or two particularly slabby horrors to be seen in the Science Area off South Parks Road and some more recent constructions may well receive short shrift from future generations.

It has been said that Oxford will never forgive Morris for what he did to Oxford. They are not prepared to accept what he did *for*

15

Oxford, let alone admit that much of what he did was good. It is easy to talk of "the great black wall of the University shadowing his life" and to say that he was able "to bolster its crumbling bastions and mortice it with gold". Rich men have been doing this for 800 years and not all were saints, nor did all of them come by their money through hard and honest work. This, at least, no-one denies of 'Motor-car Morris'.

Too many sins have been laid at his door. The age of the motor-car was imminent, even when he was building his first bicycle. He saw it coming and acted accordingly. Critics shudder at the present state of the city; they point to its bigness and brashness, to its traffic problems and the vast car parks which are never quite vast enough, to the multi-storey monster which is to hold still more cars on a site near Worcester College. They point, and with a curl of the lips say, "Morris!"

It is true that he was responsible for the unprecedented expansion of the city, for a population which doubled in his own lifetime, and for helping to create a consumer demand that has completely changed the character of the main shopping streets. But this could—and probably would—have come anyway. It has happened in remote West Country towns, in all parts of England, and in places far less well known than Oxford. The city has not really been singled out for special attention. The southward drift of industry in itself might have put paid to any hopes of preserving Oxford as some sort of unique academic shrine. Its "short and easy communications with the ports of London, Bristol and Southampton, and with the Birmingham area, are significant natural advantages . . .". It would have been too much to expect that they would have for long gone unrecognized in a naughty modern world.

The outside world moved into Oxford during the twenties, and since 1950 developers and property men have had several field days. Much of Cornmarket, the major shopping street, has been altered out of all recognition. Where there were once dozens of small, privately-owned 'individual shops full of character', there are now the multiples, the high-street barons, whose stocks and standard shop fronts are identical with those in five hundred other towns. As leases fall out, properties are snapped up, large sums of money change hands and some nominee company directed by another company and controlled by a holding company with offices in Mayfair opens up still another branch. It is the age of the *entrepreneur*, to whom Oxford is no more than a name and a source of future profits.

Nevertheless, the present state of the city—which has been called a mess—is not entirely the fault of Morris or the multiples. As late as 1954, responsible people were complaining bitterly of "the almost complete lack of control over the city's development". Since then, there has been some improvement and a serious attempt to get to grips practically with its more immediate problems. A great ring-road now encircles and protects the place like some vast defence work, helping to divert from the centre the through traffic that not so long ago was threatening to choke it to death. Heavier vehicles are now officially banned, although too many still seem to force a way in. And inevitably, as the number of vehicles increases, the benefits of earlier traffic planning are nullified. The authorities deliberate and the planners plan and periodically there are open meetings and public inquiries into this or that proposal. From time to time, somebody comes up with the bright idea of planting bollards across the bottom end of High Street, The Broad, Cornmarket and St. Aldate's. Ban all traffic from Carfax, say these fundamentalists: make the centre into a pedestrian precinct. But the shopkeepers scream and the planners say it can't be done and the council agrees and this too-simple solution is kicked into touch once again.

But traffic remains the great problem. To drive out of Oxford at 5.30 in the evening is a nightmare, and parking a car at any time during the hours of daylight costs a gallon of petrol and considerable pertinacity. For years, there has been talk of running a relief road across Christ Church Meadow; in *Oxford Replanned*, Thomas Sharp proposed this as Merton Mall, a wide freeway connecting St. Aldate's Street with The Plain below Magdalen Bridge. The advantages of such a road, he said, "stand out as plain as a hundred pikestaffs". But Christ Church is The House and what The House thinks still matters. The thought of a screeching motor road alongside the Broad Walk have given members of Christ Church and Merton a fit of the annual horrors for twenty-five years; and in this, they have many sympathizers. Few people deny that some sort of relief road in this area is necessary if the city is not to be throttled by traffic, but the Meadow is one of Oxford's greater glories. The latest plan suggests placing the hated route further to the south, leaving this marvellous space untouched. All hope that the plan is possible.

As in many ancient towns, those who are concerned for the future of Oxford are torn between the demands of re-development and the need for preservation; between the desirable and the expedient. No-one pretends that by some miracle, the two can ultimately be reconciled. It is no longer just a matter of a fight between opposing camps; both Town and Gown dispute among themselves. The conservationists want to keep much of the Banbury Road area as an example of "a perfectly preserved Victorian suburb". On the other hand, the university wants to plank down right in the middle a new, huge and splendidly modern Pitt Rivers Museum, designed by the great Italian, Pier Luigi Nervi. In such circumstances, something, somebody, has to give way. The Pitt Rivers has a vast collection, most of which is stored in wooden huts and little of which is available either to the public, or to scholars for study. The new building would be as revolutionary in its way as was Ruskin's unique Venetian-Gothic University Museum across the road from Keble College. To have, or not to have, the new Pitt Rivers? The debate continues.

Meanwhile, the city goes ahead with its £3-million re-development of St. Ebbe's and its plans to provide "a new downtown Oxford, where people will be able to shop lavishly, eat, meet and spend the evening out in an atmosphere of colour and enjoyment". Brave new words for a brave new world, and in general, most people wish the city well. St. Ebbe's has been too long a dirty, down-at-heel slum and the only ones who regret its passing are the sentimentalists who have never had the doubtful privilege of living there.

But whatever they make of St. Ebbe's, and whatever they may do in the future with ring-roads and factories, with the U.S. Air Force at Heyford and the railway station now rebuilding and the American-owned Cooper's Marmalade, one feels that somehow, Oxford, the quintessential Oxford, will survive. Cowley, almost self-sufficient with its big shopping centre and its own peculiar ethos may well become that 'second city'. Town and Gown relations may well remain for all time luke-warm. May Day at Magdalen may well develop, as in 1969, into an annual excuse for anarchists to break up the measures of the Oxford Morris Men and to wave red flags inscribed "Workers and Students—One

Struggle!" In spite of all, much of the old Oxford is bound to survive.

Customs continue, laughed at by many, but observed by the few. At Queen's, they are still occasionally summoned to Hall by the blowing of a trumpet, and on Christmas Day they still bring in the boar's head to High Table to the singing of the medieval "Boar's Head Carol". At All Souls they already look ahead to the year 2001, when the once-a-century ceremony of the All Souls' Mallard will take place and the Fellows go with lighted torches over the roofs in a futile search for this mythical bird. While Cowley sends its latest models to the Motor Show, the old boundaries of the city are beaten with rushes and ecclesiastical solemnity and little choirboys scramble for hot pennies. Choristers from Christ Church in Eton collars and birettas dash fearlessly in front of the traffic on their way to evensong in the cathedral where shortly they will sing the office like the angels they are not. Nearby, bulldozers tear down Georgian houses and throw up Anglo-Saxon remains. In summer the visitors come in tens of thousands and in winter hardly at all, wandering round the colleges like lonely ghosts as they wistfully enjoy the vicarious half-hour of an Oxford education.

People write books, read books, buy books and vaguely discuss a future when it will be all visual aids and tape cassettes and tele-recordings. In the interim, Bodley and the Radcliffe are crowded and Blackwells, Maxwells, Parkers and the rest sell more books than ever.

The river runs. Great Tom, "the loudest thing in Oxford" chimes 101 times for the original 101 members of Cardinal Wolsey's college; and this not on the hour of nine, when every self-respecting clock in Oxford does its stuff, but at five minutes past. Being 1 degree 15 minutes west of Greenwich, Oxford's true time is five minutes later than advertised and Christ Church likes to be accurate.

Oxford has been called many things in its time: "the little city of learning and laughter", "a lotus land" and "a place of medieval moods and memories". In *Lost Horizon*, James Hilton's hero told the High Lama: "To be quite frank, Shangri-la reminds me of Oxford...."

So Shangri-la it must be. Has it ever really existed?

SOME BOOKS

Thousands of books have been written about Oxford and thousands more give the place and its people more than a passing mention. Certainly, a comprehensive bibliography would in itself fill many volumes. The list which follows is no more than a sketchy indication of some of the more readily-available material consulted for *Portrait of Oxford*. Much more exists: college histories in abundance, endless academic memoirs, municipal records, the proceedings of several local historical and record societies, various Oxford magazines. And of course, the events of days past and present are covered by those two excellent newspapers, the *Oxford Mail* and the *Oxford Times*.

P. W. S. Andrews and Elizabeth Brunner, *The Life of Lord Nuffield* (1955).

W. J. Arkell, *Oxford Stone* (1947).

Dacre Balsdon, *Oxford Life* (1962), *Oxford Now and Then* (1970).

Muriel Beadle, *These Ruins are Inhabited* (1963).

John Betjeman, *An Oxford University Chest* (1938), *Summoned by Bells* (1962).

H. Bliss, *The Life of Anthony Wood* (1848).

C. W. Boase, *Oxford* (1887).

British Association, *The Oxford Region* (1954).

Vera Brittain, *The Women at Oxford* (1960).

David Cecil, *Max* (1964).

A. Clark, *The Life and Times of Anthony Wood* (1891–1900).

W. Elmhurst, *A Freshman's Diary 1911–12.* (1969).

Lewis R. Farnell, *An Oxonian Looks Back* (1934).

Ruth Fasnacht, *A History of the City of Oxford* (1954).

John Richard Green, *Oxford Studies* (1903).

V. H. H. Green, *Oxford Common Room* (1957), *The Universities* (1969).

Hamilton Gibbs, *Rowlandson's Oxford* (1912).

Thomas Hearne, *Diaries* (ed. P. Bliss) (1869).

Philip Henderson, *William Morris, his Life, Work and Friends* (1967).

Christopher Hobhouse, *Oxford* (1948).

Lord Horder, *In Praise of Oxford* (1955).

Derek Hudson, *Lewis Carroll* (1954).
Henry James, *English Hours* (1905).
C. W. Judge, *Oxford Past and Present* (1970).
Cecil King, *Strictly Personal* (1970).
Osbert Lancaster, *With an Eye to the Future* (1967).
C. S. Lewis, *Letters* (1968).
F. Madan, *Oxford Outside the Guide Books* (1923).
(Sir) Charles Mallet, *History of the University of Oxford* (1924).
Albert Mansbridge, *The Older Universities of England* (1923).
Felix Markham, *Oxford* (1968).
James Morris, *Oxford* (1965).
Leonard Mosley, *Curzon, the End of an Epoch* (1961).
(Sir) James Mountford, *British Universities* (1966).
The Oxford University Handbook (1969).
Harry Paintin, *The Oxford Mercat* (1923).
Hastings Rashdall, *Universities of Europe in the Middle Ages* (1963).
Robert Rhodes James, *Chips* (Diaries of Sir Henry Channon) (1967),
    Rosebery (1963).
L. Rice-Oxley, *Oxford Renowned* (1934).
Royal Commission on Historical Monuments, *The City of Oxford*
    (1939).
H. E. Salter, *Oxford Street Names* (1921).
W. E. Sherwood, *Oxford Rowing* (1900), *Oxford Yesterday* (1927)
R. A. H. Spiers, *Round about The Mitre* (1928).
Jack Straw, Albert Sloman, Paul Doty, *Universities: Boundaries of
    Change* (1970).
Edward Thomas, *Oxford* (1903).
G. M. Trevelyan, *English Social History* (1949).
Victoria County History of Oxfordshire, vols. 2 and 3, *The City of
    Oxford.*
W. R. Ward, *Victorian Oxford* (1965).
Windsor, H.R.H. Duke of, *A King's Story* (1951).
Philip Ziegler, *The Black Death* (1969).

GUIDE BOOKS:

Alden's Oxford Guide (1902 and 1912).
Cherwell Guide to Oxford (1968).
Clarendon Guide to Oxford, A. R. Woolley (1963).
Gardner's History, Gazetteer and Directory of Oxford (1852 and 1863).
Murray's Guide to Oxfordshire (1860 ed.).
Oxford University and City Guide (1821).
Red Guide to Oxford, Ward Lock (1962).
Traveller's Guide to Oxford and District, edited Seán Jennet (1965).

INDEX